REGENERATI**COMMON GOOD**N

*the future of community
in a permacrisis world*

CHRISTIAN SARKAR
PHILIP KOTLER
ENRICO FOGLIA

THERE IS NO ESCAPE.

THE ONLY WAY TO SURVIVE
IS TO *CHANGE EVERYTHING* –

INDIVIDUALS,
COMMUNITIES,
ORGANIZATIONS,
NATIONS,
– IN RESPECT
of
THIS ~~DYING~~
LIVING PLANET.

**WE ARE ALL
IN THIS
*TOGETHER.***

*For our children and their children
and our parents who came before us.*

*To Nonna Marcella, a true regenerative leader,
Whose power touched my heart with love.
The most precious gift she bestowed upon me
Was the love for others - a treasure for eternity.*

CONTENTS

ACKNOWLEDGEMENTS

We acknowledge these thinkers and their "ideas" as the builders of tomorrow:

- "Silent Spring" – Rachel Carson
- "The Limits to Growth" – Donella Meadows
- "Small is Beautiful" – E. F. Schumacher
- "The Death and Life of American Cities" – Jane Jacobs
- "Asset Based Community Development" – John Kretzmann & John McKnight
- "The Fortune at the Bottom of the Pyramid" – C.K. Prahalad & Stuart L. Hart
- "The Cluetrain Manifesto" – Chris Locke and gang
- "Governing the Commons" – Elinor Ostrom
- "Out of Poverty" – Paul Polak
- "Cradle to Cradle" – William McDonough
- "The Triple Bottom Line" – John Elkington
- "Biomimicry" – Janine Benyus
- "Community Wealth-building" – Ted Howard and Gar Alperovitz
- "Neighborhood Government" – Milton Kotler
- "Reconomics" – Storm Cunningham
- "The Utopia of Rules" – David Graeber
- "Social Marketing" and "De-Marketing" – Philip Kotler
- "The Great Turning" – David Korten
- "The Dream of the Earth" – Thomas Berry
- "Doughnut Economics" – Kate Raworth
- "Outcome Driven Innovation" – Anthony Ulwick
- "Rebalancing Society" – Henry Mintzberg
- "The Value of Everything" – Mariana Mazzucato
- "The Public Economy in Crisis" – June Sekera
- "Project Drawdown" – Paul Hawken
- "Reimagining Capitalism" – Rebecca Henderson
- "The Uninhabitable Earth" – David Wallace-Wells
- "Pluriversal Politics" – Arturo Escobar
- "P2P" – Michel Bauwens
- "City as Commons" – Christian Iaione and Sheila Foster
- "Degrowth" – Jason Hickel, Giorgos Kallis, Tim Jackson

In terms of regeneration specifically, we are grateful for the teachings of many, including:

- **Daniel Christian Wahl**
- **Paul Hawken**
- **Carol Sanford**
- **John Fullerton**
- **Giles Hutchins** and **Laura Storm**
- **Bill Reed**, **Pamela Mang** and **Ben Haggard**
- and the inimitable **Joe Brewer** whose adventures inspire us all.

The development of this book is also informed by a ten-year experimental initiative called the **$300 House project** (300house.com) – a design project focused on radically affordable housing.

Thanks also, to ChatGPT – don't miss the *interview* at the end of the book!

Finally, none of this would be possible without **Philip Kotler**'s work, his deep caring, mentorship, and advice.

"Destroying rainforest for economic gain is like
burning a Renaissance painting to cook a meal."
– E. O. Wilson

"The earth sings her revolution; she calls brave men and women to her defense."
– Lakota Man

"What does this Earth require of us if we want to continue to live on it?"
– Wendell Berry

"Nothing in either our theory or the data proves
the highest G.D.P. per capita is generally desirable,"
– Abhijit Banerjee and Esther Duflo

"The economists will tell you we can decouple growth from material consumption,
but that is total nonsense."
– Vaclav Smil

"Live simply so that others may simply live."
– Mahatma Gandhi

"The purpose of business is to solve the problems of people and planet profitably,
and not profit from causing problems."
– Colin Mayer

"May all live like a community where none is an outsider"
– Sikh proverb

"For every complex problem there is an answer
that is clear, simple and wrong."
– H.L. Mencken

"It's easier to imagine the end of the world
than the end of capitalism."
– Mark Fisher

"Climate change is not the problem. Climate change is the most horrible
symptom of an economic system that has been built for a few
to extract every precious value out of this planet and its people."
– Colette Pichon Battle

"Where resides the rebel heart?"
– Harry Belafonte

RELATED BOOKS

The Wicked Seven:
Why Can't We Solve the World's Wicked Problems?
by Christian Sarkar and Philip Kotler
(2023)

Losing Our Democracy
by Philip Kotler and Christian Sarkar
(2020)

Advancing the Common Good:
Strategies for Businesses, Governments, and Nonprofits
by Philip Kotler
(2019)

Brand Activism:
From Purpose to Action
by Christian Sarkar and Philip Kotler
(2018)

Democracy in Decline:
Rebuilding its Future
by Philip Kotler
(2016)

Confronting Capitalism:
Real Solutions for a Troubled Economic System
by Philip Kotler
(2015)

INTRODUCTION

What is **regeneration**? *Is sustainability over?*

How does an organization become regenerative?

What is community regeneration?

Who is a regenerative leader?

What does a regenerative economy look like?

We begin by stating the obvious - **the corporation is obsolete.** Our **institutions are not fit for purpose** - either because they are corrupt, or because they lack the imagination and will required for the tasks at hand. The same can be said for our leaders. They have betrayed the public trust.

What are the *jobs to be done* to solve the most **serious problems** facing the world today? For forty years the institutions of the world have worked to "mitigate" climate change with no results – or worse – failure to stop the rapid destruction of the ecosystems which keep us all alive. Leaders and businesses have largely ignored the cries of our dying planet. A desperate scientific community has taken up arms to spread the word, but the media won't listen. And inequality keeps growing – social, economic, climate, you name it.

Get this: *none* of the world's leading industries would be profitable if they actually *paid* for the natural capital they use!

We have moved from a polycrisis to a **permacrisis** world.

Let's face the truth. We are "greening" ourselves to extinction. *None of the institutional climate actions we're taking are on track.* And businesses are now trying to profit from the financialization of Nature. **Basta!**

In the writing of this book, we heard three distinct positions: (1) "we need a **revolution**, a system-wide transformation" (2) "**it's too late**, the elites have already decided what to do – we are powerless," and, (3) "*we do our best within the current system*, even though we know it's not going to be enough."

To these positions we say – **do not despair**. Revolutions are cruel, violent, and brutal. This is not the kind of revolution we need now. Instead, **love** is the *revolution* –

- Love for *your* children and family
- Love for *your* community
- Love for *your* work
- Love for *your* country
- Love for *your* planet
- Love for *our* Common Good

We are all waiting for change.

Our agenda is the agenda of the **Regenerative Marketing Institute** (RMI) – to promote regeneration and what it means to be regenerative.

In this book, we begin to explore the following topics:

- One, understand the various **definitions for regeneration** and develop our own – one which we think makes sense given the stakes. **Regeneration means regenerating the Common Good.** What will it take to make the Big Shift to regeneration?

- Second, how do we **regenerate a community**? Place-based regeneration is a critical capability we need now.

- Third, what is a regenerative **organization**? How can a business become responsive to the needs of the community, society, and nature?
- Fourth, what does **regenerative leadership** look like? Can politics be regenerative?

- Fifth – what is **regenerative innovation**?

- Sixth – **can our economy ever become regenerative**? What will that take?

- Finally, we look at the **lessons from Palermo.** What can we do in our neighborhoods? What is the role of the local entrepreneur in building community wealth? We highlight a number of organizations we found during our regenerative project in Palermo.

Our society, it seems, is corrupted by power and greed. Everywhere inequality grows and creates alienation – separation from each other and from the planet. Belief in the **Common Good** is fading fast. We blame each other and fight culture wars and real wars instead of fighting the only war which matters now - **the war to save our dying planet**.

Change begins with each one of us, together.

Why? *Because we are all in this together.* The billionaires who run the world don't understand that they can't eat or breathe money.

We are not separate from Nature. We are not separate from the ecosystems which give us our daily breath. We are not separate from each other, or the web of life that connects all things – surely COVID taught us that!

We are a community of communities – with the Planet as our Common Home.

Coupled with previous work with **Philip Kotler** on **Brand Activism**, **The Wicked7 Project**, and **FIXCapitalism.com**, we found ourselves examining the relationship between **local communities** and the **businesses** that remained loyal to them.

The story of this book begins when **Enrico Foglia** submitted an article to *The Marketing Journal* about trust and the story of the Phoenicians – the people who built an extensive trading network across the Mediterranean and were early pioneers in mass production. We started discussing the rising **distrust of society** in business and markets.

A zero-trust society is a society without a sense of the Common Good, without hope. How do we fight this?

A chance Zoom-call with a councilwoman from **Palermo – Cettina Martorana** – and the persuasive charm of **Mayor Leoluca Orlando** convinced **Professor Kotler** to send us down to learn more in the capital of Sicily.

We embarked on the *Palermo Rigenerativa* project, an ecosystematic learning journey which helped us develop the ideas in this book. The book shows communities that positive change is still possible, and that mutual aid can be organized across traditional boundaries to build an entrepreneurial way forward. **Profits don't come first.** Depending on what your community looks like, there are many different paths to regeneration – and we explore some of them in the pages that follow. We chose to highlight several case studies from Palermo – not only because they are **regenerative**, but because they teach us about **overcoming adversity**. We are continually inspired by the lessons we learned from the Palermitans – and the continuing efforts they are making to become once again a **Hub of Hope** in the middle of the Mediterranean.

Business must support democracy as a fundamental human right. If a few corporations are subverting the rules, then the rest of the business world must work with government to stop them. Without deep democracy, true democracy, we are finished. And what's been going on is criminal: crimes against the Planet.

Yes, *you* can reduce your *personal* impact on the environment, and take responsibility for your actions, but **together** *we* can do more. We can organize, unionize, vote, collaborate, co-create, co-own, and co-exist.

Let's start in *our* neighborhoods, our communities, our organizations, our nations.

For our Planet.

For our children and their children.

Which brings us to the final question: *Are we out of time?*

We are late, but *not too late.*

It's time to **get up, stand up.**

love and peace,

Christian Sarkar
Philip Kotler
Enrico Foglia

THE REGENERATIVE MARKETING INSTITUTE
regenmarketing.org

1. THE BIG SHIFT

We know now that ExxonMobil knew about climate change for over 40 years, and *did nothing*.

Worse than nothing, they funded *climate denial* – and undermined political leaders who were interested in stopping global warming.

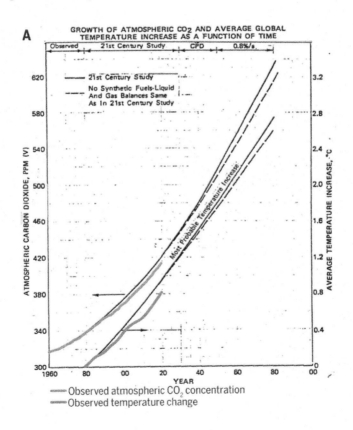

Observed atmospheric CO₂ concentration
Observed temperature change

The authors of a recent paper[1] explain:

Our findings demonstrate that ExxonMobil didn't just know "something" about global warming decades ago — they knew as much as academic and government scientists knew. But whereas those scientists worked to communicate what they knew, ExxonMobil worked to deny it — including overemphasizing uncertainties, denigrating climate models, mythologizing global cooling, feigning ignorance about the discernibility of human-caused warming, and staying silent about the possibility of stranded fossil fuel assets in a carbon-constrained world.

The charade never ends.

At COP 28 to be hosted in the United Arab Emirates, *Sultan Al Jaber, chief of Abu Dhabi National Oil Company, has been named "president" of the global climate talks.* Critics call it a "full-scale capture of the UN climate talks by a petrostate national oil company and its associated fossil fuel lobbyists."[2]

Scientists are warning privately that global temperatures will climb higher than the +1.5 degrees "Net-Zero" target even as government and business discussions prepare to "align with a 1.5°C pathway."

In their *State of Climate Action 2022* report[3], the **World Resources Institute** tells us exactly what must happen to achieve the near-term, 1.5°C-aligned targets:

---

[1] "Assessing ExxonMobil's global warming projections" by G. Supran, S. Rahmstorf, And N. Oreskes, *Science*, 13 Jan 2023 https://doi.org/10.1126/science.abk0063

[2] "UAE to launch Cop28 presidency with oil boss tipped for leading role" by Fiona Harvey, *The Guardian*, January 11, 2023 https://www.theguardian.com/world/2023/jan/11/uae-to-launch-cop28-presidency-with-oil-boss-tipped-for-leading-role

[3] *State of Climate Action 2022.* World Resources Institute. https://doi.org/10.46830/wrirpt.22.00028. Version 1.2. October 2022. (The diagram "summary of progress towards 2030 goals" is on page 168)

- Phase out coal power generation six times faster — equivalent to retiring 925 average-sized coal plants per year.
- Improve the energy intensity of building operations five times faster for commercial buildings and seven times faster for residential buildings.
- Lower the amount of carbon dioxide emitted per ton of cement produced over ten times faster.
- Expand public transportation systems, including metros, light-rail trains, and bus rapid transit networks, across the world's highest-emitting cities six times faster.
- Reduce the annual rate of deforestation 2.5 times faster — equivalent to avoiding deforestation across an area roughly equivalent to all arable land in Switzerland each year.
- Shift to healthier, more sustainable diets five times faster by lowering per capita consumption of ruminant meat to the equivalent of 2 burgers per week across Europe, the Americas, and Oceania.
- Phase out public financing for fossil fuels five times faster — equivalent to reducing subsidies by an average of $69 billion per year.

Unfortunately — and predictably —

of the 40 indicators assessed in the report, **none** are on track to reach their 2030 targets!

And still the mainstream media is silent.

The report warns[4]:

*Even if current 2030 climate pledges are fully implemented, scientists estimate that we will face warming of roughly **2.4°C to 2.8°C** by the end of the century (IPCC 2022b; Climate Action Tracker 2021). This future represents an unrecognizable world of hardship in which some regions are no longer habitable, agricultural fields either dry up or are inundated with floodwaters, greater swaths of forests burn for longer, an increasing number of species face extinction, and rising seas swallow coastlines. In this world, climate impacts perpetuate injustice and inequity, with those who often have the fewest resources to adapt, namely historically marginalized communities, bearing the brunt of costs and impacts.*

Here's the dismal report card (see facing page)!

What would you do if your child brought this progress report home?

We can't blame COVID, the War in Ukraine, or natural disasters. The world-as-we-know-it is ending because of a startling failure of our leaders and our institutions.

Our economic system is disconnected from reality – from Nature, from the needs of the people, and from the next generation, many of whom know that they are facing dire prospects through no fault of their own.

---

[4]*State of Climate Action 2022*. World Resources Institute. https://doi.org/10.46830/wrirpt.22.00028. Version 1.2. October 2022. (The diagram "summary of progress towards 2030 goals" is on page 168)

Summary of progress towards 2030 targets

TRAJECTORY OF CHANGE   ACCELERATION FACTOR*

>10x   **Exponential Unlikely**   2x   **Exponential Likely**   5x   **Exponential Possible**

Note: We use "exponential" as shorthand for various forms of rapid, non-linear change. But not all non-linear change will be perfectly exponential.

ON TRACK: Change is occurring at or above the pace required to achieve the 2030 targets.

None

OFF TRACK: Change is heading in the right direction at a promising, but insufficient pace

6x*	Share of zero-carbon sources in electricity generation
1.7x	Share of electricity in the industry sector's final energy demand
5x*	Share of electric vehicles in light-duty vehicle sales
>10x*	Share of battery electric vehicles and fuel cell electric vehicles in bus sales
1.5x*d	Reforestation
1.3x	Ruminant meat productivity

WELL OFF TRACK: Change is heading in the right direction, but well below the required pace

5x	Carbon intensity of electricity generation
6x	Share of unabated coal in electricity generation
5x Commercial 7x Residential	Energy intensity of building operations*
>10x	Carbon intensity of global cement production
>10x	Green hydrogen production
6x*	Number of kilometers of rapid transit (metro, light-rail and bus rapid transit) per 1M inhabitants (in the top 50 emitting cities)
>10x*	Number of kilometers of high-quality bike lanes per 1,000 inhabitants (in the top 50 emitting cities)
>10x	Share of electric vehicles in the light-duty vehicle fleet
Ins. data*	Share of battery electric vehicles and fuel cell electric vehicles in medium- and heavy-duty vehicle sales
Ins. data*	Share of sustainable aviation fuels in global aviation fuel supply
Ins. data*	Share of zero-emission fuel in maritime shipping fuel supply
2.5x*	Deforestation
6x	Crop yields
5x	Ruminant meat consumption*

WELL OFF TRACK: Change is heading in the right direction, but well below the required pace

>10x!	Technological carbon removal
>10x	Global total climate finance
>10x	Global public climate finance
>10x	Global private climate finance
>10x	Share of global emissions under mandatory corporate climate risk disclosure
8x	Median carbon price in jurisdictions with pricing systems
5x*	Total public financing for fossil fuels

WRONG DIRECTION: Change is heading in the wrong direction, and a U-turn is needed

N/A	Share of unabated fossil gas in electricity generation
N/A	Carbon intensity of global steel production
N/A	Share of kilometers traveled by passenger cars
N/A*	Mangrove loss
N/A	Agricultural production GHG emissions

INSUFFICIENT DATA: Data are insufficient to assess the gap in action required for 2030

Ins. data	Carbon intensity of building operations*
Ins. data	Retrofitting rate of buildings
Ins. data	Carbon intensity of land-based passenger transport
Ins. data*	Peatland degradation
Ins. data*	Peatland restoration
Ins. data*]	Mangrove restoration
Ins. data	Share of food production lost
Ins. data	Food waste

And incremental changes won't make a difference – not any more.

In 2021, only 26% of our electricity production came from renewables. And fossil fuel expansion continues. Even Germany, long considered an environmental leader, has given the green light to a *coal mine expansion* in the city of Lützerath!

What's going on?

Paul Polman asks – *"Can leadership levels rise faster than sea levels?"*[5] His point is that the thing that still isn't being given enough attention is actually what we need most of in the year ahead: **courageous leadership**. For Polman, three of the most needed leadership characteristics are:

1) **setting targets the world needs**, not just the ones they know they can deliver.
2) asking **greater responsibility for impacts** of their business that are beyond their immediate control.
3) **CEOs collaborating** to collectively drive the transformative changes no company can deliver alone.

Waiting for flashes of "leadership courage" to break through the darkness is not enough. And the history of corporate leadership is not very encouraging either.

Capitalism – the driving ideology behind how our world functions – is itself in dire need of regeneration (or outright replacement). In his book *Confronting Capitalism: Real Solutions for a Troubled Economic System*, our co-author - **Philip Kotler** - lists 14 critical flaws of Capitalism[6]:

---

[5] "Can leadership levels rise faster than sea levels?" by Paul Polman, *LinkedIn*, January 17, 2023, https://www.linkedin.com/pulse/2023-can-leadership-levels-rise-faster-than-sea-paul-polman-/
[6] For more information visit www.fixcapitalism.com

1. Proposes little or no solution to persisting poverty

2. Generates a growing level of income and wealth inequality

3. Fails to pay a living wage to billions of workers

4. May not provide enough human jobs in the face of growing automation

5. Doesn't charge businesses with the full social costs of their activities

6. Exploits the environment and natural resources in the absence of regulation

7. Creates business cycles and economic instability

8. Emphasizes individualism and self-interest at the expense of community and the commons

9. Encourages high consumer debt and leads to a growing financially driven rather than producer-driven economy

10. Allows politicians and business interests to collaborate and subvert the economic interests of the majority of citizens

11. Favors short-run profit planning over long-run investment planning

12. Should have regulations regarding product quality, safety, truth in advertising, and anti-competitive behavior

13. Tends to focus narrowly on GDP growth

14. Needs to bring social values and happiness into the market equation

We have run out of easy choices.

Colonialism evolved into Capitalism and Globalization, but the fundamentals of exploitation and extraction have not changed. It's time to look outside the bubble of the **dominant mindset** of the "market." Markets aren't regenerative. They're extractive and destructive.

What about our institutions? Our governments? The UN? The World Economic Forum?

They are guilty of **institutional betrayal**.

What's that, you ask? According to psychologist **Dr. Jennifer Freyd**,[7] *institutional betrayal* refers to wrongdoings perpetrated by an institution upon individuals dependent on that institution, including failure to prevent or respond supportively to wrongdoings by individuals committed within the context of the institution. This includes:

1) Institutions harming those dependent on the institution.
2) the failure to prevent or respond supportively to wrongdoings within the institution when there is a reasonable expectation of protection.
3) The effects of institutional betrayal are both pragmatic and psychological.

Surely, we know by now that the governments, companies, institutions, and "leaders" who brought us to this mess are *least* qualified to lead us out of it.

Dr. Freyd defines **institutional courage**[8] as well: the *commitment to seek the truth and engage in moral action, despite unpleasantness, risk, and short-term cost. It is a pledge to protect and care for those who depend on the institution. **It is a compass oriented to the common good of individuals, the institution, and the world.** It is a force that transforms institutions into more accountable, equitable, healthy places for everyone.*

WELCOME TO THE ZERO-TRUST SOCIETY

The USA, and increasingly the rest of the world, is becoming more and more fragmented – with COVID being blamed[9], in part, for the *death of the Common Good.*

---

[7] https://dynamic.uoregon.edu/jjf/institutionalbetrayal/
[8] *Institutional Betrayal and Institutional Courage* by Jennifer J. Freyd, PhD
website: https://dynamic.uoregon.edu/jjf/institutionalbetrayal/
[9] "The pandemic killed the common good" Samuel Goldman, *The Week* July 21, 2021
https://theweek.com/feature/opinion/1002821/the-common-good-is-a-pandemic-casualty

If we cannot agree – as nations, as institutions, and as individuals – on actions to save the Planet, then *what hope can we have at all?*

We have been betrayed by our leaders, misleaders and the institutions they lead. How did this happen?

Robert Reich traces the roots of America's disenchantment with the Common Good[10], with government in particular:

Watergate represented something of a turning point for America, in terms of our faith in the presidency. Nixon was a scoundrel, by almost any definition of the term. He was worried far more about his own power, and maintaining it, than the institutions of government. Other presidents before him had also put a greater priority on their political survival than on the institutions of democracy, but Nixon was an extreme example. No one in the post-war era had so abused government. Because of that, the generation of Baby Boomers were shocked into a form of cynicism that was very different from the belief in government and the social contract up to that point.

Reich elaborates:

Trump has been a wake-up call to many people that cynicism is a self-fulfilling prophecy. It can be very destructive. We need to rebuild our institutions and find a common good.

In our book[11], *Brand Activism: From Purpose to Action*, we discussed the "trust crisis," and referred to the **Edelman Global Trust Barometer**. Unfortunately, **we no longer trust the trust barometer!**

---

[10] "Robert Reich: How to Resurrect the Common Good" interview by Hope Reese, *JSTOR Daily* March 16, 2018 https://daily.jstor.org/robert-reich-interview/?utm_source=pocket_reader

[11] *Brand Activism: From Purpose to Action* by Christian Sarkar and Philip Kotler, IDEA BITE PRESS, 2018

Why? *The Guardian* revealed[12] that Edelman has signed about \$9.6m worth of deals with the Saudis, while simultaneously urging businesses to stand up for human rights. Incidentally, *The Guardian* also states that Edelman is *not* the only US firm doing business for the government of Saudi Arabia. **McKinsey & Company**, **Boston Consulting Group**, **Hogan Lovells** and **Qorvis Communications** are a few named, and there are many more. Remember **Jared Kushner**? He pocketed \$2 billion to start up his own private-equity company[13].

Richard Edelman has called climate change "the biggest crisis we face as a society," proclaiming that "we think very carefully about which businesses we work for." Apparently, that advice doesn't apply to his company. Edelman's clients have included ExxonMobil, Shell, Chevron, the pro-coal National Mining Association and the American Petroleum Institute (API), a lobbying group for some of the biggest fossil fuel companies.

The Guardian once again:

Edelman's work for API has proven particularly lucrative, netting the PR firm nearly \$440m since 2008. Energy Citizens, an astroturf group that Edelman helped launch for API, contributed to the defeat of climate efforts in Congress. One study found that between 1989 and 2020 Edelman conducted at least 60 "engagements" for oil, gas, coal, steel, and rail clients–more than any other PR firm.

Even as we write these words, **Exxon Mobil Corp** posted a \$56 billion net profit for 2022, taking in about \$6.3 million per

---

[12] "The American PR firm helping Saudi Arabia clean up its image" by Adam Lowenstein, *The Guardian*, Dec 22, 2022 https://www.theguardian.com/world/2022/dec/22/edelman-saudi-arabia-pr-image
[13] "REPORT: JARED KUSHNER'S \$2 BILLION SAUDI CHECK APPEARS EVEN MORE COMICALLY CORRUPT THAN PREVIOUSLY THOUGHT" by Bess Levin, Vanity Fair, May 23,2022
https://www.vanityfair.com/news/2022/05/jared-kushner-affinity-partners-saudi-arabia

hour last year, and setting not only a company record but a *historic high* for the Western oil industry.

This sort of institutional betrayal accelerates us on the path to a **zero-trust world**.

What does a zero-trust world look like? **The core concept of zero trust is simple: assume everything and everyone is hostile by default.**
Another way to see it is to view it as *social collapse*.

In a zero-trust world, there is no Common Good. There is **no Truth** either. It's every individual for themselves, and at best, their families. Threats – real and non-existent – are everywhere. Violence is the way of life. There is no collective security, or even trash pickup. Conflict is embraced as a model for everyday living. Threats and bullying are everyday occurrences. Think of a society run by warlords, by mafia bosses, by autocrats. Guns everywhere. Governance is by fear, intimidation and militarization. The state is a man with an ideology and a "plan."

Sound familiar? We are at a fork in the road. Either civilization goes down in hate, war, violence, and collapse, or we turn, finally, to a path of peaceful **regeneration**, beginning with the **Common Good**.

But what is the Common Good?

In ordinary political discourse, the "common good" refers to those facilities – whether material, cultural or institutional – that the members of a community provide to all members in order to fulfill a relational obligation they all have to care for certain interests that they have in common. Some canonical examples of the common good in a modern liberal democracy include: the road system; public parks; police protection and public safety; courts and the judicial system; public schools; museums and cultural institutions; public transportation; civil liberties, such as the freedom of speech and the freedom of association; the system of property; clean air and clean water; and national defense.[14]

	PUBLIC GOODS	COMMON GOODS	GLOBAL COMMON GOODS
FEATURES	· Available to all; others cannot be prevented from enjoying them (non-excludable); · Equally beneficial for users who have paid and those who have not contributed to their financing or have contributed to a lesser extent; · Use of public goods does not diminish their value or availability (non-rivalrous); · Requires mediation; ownership is with the state, not markets; · Provision corresponds with the state but can be delegated to third parties (private companies); · In contrast to common goods, does not convey a sense of commonality among a group of individuals, but rather a political binding constituted collectively within a particular society (usually a country); · The economic framing has been criticized for centering on individual wellbeing. One different approach is 'global public goods' that benefit everyone in the world in the present and future and focus on planetary wellbeing.	· Available at no cost to anyone who wishes to make use of them (non-excludable); · Promotes benefit for all (not advantaging any one group or class), but if one person uses these resources, it reduces another person's ability to use them (rivalrous); · Ownership belongs to everyone – shared resources; managed by custom, tradition, grassroots practices etc.; · However, when they become scarcer, governments may exercise their sovereignty within their jurisdictional borders and intervene (e.g. establishing quotas, regulations and other control and distribution mechanisms); · Can be created by public or private goods (e.g. research can create common goods); · In the singular, the term is understood as the collective requirement/desire of any society. Yet, more difficult to define as its meaning has changed over time; · A new framework of 'common good' is needed, but this is difficult to achieve in today's large and pluralistic societies. The politics of the common good has been reduced to the level of communities or, at most, to a country level.	· Like public goods, GCGs are also non-excludable and non-rivalrous, but are differentiated by having benefits that cross borders and being global in scope; · Like common goods, GCGs have a shared or common interest; · When such commonality is related to shared values of enforcement, production, distribution, access, preservation, protection etc. for GCGs, we are also talking about global citizenship; · States cannot act extraterritorially on GCGs without global consensus; · States might recognize the rights of the world citizens to their commons, but a 'global guardian' to provide or guarantee GCGs would be difficult to set up because States can only exercise coercive power within the limits of their territory; · To construct a framework for the GCG thus remains highly aspirational. Even though the UN exists, almost all of its actions on GCGs (e.g. conventions) are soft law and not legally binding.
EXAMPLES	Street lighting National defense	Fishing Forests Beaches	Human Rights Oceans Ozone layer Antarctica (the only asset protected by international treaty)
USE IN HIGER EDUCATION	The right to access to higher education is a public good. We cannot prevent other people from being holders of the same right (non-excludable), nor can the exercise of such right by one person reduce the ability of another to exercise it (non-rivalrous).	Higher education as a whole is also a common good. For example, according to Argentine law, all people after completing secondary studies have the right to enter the University (the grade point average does not matter and there are no entrance exams). It is not excludable, but it is rival because public supply does not grow at the same rate as demand.	Knowledge drives the generation of further knowledge and is key to human development. For that reason, it is considered a GCG. That said, some knowledge may be protected by the Intellectual Property Right (IPR) e.g. a patent placed on a new drug. However, the belief that knowledge, in a broad sense, is a GCG is so ingrained that certain products protected by IPRs are being contested by social movements.

---

[14] *Stanford Encyclopedia of Philosophy,* https://plato.stanford.edu/entries/common-good/

This diagram explains the difference between "public goods," "common goods," and "global common goods":[15]

The Common Good thus is the pathway to us working together. **Without the Common Good, there is no regeneration.**

We should also clarify here that **the Common Good is not the same as "shared value"**[16] - *the corporate mantra that seems to have gone nowhere.*

The idea of **regeneration** is not a new one.[17] It is Nature's way. In business, we already see it in use, almost as a replacement for "sustainability," and yet there is a growing sense of unease, a fear that, this too will be turned into another *buzzword* that distracts us from what we need to do now – which is to **act decisively** to save our lives and life on Earth, our **Common Home.**

---

[15] Sabzalieva, E., & Quinteiro, J. A. (2022). Public goods, common goods and global common goods: A brief explanation. UNESCO IESALC. https://www.iesalc.unesco.org/en/2022/01/07/public-goods-common-goods-and-global- common-goods-a-brief-explanation/

[16] "Creating Shared Value" by Michael Porter and Mark R. Kramer Harvard Business Review Jan-Feb 2011 https://hbr.org/2011/01/the-big-idea-creating-shared-value

[17] In the *medical* field regeneration usually refers to the "process of replacing, engineering or regenerating human or animal cells, tissues or organs to restore or establish normal function."

Wendell Berry describes the soil as "the great connector of lives, the source and destination of all. It is the healer and restorer and resurrector, by which disease passes into health, age into youth, death into life. Without proper care for it we can have no community, because without proper care for it we can have no life." Thus, the soil is connected to the life of the community and life itself. **Mother Nature is the regenerative force** – replacing, restoring, renewing, and regenerating itself, as it dances the seasons of life.

The Ellen MacArthur Foundation describes **regenerative agriculture** as "a broad set of food production methods with two clear and complementary outcomes: the production of high-quality food and the improvement of the surrounding natural ecosystem." The principal idea is a shift "from extractive, linear thinking that prioritizes high yields above all else, to establishing cycles of regeneration." " Regenerative agriculture" - website Ellen MacArthur Foundation https://ellenmacarthurfoundation.org/articles/regenerative-agriculture

The deliberate destruction of Public Trust, through well-funded political tactics of polarization, is a deliberate way to create chaos, subvert democracy, and create a society where only the powerful get (or take) what they want.

Regeneration is too important, too crucial, to leave to the corporate consultants or the non-profits that profit from the status quo.

We must pay special attention to **community** activities at the local level because regeneration is *place-based*.

It is *our* neighborhood, after all. **Douglas Rushkoff**, whose latest book *Survival of the Richest: Escape Fantasies of the Tech Billionaires,* is about the absurd mindset and dystopian strategies of the hyper-rich, explains[18]:

"You live in a bad neighborhood. What do you do? Make enough money to get out of the bad neighborhood and get somewhere better. That was good. I get it. It's beautiful. Now, I look at it and go, "Wait a minute. The whole world is becoming a bad neighborhood." You can't earn enough money to get out of this neighborhood. It's like, 'No, we're finally at that place. Don't move.' You can't move. You got to actually make the neighborhood a place that's livable."

There is no place to run away to.

Places need regeneration now more than ever – thanks to the impact of Globalization and marginalization of local communities which has played out over the past thirty years.

Add to this the effects of climate change, food insecurity, economic disruption, and the lingering effects of COVID, and it

---

[18] Douglas Rushkoff: "The Ultimate Exit Strategy" on *The Great Simplification with Nate Hagens* podcast, Episode 36, September 14, 2022 https://www.thegreatsimplification.com/episode/36-douglas-rushkoff

is clear that **regeneration is an imperative for all** – from neighborhood and street regeneration, to the city, to the region and state level, all the way to national and cross-border institutions.

Instead of allowing the Common Good to die, we must work to regenerate it – **one community at a time**.

Bottom up, top-down, working together, to make the *Big Shift* – from a World of Extraction to a World of Regeneration. A world driven by justice, not profits.

REGENERATION IS THE BIG SHIFT

So where do we find other paths? Where do we find institutions *with* institutional courage?

Our search for regeneration led us to a **model for regeneration** developed by a conclave of 64 grass-roots organizations and 80 leaders in the summer of 2019 – the **United Frontline Table** (UFT). Their work – which proposes a **Regenerative Economy**, is based on *deep listening* and *collaboration* from *frontline communities*[19]. This thinking is not generally encountered in the board room.

Here's what they say:

We must build visionary economy that is very different than the one we now are in. This requires stopping the bad while at the same time as building the new. We must change the rules to redistribute resources and power to local communities. Just transition initiatives

---

[19] The United Frontline Table (UFT) is comprised of the following networks, alliances, coalitions, and their members, with the cooperation of movement support organizations: Asian Pacific Environmental Network, Center for Economic Democracy, Climate Justice Alliance, Dēmos , Grassroots Global Justice Alliance, Gulf Coast Center for Law and Policy, Indigenous Environmental Network, It Takes Roots, Kentuckians for the Commonwealth, Labor Network for Sustainability, New Economy Coalition, People's Action, Right to the City Alliance, The Rising Majority, Trade Unions for Energy Democracy, and UPROSE.
READ: *A People's Orientation to a Regenerative Economy*, United Frontline Table, June 2020
https://climatejusticealliance.org/wp-content/uploads/2020/06/ProtectRepairInvestTransformdoc24s.pdf

are shifting from dirty energy to energy democracy, from funding highways to expanding public transit, from incinerators and landfills to zero waste, from industrial food systems to food sovereignty, from gentrification to community land rights, from military violence to peaceful resolution, and from rampant destructive development to ecosystem restoration. Core to a just transition is deep democracy in which workers and communities have control over the decisions that affect their daily lives.[20]

	EXTRACTIVE ECONOMY	**REGENERATIVE ECONOMY**
WORLDVIEW	Consumerism, Colonial Mindset	Caring & Sacredness
PURPOSE	Enclosure of Wealth & Power	Ecological & Social Well-being
GOVERNANCE	Militarism	Deep Democracy
RESOURCES	Extraction - Dig, Burn, Dump	Regeneration
WORK	Exploitation	Cooperation

source: Climate Justice Alliance

The job-to-be-done? A **transformation to total regeneration.** This is nothing short of a revisioning of the past 400 years. It means regenerating our worldview (mindsets), the purpose of the economy, our government, work, how we use resources, the place of the individual, and the common infrastructure needed – all in the context of the **Common Good** and **place** – our communities, the space we live in.

---

[20] https://climatejusticealliance.org/just-transition/

An illustration of the "just transition" from an **extractive economy** to a **regenerative economy** looks like this:

The shift to a true regenerative economy means **everything must change**.

Justice is *the* guiding strategy. So just imagine the word "regenerative" used as an *adjective*, added in front of every activity, industry, or domain of knowledge we hold dear. For example: regenerative agriculture, regenerative health, regenerative industry, regenerative business, regenerative leadership, regenerative economics, regenerative ideology, regenerative justice... the list is endless.

THE
BIG *SHIFT*

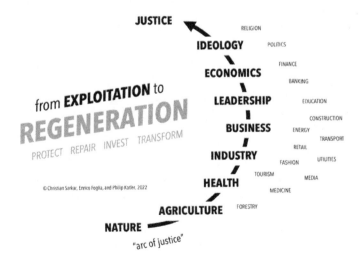

JUSTICE
RELIGION
IDEOLOGY
POLITICS
FINANCE
ECONOMICS
BANKING
from **EXPLOITATION** to
LEADERSHIP
EDUCATION
REGENERATION
CONSTRUCTION
BUSINESS
ENERGY
TRANSPORT
PROTECT REPAIR INVEST TRANSFORM
RETAIL
INDUSTRY
FASHION
UTILITIES
TOURISM
© Christian Sarkar, Enrico Foglia, and Philip Kotler, 2022
MEDIA
HEALTH
MEDICINE
AGRICULTURE
FORESTRY
NATURE
"arc of justice"

What will make the adjective true?

Can every human activity be more regenerative? And if so, how?

In theory, every human activity has the potential to be made more regenerative, meaning that it can be designed in a way that supports the health and restoration of natural and social ecosystems and communities, rather than causing harm.

In practice, making all our activities fully regenerative is a frustrating, complex and even life-threatening task that requires systemic changes in the way we live and work.

A DECLARATION OF INTERDEPENDENCE

What is needed now more than ever is a **declaration of interdependence**, according to **Henry Mintzberg**, who rightly worries that our world has reached the limits of growth driven by the pursuit of individual rights at the expense of shared responsibilities.

He proposes the following resolutions[21]:

- Balance begins when each of us decides how we shall become part of the solution. By doing nothing, we remain part of the problem.
- We advance to **action in our communitie**s, networked to consolidate a global movement for *peaceful reformation.*
- We commit to the ideals of social conscience, fair trade, and good government, to replace the dogma of imbalance—that greed is good, markets are sufficient, and governments are suspect. We explore our human resourcefulness by resisting our exploitation as human resources.

---

[21] *The Declaration of Our Interdependence*, Henry Mintzberg https://ourinterdependence.org/

- We build **worthy institutions** in all three sectors of society — departments in government, enterprises in business, associations in communities — from the ground up, with widespread engagement that carries *individual* leadership into *collective* communityship.
- At the tables of public policy, we strive to replace the compromises of self-interest with the coalescing of common interest.
- We challenge the rampant **corruption** that is legal as vigorously as we expect our governments to prosecute the overt corruption that is criminal.
- Sustainable global balance requires substantial global government. We call on all **democratic nations to rally for lasting peace**, by *containing* any power that aims to dominate while holding economic globalization in its place, namely the marketplace.

Mintzberg tells us:

*These resolutions require concerted action, **not** by centrally orchestrated planning so much as through a **groundswell** of initiatives by concerned citizens the world over, to restrain our worst tendencies while encouraging our best. For the future of our planet and our progeny, this is the time to get our collective act together.*[22]

The **Declaration of Interdependence** is thus a call for a **peaceful revolution**. Mintzberg declares[23]: "**businesses** have to contribute in a constructive way, **governments** have to do the work of protecting us from imbalance, and the **plural sector** associations have to help drive the changes in government and

---

[22] *The Declaration of Our Interdependence*, Henry Mintzberg https://ourinterdependence.org/

[23] "The Declaration of Interdependence – an interview with Henry Mintzberg" by Christian Sarkar *Activistbrands.com* January 30, 2020 https://www.activistbrands.com/the-declaration-of-interdependence-an-interview-with-henry-mintzbeg/

business. Let's read the declaration, and note the emphasis on **fighting corruption**.

THE DECLARATION *of* INTERDEPENDENCE

We hold these truths to be self-evident, that all people are created dependent —on each other, our earth, and its climate—endowed with the inalienable responsibility to maintain justice, liberty, and affiliation for all. Thus our societies must sustain balance across public sector governments that are respected, private sector businesses that are responsible, and plural sector communities that are robust. Some societies retain this balance; others have lost it; many never had it. We propose the following resolutions to guide the rebalancing of society:

➤ **Balance begins** when each of us decides how we shall become part of the solution. By doing nothing, we remain part of the problem.

➤ **We advance to action in our communities**, networked to consolidate a global movement for peaceful reformation.

➤ **We commit to the ideals** of social conscience, fair trade, and good government, to replace the dogma of imbalance—that greed is good, markets are sufficient, and governments are suspect. We explore our human resourcefulness by resisting our exploitation as human resources.

➤ **We build** worthy institutions in all three sectors of society— departments in government, enterprises in business, associations in communities—from the ground up, with widespread engagement that carries individual leadership into collective communityship.

➤ **At the tables of public policy**, we strive to replace the compromises of self-interest with the coalescing of common interest.

➤ **We challenge the rampant corruption that is legal** as vigorously as we expect our governments to prosecute the overt corruption that is criminal.

➤ Sustainable global balance requires **substantial global government**. We call on all democratic nations to rally for lasting peace, by containing any power that aims to dominate while holding economic globalization in its place, namely the marketplace.

These resolutions require **concerted action**, not by centrally orchestrated planning so much as through a groundswell of initiatives by concerned citizens the world over, to restrain our worst tendencies while encouraging our best. **For the future of our planet and our progeny, this is the time to get our collective act together.**

ourinterdependence.org

In Indian Vedic tradition, the idea of interdependence is contained in the Sanskrit phrase: वसुधैव कुटुम्बकम् (**Vasudhaiva Kutumbakam**) which means "The Entire World is a Family."

Why is this so difficult to comprehend and embrace?

REGENERATION OF THE COMMON GOOD

Here are 7 questions we seek to answer:

1) How do we define regeneration?
2) What does the **process of regeneration** look like?
3) **What** specifically do we plan on regenerating?
4) **Where** does regeneration take place?
5) **Who** does the regenerating?
6) **Where** should *we* begin?
7) How can *you* **make a difference?**

The etymology of the word **regeneration** is traced to the mid-14 century, *regeneracioun*, "act of regenerating or producing anew," originally spiritual, also of the Resurrection, from Old French *regeneracion* (Modern French *regénération*) and directly from Late Latin *regenerationem* "a being born again," noun of action from past participle stem of Latin *regenerare* "make over, generate again," from *re-* "again" + *generare* "bring forth, beget, produce," from *genus* "race, kind."[24] Originally theological, "radical spiritual change in an individual accomplished by the action of God;" of animal tissue, "power or process of growing again," early 15c.; of forests, 1888.

Here are some other traditional definitions of **regeneration**:

- "the act of improving a place or system, especially by making it more active or successful" [25] – *Cambridge dictionary*

---

[24] https://www.etymonline.com

[25] https://dictionary.cambridge.org/dictionary/english/regeneration

- the process of being "restored to a better, higher, or more worthy state"[26]

It was **Bill Reed**[27] who emphasized the regenerative role of designers and stakeholders in creating a whole system of mutually beneficial relationships. His diagram on the "Trajectory of Environmentally Responsible Design" is a classic – which has been beautifully adapted by others, including **Daniel Christian Wahl**. Our **adaptation** focuses on the **Common Good**, because, frankly, without it, regeneration is destined to become just another green-washing buzzword.

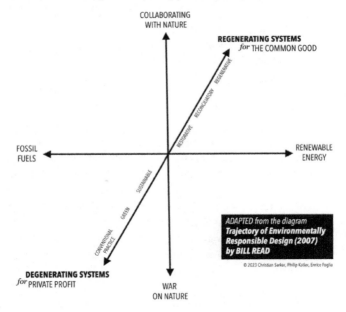

[26] https://www.merriam-webster.com/dictionary/regenerating

[27] "Shifting from 'sustainability' to regeneration" by Bill Reed 2007 *Building Research & Information*, 35:6, 674-680, DOI: 10.1080/09613210701475753

https://www.tandfonline.com/doi/full/10.1080/09613210701475753

NOTE: Daniel Christian Wahls' adaptation of Reed's work is important because it situates this regenerative design framework as a tool for redesigning culture. SEE: "Sustainability is not enough: we need regenerative cultures" by Daniel Christian Wahl, March 15, 2017 https://designforsustainability.medium.com/sustainability-is-not-enough-we-need-regenerative-cultures-4abb3c78e68b

Regeneration is a *process* of rebuilding or renewal of the **Common Good** – taking an **asset**, **resource**, **ecosystem**, **individual**, **family**, **organization**, **community**, or **place**, from crisis and collapse to recovery and regeneration. There are **9 Domains** *of* the **Common Good**: Social, Economics, Nature, Work, Culture, Media, Law, Technology, and Politics. The *process* *of* *regeneration* follows **indigenous traditions**: to *protect*, *repair*, *invest*, *transform* and *learn* – rooted in the past and *looking forward*, **seven generations** ahead. Regeneration includes **5 Worlds**, interconnected and interdependent, the **individual**, **community**, **work**, the **Nation**, and the **Planet**.

REGENERATION *of* **THE COMMON GOOD**

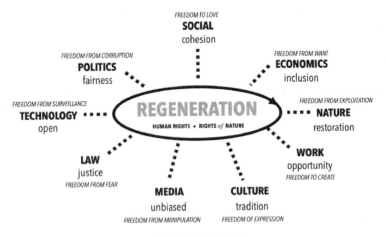

© Christian Sarkar, Enrico Foglia, and Philip Kotler, 2022

Our position is this. The Climate Crisis and the Collapse of Society are both symptoms of the same fatal sickness: *the destruction of the Common Good.* We cannot compartmentalize the climate and separate it from the rest of society or our activities.

Even Bill Gates[28] gets this - to an extent:

When I started this work, my biggest focus was global health, because it's the worst inequity in the world and it's a solvable problem. That's still the case today. But as time went on — and as the disastrous consequences of a warming world became more evident — it became clear that you can't improve life for the world's poorest without also tackling climate change.

Climate change and global health are inextricably linked. Hotter temperatures will make poverty reduction harder by increasing food insecurity and the prevalence of infectious diseases and diverting resources away from those who need them the most. It's a vicious cycle. The poorer a community is, the more vulnerable it is to climate change. And the more impacted a community is by extreme weather events, the more entrenched in poverty it becomes. To break the cycle, we need to make progress on both problems at the same time.

When I talk to people about this, I often hear the same response: "There isn't enough time or money to solve both at the same time." But this idea that we can only tackle one thing at a time is just wrong. I'm stubborn in my belief that with the right innovations and delivery channels to get them to the vulnerable, we're capable of making progress on lots of big problems at once — even at a time when the world faces multiple crises.

Why stop there, Bill? Why not look at *all of it*? What is stopping us from addressing the world's most urgent challenges? Why can't billionaires support the Common Good?

---

[28] "My message in India: To fight climate change, improve global health" by Bill Gates, *GatesNotes* February 22, 2023 https://www.gatesnotes.com/My-message-in-India

Let's introduce the **9 Domains of the Common Good** – each ripe for regeneration. We cannot regenerate these domains independently – rather they feed each other. Each community will have to discuss, debate, and define their own views on the Common Good, taking into account the *place* they call home.

- **Social regeneration:** creating a vibrant and thriving local community which values tolerance, respect, and justice for all its members. It aims to restore social trust and strengthen the bonds within a neighborhood, including through community wealth-building initiatives. To achieve this, efforts are made to increase access to education and encourage inclusiveness within the community. The ultimate goal is to build resilient communities with a high quality of life. The community has a right to have a say in the decisions that affect it and to have its views and concerns taken into account. Social regeneration includes the *needs of the community*: food, housing, healthcare, education, infrastructure, and good governance.

- **Economic regeneration:** an economy which fosters community wealth-building. Investments are made to foster local economic development, creating job opportunities for community members. The "economy of essentials" is focused on delivering on local needs, shortening the supply chain of essential goods and services, and reducing the impact on both humans and the environment. It prioritizes local production and manufacturing, while improving workers' lives. It also includes local infrastructure development, targeted community level education and training, and support for small, local businesses and startups. Economic regeneration also includes *just* taxation of the rich and corporations.

- **Regeneration of Nature**: comprehensive protection of the wild and cessation of activities that damage the ecosystems we depend on for life (air, water, land). The *Rights of Nature* are recognized, but not financialized. The regeneration of nature refers to efforts to restore and revitalize natural environments that have been damaged or degraded, and includes activities like reforestation, habitat restoration, pollution abatement and cessation, species recovery, climate change mitigation and adaptation, and rewilding.

- **Work regeneration:** a fair workplace which creates opportunity for *all* workers and is not extractive or exploitative. Workplace regeneration refers to efforts to revitalize and improve the work environment in order to create a more positive and fulfilling experience for employees; this begins with recognizing the worker as a partner in the company, not as "our most valuable asset" who is laid off at the first sign of economic difficulty. Of significance is the idea of a *workplace without fear*, where open and honest communication is rewarded, and employees are involved in decision-making processes, even perhaps in co-ownership.

- **Cultural regeneration:** the Cultural regeneration refers to efforts to revitalize and promote the cultural traditions, heritage, and identity of a community or region. This can involve a wide range of activities, such as: protecting, preserving and **regenerating cultural heritage**, traditions, languages, cultural artifacts, landmarks, and other elements of cultural heritage; promoting cultural traditions and supporting cultural organizations by funding museums, galleries, and performing arts groups; encouraging the continuation and celebration of traditional cultural practices, such as art, music, dance, and festivals; creating cultural education and outreach to help the public learn about and appreciate the cultural traditions of the community; developing regenerative tourism initiatives to attract "slow tourists" and showcase local cultural heritage. The goal of cultural regeneration is to help preserve and promote the cultural traditions and heritage of a community, and to contribute to the social and economic well-being of the region.

- **Media regeneration:** the demand that media serve the public interest. To make the media more impartial, several factors must be addressed: for starters, truth and objectivity must be primary drivers of coverage. Coverage should strive to present a variety of perspectives and voices, to ensure that a range of opinions is heard. The media should be free from any political or commercial influence and maintain its independence to report objectively. Media outlets should be diligent in verifying the information they report, and transparent about their sources. Community-owned media should be a priority, with transparency about funding sources, ownership structure, and any potential conflicts of interest. Media personnel should receive regular training on ethical and impartial journalism.

- **Regenerative Law:** where laws and the justice system create a society of hope for the future; Regeneration must embrace **Human Rights** *and* the **Rights of Nature**. Regenerative law is a framework for legal practice that is focused on creating positive change in individuals, organizations, and communities. It is based on the principles of regenerative justice and seeks to promote the well-being and growth of *all* stakeholders. Regenerative law may involve a variety of approaches, such as regenerative and restorative justice, transformative justice, and community-based justice.

- **Regenerative Technology:** is technology used in service of the common good – like a "public-value" digital platform which is owned by the community, rather than private VC-backed extractive companies. It focuses on open-source and co-creation rather than enclosure of the digital commons. Digital utility services may be owned by co-ops and the state, not by rent-seeking profiteers.

- **Regenerative Politics:** a political arena where politicians focus on solving problems for the common good. The approach prioritizes the well-being of the community and its members, along with Nature and the planet. It creates systems and policies that are restorative and regenerative, rather than extractive and destructive. Regenerative politics serves the needs of the community – and decisions are made with transparency and the engaged, deep participation of citizens.

Underlying these **9 domains** of regeneration is the **mind-shift** to regeneration– *a change in how we view the world*, our ideology, our identity, our thinking.

In 1965, **James Baldwin**[29] debated William F. Buckley Jr. at Cambridge University on the topic of racism and the American Dream. Baldwin explains that "reality" depends on our point of view – *"how you view the world is largely shaped by where you are in it."*

This makes our understanding of the world and our place in it dependent on the dominant narrative of the country, region, even family, that we live in. The banker and the board member

---

[29] https://youtu.be/mnYwcSxqhJc

may not be able to see the path to regeneration, because, in the words of **Upton Sinclair**: *"It is difficult to get a man to understand something, when his salary depends on his not understanding it."*

The shift from **self-interest** to **common-interest** is the pre-requisite for the shift to regeneration. There are two ways to achieve this shift – either intellectually, *followed by action*, or behaviorally, where we **act first**, and our thinking follows. For some, actions speak louder than words. For them it is better to get started on a regenerative project, and the mindset of regeneration will follow.

The Common Good is also about **freedom**. Not the freedom to loot and pollute, as Big Oil desires, but these 9 essential freedoms:

1) Freedom to love
2) Freedom from want
3) Freedom from exploitation
4) Freedom to create
5) Freedom of expression
6) Freedom from manipulation
7) Freedom from fear
8) Freedom from surveillance
9) Freedom from corruption

These 9 freedoms require a balance between the needs of society and the needs of the individual.

The key to building the Common Good is **Trust**, which is built through actions, behavior, and accountability. It also requires **deep democracy**.

The **Native Americans** had **no word for ownership** because the Great Plains were the roaming grounds of the buffalo, not land to be parceled, fenced, and sold off. Before Europeans colonized the West, there were an estimated 65 million buffalo roaming the plains. By the end of the century, there were fewer than a thousand – cut off from water and migration paths by *barbed wire.*

The privatization of Nature continues around the world to this day – with new proposals being made to financialize the ecosystem services provided by the Planet. Nature is being destroyed for the benefit of a few wealthy speculators. It is time to stop the private looting of the Commons.

We repeat:

Regeneration means *regenerating the Common Good.*

THE PROCESS OF REGENERATION

Regeneration is a process – applied to these 9 domains. Again, we turn to the **United Frontline Table**, the collective made up of grass roots and indigenous organizations, to define the process of regeneration[30]:

(1) **PROTECT**: to save, conserve, prevent collapse, or extinction; solutions must protect, not harm, our

---

[30] *A People's Orientation to a Regenerative Economy*, United Frontline Table, June 2020

communities – the people and the natural ecosystems around them.

(2) **REPAIR**: to restore or fix the damage; solutions must repair the harms of our extractive economy.

(3) **INVEST**: to dedicate resources to improvement; solutions must move non-extractive and equitable investments to our communities and workers; create/nurture new capabilities and skills that are required; and

(4) **TRANSFORM**: to enliven, make successful – with the final stage being one of thriving and flourishing – a state of stability and resiliency. Solutions must provide the foundation to transform relationships and structures so that they are rooted in respect, equity, and justice.

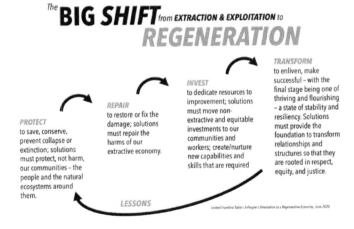

The **BIG SHIFT** from *EXTRACTION & EXPLOITATION* to *REGENERATION*

PROTECT
to save, conserve, prevent collapse or extinction; solutions must protect, not harm, our communities – the people and the natural ecosystems around them.

REPAIR
to restore or fix the damage; solutions must repair the harms of our extractive economy.

INVEST
to dedicate resources to improvement; solutions must move non-extractive and equitable investments to our communities and workers; create/nurture new capabilities and skills that are required

TRANSFORM
to enliven, make successful – with the final stage being one of thriving and flourishing – a state of stability and resiliency. Solutions must provide the foundation to transform relationships and structures so that they are rooted in respect, equity, and justice.

LESSONS

United Frontline Table's A People's Orientation to a Regenerative Economy, June 2020

Regeneration is a *dynamic process* – an extension of the famous *S-curve*.[31] In fact, there's a double, even triple S-curve.

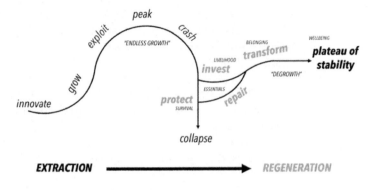

THE BIG SHIFT *to* REGENERATION

© 2022 Christian Sarkar, Enrico Foglia, and Philip Kotler

WHERE DOES REGENERATION HAPPEN?

Regeneration operates at five levels of **impact** – the **5 nested worlds** or *lifespaces* we live in:

1. **Individual:** the world of our personal lives – along with our families, relatives, and friends.
2. **Community:** the community we belong to – based on place but also in terms of interests and identity.
3. **Work**: the organizational world in which we earn our livelihoods. Before COVID, many people spent more time at work with their co-workers than with their immediate families!

---

[31] The sigmoid function used by Everett Rogers in his book *Diffusion of Innovations* (1962, Simon and Schuster)

4. **State**: the country or state we live in and feel allegiance to. Taking pride in our country is part of being a responsible citizen.

5. **Planet**: what does it mean to be a citizen of the planet? The state of the planet is now inextricably linked to the four other worlds we live in.

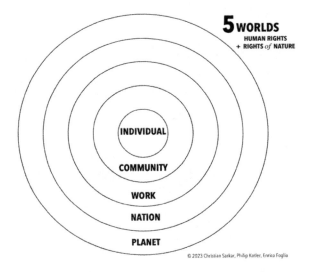

© 2023 Christian Sarkar, Philip Kotler, Enrico Foglia

Total regeneration integrates all 5 worlds:

- What does **individual** regeneration mean?
- What does **community** regeneration entail?
- How does **work** (a business, for example) become regenerative?
- What might **national** regenerative policies look like?
- What will it take to **stop the death of our planet**?
- How do we **integrate** these worlds?

It is the **world of work** and business that has dominated our economic and social lives – with the absurd measure of shareholder value-creation used as a yardstick for societal wellbeing.

Most of all, we must learn to view regeneration for what it really is – a process of transformation, of real change.

22 TESTS FOR REGENERATION

We've compiled a list of the **attributes of regeneration** as they apply to a **community.**

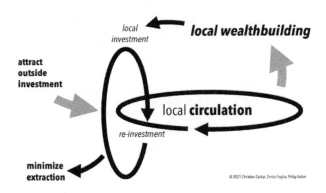

Here are our *22 Tests for Regeneration:*

1. Regeneration is **local** – it must be place-based.
2. Regeneration begins with **jobs to be done** – it starts with the urgent needs of the community. What does the community *value* most? What needs to happen to *create value for the community?*
3. Regeneration goes beyond **sustainability** – it cannot be a proponent or neutral to the Death of Nature; it must seek and employ renewable sources of energy and reverse the death-spiral our natural ecosystems are facing

4. Regeneration **creates community wealth** – it cannot enrich private shareholders while destroying public value

5. Regeneration strengthens existing community **assets, talents,** and **capabilities**

6. Regeneration **builds trust** – the relationships of the members of the community are strengthened by participation in community regeneration projects

7. Regeneration is **inclusive** – it includes all sectors and members of society without discrimination; it empowers and supports the young and marginalized

8. Regeneration takes **time** – progress can be gradual and requires patience (trust is not built overnight)

9. Regeneration requires **collaboration** – it drastically reduces the *distance* between Nature, organizations, and peoples – to build a **climate of solidarity** and interdependence and brings people and institutions (public, private, and plural) together to work on the **Common Good**

10. Regeneration is a function of **deep democracy** *and* **consensus building**

11. Regeneration builds **resilience**. At the end of a regenerative project, the project is able to maintain itself and continue doing good work without its original founders

12. Regeneration respects **Human Rights** starting with the **rights of indigenous communities** and an honest accounting for the atrocities of history (colonialism, genocide, ethnocide, slavery, incarceration, and exploitation)

13. Regeneration respects the **Rights of Nature**

14. Regeneration takes the **long-view** – it focuses on short-term impact but only in alignment with a long-term vision

15. Regeneration is **non-ideological** – decisions are based on evidence, facts, and *desired outcomes* which promote the common good

16. Regeneration **shares power** among all sectors of the community. Unions, for example, are embraced as part of a company and not viewed as "socialist"
17. Regeneration requires **accountability** at all levels – the traceability of all flows, particularly economic and monetary benefits is transparent and open to all
18. Regeneration may require **radical innovation** – because many of the changes required are institutional as well as procedural.
19. Regeneration is built on nurturing and strengthening local **ecosystems** – natural, social, and *economic*
20. Regeneration challenges existing **economic models** to establish *justice as a strategy*
21. Regeneration is **not isolationist** – it adopts a **cosmo-local** perspective and nurtures and facilitates **collaboration** between places – based on respect for local values and shared learning
22. Regeneration is a **paradigm shift**

Michel Bauwens and **Vasilis Niaros** call it a **value shift**[32]:

The current value regime rewards 'extractive' production and consumption activities. Indeed, issues like the free labor of digital workers and social media users, the non-recognition of care work, and the ongoing ecological degradation of our planet and its resources are interlinked to the dominance of a system based on extractivism. Therefore, the key underlying shift needed is one from extractive models, practices that enrich some at the expense of the others (communities, resources, nature), to generative value models, practices that enrich the communities, resources etc., to which they are applied. This is what we could call the Value Shift.

Endless growth doesn't compute. As Greta Thunberg says, it's a fairy tale. Except that it's real and deadly. It's time to focus on **community regeneration**.

For those who say that regeneration is *what comes next after sustainability*, we ask a simple question: **Is the community better off because your organization operates in the community?** If so, your organization may be regenerative.

---

[32] *Value in the Commons Economy: Developments in Open and Contributory Value Accounting* by Michel Bauwens and Vasilis Niaros February 2017 Heinrich-Böll-Foundation & P2P Foundation https://www.boell.de/en/2017/02/01/value-commons-economy-developments-open-and-contributory-value-accounting

2. COMMUNITY REGENERATION

Business schools focus on teaching "business value creation." Nowhere do they teach **community value creation**.

What might that look like? In the past, we've seen many approaches to **community development** come and go – many of them as real estate projects to bring back economic life to dying neighborhoods. Results have often led to gentrification and displacement of the very population that was the intended beneficiary.[33]

Wendell Berry spoke[34] about **community value** back in the 90s. Here are his key insights which are timelier than ever:

1. Ask of any proposed change or innovation: What will this do to our community? How will this affect our common wealth?
2. Include local nature — the land, the water, the air, the native creatures — within the membership of the community.

---

[33] A WARNING FROM HISTORY: Without deep democratic engagement of the local population, community development becomes a negative, exploitative, even destructive practice, not unlike the forced eviction of Native Americans from their ancestral lands. In the past, "urban renewal" was a term often used for the various strategies to restore profitability and/or repopulate areas of the city deemed to be in decline. Also termed 'reconstruction', urban renewal describes a broad range of interventions in the built environment and in communities facilitated by the state, the private sector, public-private partnerships, or less commonly, by community-level agencies. In essence, urban renewal promised physical, material, or spatial solutions to social and economic problems. This is a reductive and destructive way of thinking of the whole ecosystem – especially in the US, where the criticism of urban renewal programs is not new. Urban renewal in the US, has not helped the poor. It was primarily a mid-20th century phenomenon that decimated the cores of America's cities. More than two thousand urban renewal construction projects were undertaken between 1949 and 1973, when the urban renewal program officially ended. Over two million inhabitants to displaced and moved. Urban renewal provided local "agencies" with federal funds and the power of eminent domain to condemn slum neighborhoods, tear down the buildings, and resell the cleared land to private developers at a reduced price. In the end, more than 40 state legislatures in the US ended up passing laws restricting or banning the use of eminent domain for economic rejuvenation.

[34] Wendell Berry - from a speech delivered November 11, 1994 at the 23rd annual meeting of the Northern Plains Resource Council. https://sustainabletraditions.com/2010/10/wendell-berry-17-rules-for-a-sustainable-local-community/

3. Ask how local needs might be supplied from local sources, including the mutual help of neighbors.

4. Supply local needs first (and only then think of exporting their products, first to nearby cities, and then to others).

5. Understand the ultimate unsoundness of the industrial doctrine of 'labor saving' if that implies poor work, unemployment, or any kind of pollution or contamination.

6. Develop properly scaled value-adding industries for local products in order not to become merely a colony of the national or the global economy.

7. Develop small-scale industries and businesses to support the local farm or forest economy.

8. Strive to produce as much of their own energy as possible.

9. Strive to increase earnings (in whatever form) within the community, and decrease expenditures outside the community.

10. Circulate money within the local economy for as long as possible before paying it out.

11. Invest in the community to maintain its properties, keep it clean (without dirtying some other place), care for its old people, and teach its children.

12. Arrange for the old and the young to take care of one another, eliminating institutionalized 'child care' and 'homes for the aged.' The young must learn from the old, not necessarily and not always in school; the community knows and remembers itself by the association of old and young.

13. Account for costs that are now conventionally hidden or 'externalized.' Whenever possible they must be debited against monetary income.

14. Look into the possible uses of local currency, community-funded loan programs, systems of barter, and the like.

15. Be aware of the economic value of neighborliness — as help, insurance, and so on. They must realize that in our time the costs of living are greatly increased by the loss of neighborhood, leaving people to face their calamities alone.
16. Be acquainted with, and complexly connected with, community-minded people in nearby towns and cities.
17. Cultivate urban consumers loyal to local products to build a sustainable rural economy, which will always be more cooperative than competitive.

Berry's vision is **regenerative** in all aspects – it's based on a vision of community – a vision of the **Common Good**.

ASK: *What are the "commons" for my community? What is the best way to manage the Common Good?*

What is the community ecosystem of everyday living? Is it a system of mutual understanding and purpose? A **common vision** is a vision of the future – of how we want to live as a community. Building a common vision is a process that must be *inclusive, transparent,* and *participative*. Unfortunately, our political processes have strayed too far from these principles, and are often dictated by special interests who exert undue influence on our elected politicians. At a local level, that weakness can be overcome by **deep democracy** – active and inclusive participation in decision-making by concerned and engaged members of the community.

There is not "one way" to do this. Everything depends on the community, its leaders, and the support regeneration projects get from the community and local government leaders. **Entrepreneurial learning** – the ability to think around constraints – becomes a key success factor in as well.

THE PRIVATIZATION OF EVERYTHING

Unfortunately, our society has largely been conditioned to **eliminate the concept of the common good**.

In their book, *The Privatization of Everything: How the Plunder of Public Goods Transformed America and How We Can Fight back*, Donald Cohen and Allen Mikaelian explain how the US-approach to fighting COVID was based not on effective public health policy, but rather on letting the markets decide. Public health is a public good, but the Trump administration handed it over to corporations. Cohen and Mikaelian tell us that **our theory of public goods sidelines the public almost completely:** [35]

It assumes that the market can and will provide just about everything. According to conservative economists, the government should step in only when markets fail. In those rare instances where someone can't make money from a particular good or service, it becomes permissible for the government to take it on. In this framing, the market decides what is public and what is private, and the public must follow the market's dictates. Privatization is often a logical outcome. When a good or service is privatized, it means that someone has figured out how to make money from it or that they want to exclude segments of the public. And when that happens, according to free-market adherents, the public needs to get out of the way.

This classic and narrow definition of public goods is fundamentally opposed to democracy and leaves decision-making about vital issues to the whims of the market.

The authors argue that **in a democratic society public goods should not be defined by the market.** Instead, they should be defined by the *public* and its values.

---

[35] *The Privatization of Everything: How the Plunder of Public Goods Transformed America and How We Can Fight back*, Donald Cohen and Allen Mikaelian, The New Press (November 23, 2021)

In 1981, the Business Roundtable – a group that represents large American firms – said that companies "have a responsibility, first of all, to make available to the public quality goods and services at fair prices, thereby earning a profit that attracts investment to continue and enhance the enterprise, provide jobs, and build the economy." By 1997, the Roundtable declared that the "principal objective of a business enterprise is to generate economic returns to its owners."[36]

The change from focusing on "public good" to believing that the sole mission of business was to maximize shareholder value, leads to executives pocketing more and more profit for themselves, rather than investing in their workforce.

Similarly, when governments are driven by ideology and promote policies dictated by powerful financial interests, and refuse to confront the realities facing their citizens, then we must challenge our assumptions and rethink what it is we want from our leaders. We may discover that our leaders do not represent us. Perhaps they have lost our trust. What can be done? Already there is a visible turn to local leadership, to community-leaders who stand for the local interests of the community. It is these leaders who inspire trust. We'll address the topic of *regenerative leadership* in a separate chapter.

COMMUNITY TRUST BUILDING

One of the key attributes of community strength is the ability to collaborate. **Trust** – a so-called intangible value – is the critical component of collaboration. In low-trust environments, the following behaviors are observed[37]:

- Facts are manipulated or distorted
- Information and knowledge are withheld and hoarded
- People spin the truth to their advantage

---

[36] See: https://www-vice-com.cdn.ampproject.org/c/s/www.vice.com/amp/en/article/a3xqze/shell-ceo-ben-van-beurden-climate-change

[37] *Interview: Stephen M. R. Covey on "The Speed of Trust"* (2007 interview by Christian Sarkar) https://christiansarkar.com/2008/02/my-interview-with-stephen-m-r/

- Getting the credit is very important
- New ideas are openly resisted and stifled
- Mistakes are covered up or covered over
- Most people are involved in a blame game, badmouthing others
- There is an abundance of "gossip" and "rumor" talk
- There are numerous "meetings after the meetings"
- There are many "undiscussables"
- People tend to over-promise and under-deliver
- There are a lot of violated expectations for which people make many excuses
- People pretend bad things aren't happening or are in denial
- The energy level is low
- People often feel unproductive tension–sometimes even fear

Why are these attributes present in a community? The reasons are usually historical, based on past conflicts. They lead to a critical problem: **the inability to collaborate**.

Trust has two components – *character* and *competence*, and both are equally important. Character is about doing the right thing, and competence is about doing things right. A cliché, but still important.

No community project can be successful without trust. And **trust is a slow process of relationship-building.** Trust is about trusting others – building a shared sense of purpose, and starting small. Trust must be inclusive, and welcome new voices and participants.

For **individuals** and **organizations**, we ask: is there a genuine concern for people, purposes and the community as a whole or is profit your sole motive? Those that are operating "by themselves, for themselves" are not good community partners, and are often non-participants in the planning or support of community projects.

In business, this mindset can be traced back to the mindset of the founder, and cannot be changed without a "transformation" process for the founder and/or senior executive team. What must be done to help them engage and participate in community regeneration?

Non-profits and cooperatives must also ask themselves the same questions – how do we work together to build trust in our institutions and the future? The same applies to religious organizations as well.

And finally, we must ask city and regional **government administrators** to rise above the petty politics and build "bridges of trust" by encouraging boundaryless thinking – by getting the various administrative institutions to work together around serving the citizens, not the other way around.

A common misperception is that trust is a social virtue, and that it either exists or doesn't.

This fallacy prevents communities, businesses, and organizations from viewing trust as a capability – a competence which can be systematically developed, nurtured, and cultivated.

The future of any community depends on rethinking how the various constituents work *together*. We must foster "cross-boundary thinking" – by getting individuals to begin working together to create opportunities for the next generation. *How will public officials and private leaders create a culture of collaboration and entrepreneurship to encourage and nurture the young?*

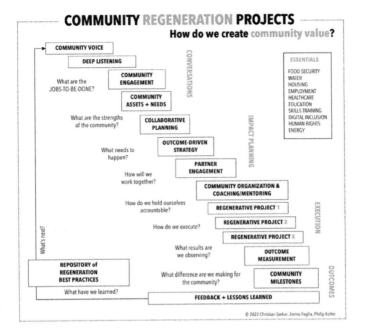

In different communities the sources of leadership will vary. In cities, it may be the administration – the mayor, for example. In neighborhoods, it might be a local, anchor entrepreneur, or a social worker. That is why it is critical to build a *team of community leaders* who work together to create community value.

The other obvious question is: *who benefits?* If the project does not deliver universal, common benefits to the entire community, it can still be regenerative by creating value for specific recipients. The litmus test is *inclusion.* Who is included/excluded and why?

BRINGING THE COMMUNITY TOGETHER

The path to community regeneration is unlikely to be a top-down aid-driven approach. In fact, that is a recipe for failure. It must be community-based, and community-led.

We'll look at two examples of community regeneration[38]:

- Palermo, Sicily
- Eskişehir, Turkey

PALERMO, SICILY

The story of Palermo's renaissance is in large part the story of **Leoluca Orlando** – the mayor who declared war on the Mafia and transformed the city in the process – using what he calls the "culture and economy of human rights."

Leoluca Orlando started his political journey as a legal advisor for Piersanti Mattarella, the president of Sicily. However, this came to an end when Mattarella was tragically killed by the Mafia in 1980. But in 1985, Orlando took on a new challenge and became the mayor of Palermo. This marked the beginning of what was called the "Palermo Spring," a time of hard work and achievements aimed at freeing the city from the grip of organized crime.

He struggled to remove the Mafia's influence on every dimension of the city – beginning with the restoration of the City's historical center. Before Orlando, previous mayors either ignored or aided the Mafia, which led to the decline of the city center, a decrease in cultural events and businesses, and a weakened education system. But with the support of the nationwide efforts to fight organized crime, Orlando during his second and third terms as mayor (1993–1997 and 1997–2000), got the community and businesses involved in reviving Palermo.

---

[38] For more examples, visit the Regenerative Marketing Institute at www.regenmarketing.org

The importance of civic groups and businesses in revitalizing the city cannot be understated.

Orlando's indefatigable style helped reawaken civic pride by renovating or reacquiring hundreds of public buildings and monuments, building a cultural center and founding a downtown concert series, kick-starting entrepreneurial activity and tourism, building schools, and incorporating civic consciousness into the education system.

The Teatro Massimo reopened in 1997 after a lengthy restoration process. The theater, which is one of the largest opera houses in Europe, had been closed for several years due to safety concerns and the need for renovation. The restoration project, which was led by Orlando, involved the rehabilitation of the theater's interior and exterior, as well as the installation of modern technical facilities. The reopening of the Teatro Massimo was a major event in Palermo's cultural life and symbolized the city's rebirth as a center of art and culture.

Similarly, the port of Palermo had fallen into disrepair and had become a symbol of the city's decline. The entire port area was cluttered with cargo containers, abandoned buildings, and other eyesores, and was seen as a hindrance to the city's economic and cultural development.

In the 1990s, under the leadership of Orlando, the port of Palermo was renovated and transformed into a modern and attractive transportation and commercial hub. The renovation project involved the removal of many of the cargo containers and other obstacles that had cluttered the port area, and the construction of new facilities, such as terminals and warehouses. The renovated port was equipped with state-of-the-art technology, including computerized systems for tracking cargo and managing traffic, and was designed to be more efficient and user-friendly.

Orlando's Rules of Order

HOW TO FIGHT ENTRENCHED INTERESTS

- Break the identity trap. Find ways to break the Mafia's hold on community members.
- Demonstrate confidence and community trust - the culture of the Mafia is a perversion of the culture of belonging.
- Create a common language - based on values.
- Establish common space. The parks, schools, theater, streets, the square, arena - these all belong to the community.
- Culture and economy go together, but culture comes first. Human rights are foundational.
- Social services are for all.
- Jobs come from legality, not the other way around.
- Return schools to a culture of learning - especially in Mafia neighborhoods.
- Restore the historical center of the city. Without art and culture, there is no city, only a mall.
- Public services must compete to win the citizens approval. No contracts are given. They must be won as public tender. Get rated by Moody's.
- Eliminate violence by cutting the connections between criminals and politicians. Make jail time stick.
- Change the minds of the next generation to break the cycle of killing.
- Pay invoices in 30 days.
- Appoint heads of departments for results, not for their connections.
- Encourage leadership at all levels - including outside the city government.
- Human mobility is an inalienable human right. An "open city" discourages Mafia activity.

The renovation of the port of Palermo was another key component of the city's revitalization effort and helped to jumpstart the city's economic growth and attract new investment. The improved port has also helped to boost the city's reputation as a major transportation hub and has made Palermo a more attractive destination for tourists and business travelers alike.

Orlando's fourth and fifth terms as mayor in 2012 and 2017 were a continuation of the regeneration process with an emphasis on cultural regeneration. For Orlando this included the promotion of Palermo on the word stage. The 2015 **Charter of Palermo** recognized international *human mobility as an inalienable human right.*[39] One of Orlando's favorite phrases went something like this: "In Palermo we have no migrants, whoever lives in Palermo is Palermitan."

Orlando was instrumental in setting the stage for numerous awards and worldwide recognition of the city's rich cultural legacy – including UNESCO's world heritage recognition for the Arab-Norman architecture of Palermo, Cefalù and Monreale. **Manifesta 12**, the European Nomadic Biennial, was held Palermo in 2018. A major international art event, it attracted visitors from all over the world – and opened Palermo to new visitors and investors. Also, in 2018 – Palermo was named the Italian Capital of Culture.

Perhaps the most important change in Palermo was the shift in mindset – which allowed the people to think beyond the Mafia, and engage in acts of community regeneration and open the doors to tourism and cultural travel. Palermo is a *mosaic* of cultures and people – and this natural identity was subverted by the Mafia. Many small businesses grew in spaces formerly controlled by the Mafia. The city went from a hotbed of violence to becoming one of the safest cities in Europe. The Palermo renaissance continues.

When the Mayor asked us to visit Palermo to see what should be done in terms of future regeneration, he asked us to

---

[39] https://www.fondazionemosaico.org/wp-content/uploads/2023/03/CharterofPalermo2015.pdf

undertake the project independently – for the future of the city – *not* for his administration. A summary of our *Palermo Rigenerativa* project recommendations is at the end of this book. Many of the case studies for regenerative business came out of our Palermo experience. Most cities have these types of enterprises at the edge of the business community – you simply have to *look for them*.

ESKİŞEHIR, TURKEY

One of the best examples of community regeneration is the 11th largest city in Turkey, **Eskişehir**[40].

In 1999, the newly-elected mayor **Yılmaz Büyükerşen** faced the challenges that had festered over the years to make life in the city almost unbearable. The Porsuk river was choked with trash and repeatedly flooded the city with dangerous toxic waste. The traffic congestion was unbearable, with car pollution and bottle-necks slowing transportation to a crawl. And to make matters next-to-impossible, 6 months into the mayor's term, a 7.8 magnitude earthquake killed 37 people and damaged several of bridges, along with critical city infrastructure.

The mayor and his team, many from Eskişehir's Anadolu University, sprang into action, bringing together a wide cross-section of community members: academics, industry representatives, the chamber of commerce, and advocates of those with mobility needs. The job? To conceptualize and prioritize community projects to regenerate the city. The Eskişehir Urban Development Project was on!

The first community project was dredging and restoring the river – from removing the toxic refuse and trash that was piled high in the river, to building flood protection embankments and rebuilding the failing wastewater infrastructure.

---

[40] "Urban Transformations: The Reinvention of Eskişehir, Turkey from Dump to Destination" by Madeleine Galvin and Anne Maassen, *World Resources Institute*, Insights March 28, 2019
https://www.wri.org/insights/urban-transformations-reinvention-eskisehir-turkey-dump-destination

Second, the team designed and built a new public transportation network, which increased mobility while creating new pedestrian-only community spaces. The bridges were rebuilt and renovated, with new sidewalks throughout the historical center. New, wheelchair-accessible parks were inaugurated on the banks of the Porsuk, to host art and cultural events.

Business and tourism boomed. The riverwalk became a hub with new cafes, bookstores, and bars. The change in the attitude of its residents became a driver of further change – women entrepreneurs emerged and were included in the culture of renewal. Now, with the recent devastating earthquakes in Turkey, the Eskişehir Metropolitan Municipality workshops is producing and installing portable toilets which is one of the most urgent needs in the earthquake hit regions. It is our sincere hope that, for Turkey, we see an emergence of community-based regeneration similar to Eskişehir.

PATHS TO REGENERATION

Each community must decide the regeneration approach which works best for them. We present a number of methods and tools in this chapter which we hope will be useful:

- The Pyramid of Community Value
- Asset Based Community Development (ABCD)
- Community Wealth-building
- Worksharing
- Base of the Pyramid + Green Leap
- Missions
- Resilient Cities
- Complete Communities
- City as Commons
- Community as a Platform
- Ecosystematic

- Cultural Regeneration

THE PYRAMID OF COMMUNITY VALUE

Patterned after the "elements of value"[41] the **community value pyramid** is a simple tool we developed to help community members identify what the most important jobs-to-be-done in their community might look like. Of course, each community can build their own pyramid by modifying the elements.

We recognize that our pyramid of value is a reflection of Maslow's hierarchy of needs, and that this hierarchy may be misplaced. Community members can use the pyramid to ask themselves five questions:

---

[41] "The Elements of Value" – An Interview with Jamie Cleghorn, *The Marketing Journal*, April 11, 2018
https://www.marketingjournal.org/the-elements-of-value-an-interview-with-jamie-cleghorn/

1. What do the people say we need most urgently?
2. How do our community value propositions compare with other communities we admire?
3. How do we bridge the gaps to create local value for our community?
4. What essential services do we need for the common good?
5. How will we plan, execute, maintain, and measure impact?

The community value pyramid becomes a tool to help decide which areas need regeneration the most. Note that the *foundational* community values of **human rights**, **tolerance**, and **justice** are represented on the sides of the pyramid. These are first principles. And of course, the hierarchy is based on requirements for survival – but most of our daily lives cut across this hierarchy.

ASK: *What are the most urgent and important jobs to be done[42]? These are the "**unmet needs of the community.**"*

Once you ask this question, you'll want to think of the following:

- *what* – the type of need: describe it as clearly as possible
- *who* – is being impacted? Individual, community, work, national, planet? who decides what is to be done? for whom?
- *where* – is the need observed?
- *when* – does the need occur – is it continuous or sporadic?
- *who/what* – should be held accountable? is blocking the solution?

---

[42] *Jobs to be Done: Theory to Practice* by Anthony Ulwick, IDEA BITE PRESS, 2016

Discussions work best in an environment of caring and trust. **Fear must be eliminated**. The first step must be to create a *safe space* for open and frank exchange and deliberation – without fear of reprisal.

In most communities there is a hegemony – a power structure that upholds and protects the cultural norms of the community. How do you create a system for collecting input: suggestions, requests, and concerns which does not penalize the least powerful?

HUMAN SCALE DEVELOPMENT

Max-Neef, the Chilean economist, created a spectrum to describe the **fundamental needs**[43] of human beings. He attempted to describe why many of the countries in South America were failing.

Fundamentally, these countries did not help their citizens meet their most basic needs. Without meeting these basic needs, it was nearly impossible for these countries to grow their economies.

This created a vicious cycle where citizens weren't receiving proper care, and as a result, the countries' infrastructures were failing due to the lack of secure, healthy, and strong citizens to support them. Neef also made some remarkable statements, more relevant today than ever:

This crisis is not just economic, nor just social, cultural or political. On the contrary, it is the convergence of all these, which, added together, become an entirety exceeding the sum of its parts.

---

[43] *Development Dialogue* 1989, 1 a journal of international development cooperation published by the Dag Hammarskjöld Foundation, Uppsala. http://www.daghammarskjold.se/wp-content/uploads/1989/05/89_1.pdf

FUNDAMENTAL NEEDS
Max-Neef 's Human Scale Development

	BEING	HAVING	DOING	INTERACTING
SUBSISTENCE	physical health, mental health, equilibrium, sense of humor, adaptability	food, shelter, work	feed, procreate, rest, work	living environment, social setting
PROTECTION	care, adaptability, autonomy, equilibrium, solidarity	insurance systems, savings, social security, health systems, rights, family, work	cooperate, prevent, plan, take care of, cure, help	living space, social environment, dwelling
AFFECTION	self-esteem, solidarity, respect, tolerance, generosity, receptiveness, passion, determination, sensuality, sense of humor	friendships, family, partnerships, pets, relationships with nature	make love, caress, express emotions, share, take care of, cultivate, appreciate	privacy, intimacy, home, space of togetherness
UNDERSTANDING	critical conscience, receptiveness, curiosity, astonishment, discipline, intuition, rationality	literature, teachers, method, educational policies, communication policies	investigate, study, experiment, educate, analyze, meditate	settings of formative interaction, schools, universities, academies, groups, communities, family
PARTICIPATION	adaptability, receptiveness, solidarity, willingness, determination, dedication, respect, passion, sense of humor	rights, responsibilities, duties, privileges, work	become affiliated, cooperate, propose, share, dissent, obey, interact, agree on, express opinions	settings of participative interaction, parties, associations, churches, communities, neighborhoods, family
IDLENESS	curiosity, receptiveness, imagination, recklessness, sense of humor, tranquility, sensuality	games, spectacles, clubs, parties, peace of mind	daydream, brood, dream, recall old times, give way to fantasies, remember, relax, have fun, play	privacy, intimacy, spaces of closeness, free time, surroundings, landscapes
CREATION	passion, determination, intuition, imagination, boldness, rationality, autonomy, inventiveness, curiosity	abilities, skills, method, work	work, invent, build, design, compose, interpret	productive and feedback settings, workshops, cultural groups, audiences, spaces for expression, temporal freedom
IDENTITY	sense of belonging, consistency, differentiation, self-esteem, assertiveness	symbols, language, religion, habits, customs, reference groups, sexuality, values, norms, historical memory, work	commit oneself, integrate oneself, confront, decide on, get to know oneself, recognize oneself, actualize oneself, grow	social rhythms, everyday settings, settings which one belongs to, maturation stages
FREEDOM	autonomy, self-esteem, determination, passion, assertiveness, open-mindedness, boldness, rebelliousness, tolerance	equal rights	dissent, choose, be different from, run risks, develop awareness, commit oneself, disobey	temporal/spatial plasticity

At a political level, the crisis becomes very acute owing to the inefficiency of the existing representative political mechanisms in coping with the actions of the financial power elite, the increasing inter-nationalization of political decisions and the lack of control of the citizenry over public bureaucracies. The increase in technological control over society, the arms race and the lack of a deep-rooted democratic culture in Latin American societies also contributes to the configuration of a political universe which does not have an ethical foundation.

Today, we see that Max-Neef's assessment is not only relevant, but is still the fundamental reason why we cannot move forward and meet the existential challenges facing us today.

ASSET BASED COMMUNITY DEVELOPMENT (ABCD)

The fundamental problem of development was tackled head-on by **John (Jody) Kretzmann** and **John McKnight** in their seminal book *Building Communities from the Inside Out: A Path Toward Finding and Mobilizing a Community's Assets (1993)*. Their innovative approach called **"asset-based community development"** (ABCD) reset the *assumptions* of the development industry.

Instead of viewing the community through a lens of **"needs"** - as needy and problematic and deficient neighborhoods populated by needy and problematic and deficient people, asset-based community development supports community policies and activities based on the **capacities, skills** and **assets** of lower income people and their neighborhoods.

A **"needs-based"** strategy can guarantee only *survival*, explain the authors, and can "never lead to serious change or community development.[44]" Thus, this orientation is one of the major causes of a sense of hopelessness.

Conversely, they tell us – "significant community development takes place only when local community people are

---

[44] *Building Communities from the Inside Out: A Path Toward Finding and Mobilizing a Community's Assets* by John Kretzmann and John McKnight (1993)

committed to investing *themselves* and their resources in the effort."

COMMUNITY "NEEDS"

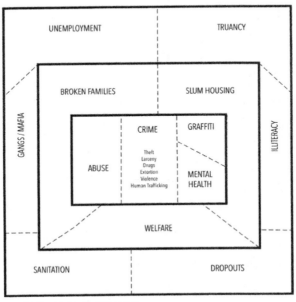

adapted from: John Kretzmann and John McKnight
Building Communities from the Inside Out: A Path Toward Finding and Mobilizing a Community's Assets (1993)

That is why *communities are never built from the top down*, or from the outside-in.

Furthermore, they emphasize, "it is increasingly futile to wait for significant help to arrive from outside the community... so wherever there are effective community development efforts, those efforts are based upon an understanding, or map, of the community's assets, capacities and abilities."

COMMUNITY "ASSETS"

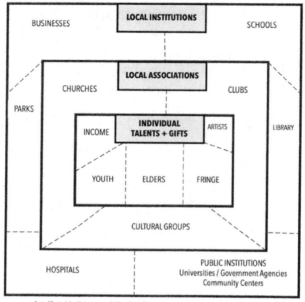

adapted from: John Kretzmann and John McKnight
Building Communities from the Inside Out: A Path Toward Finding and Mobilizing a Community's Assets (1993)

This asset-based approach requires a mapping of community assets, beginning with an inventory of the gifts, skills and capacities of the community's residents. The authors are clear: "Household by household, building by building, block by block, the capacity mapmakers will discover a vast and often surprising array of individual talents and productive skills, few of which are being mobilized for community-building purposes."

For Kretzmann and McKnight, the asset-based approach is the foundation of regeneration. One has to look at the state of the current assets in the community and begin to draw out a process of regeneration for those assets – from the inside-out. The authors again: "One of the central challenges for asset-based community developers is to constantly build and rebuild the relationships between and among local residents, local associations and local institutions.[45]" These relationships must be "built upon the strengths and capacities of the parties involved, never on their weaknesses and needs."

The principles[46] that guide ABCD include:

- *Everyone has gifts*: Each person in a community has something to contribute.
- *Relationships build a community*: People must be connected in order for sustainable community development to take place.
- *Citizens at the center*: Citizens should be viewed as actors — not recipients — in development.
- *Leaders involve others*: Community development is strongest when it involves a broad base of community action.
- *People care*: Challenge notions of "apathy" by listening to people's interests.
- *Listen*: Decisions should come from conversations where people are heard.
- *Ask*: Asking for ideas is more sustainable than giving solutions.
- *Inside-out organization*: Local community members are in control.
- *Institutions serve the community*: Institutional leaders should create opportunities for community-member involvement, then "step back."

Most importantly, ABCD stresses the power of social relationships and the primacy of the community member. Institutions, like hospitals and NGOs must focus on the "unmet needs" of the citizen, not the needs and wants of the institution.

---

[45] *Building Communities from the Inside Out: A Path Toward Finding and Mobilizing a Community's Assets* by John Kretzmann and John McKnight (1993)
[46] "What is Asset Based Community Development (ABCD)" Rowland, Stan *Collaborative of Neighborhood Transformation* (26 April 2008)

One more thing. Kretzmann and McKnight have an answer to an important question:

Does development from the "inside out" mean that outside resources don't really count?[47]

No. Especially in lower income inner-city neighborhoods, outside resources are essential to the renewal process. There are, nonetheless, two critical qualifications to this answer.

First, outside resources will largely be wasted if the internal capacity of the community is not developed. Here, the question is the order. The inside capacity must be there before the outside resource can be effectively leveraged. That is why this guide is described as focusing on development "from the inside out." It is a process from the inside to the outside.

Second, outside resources that overwhelm, dominate or replace the work and potential of local citizens, their associations and the institutions they control will weaken rather than enhance the development process. We can see this most clearly in a few neighborhoods and housing developments that are virtual colonies dominated by local outposts of outside systems. These places have become very powerless in citizen and associational capacity. We can easily recognize this kind of powerlessness. The name for it is dependency.

---

[47] *Building Communities from the Inside Out: A Path Toward Finding and Mobilizing a Community's Assets* by John Kretzmann and John McKnight (1993) The best compilation of John McKnight's thinking is available online at McKnight's own website at https://johnmcknight.org/learnings/ and at the Asset Based Community Development Institute at DePaul University: https://resources.depaul.edu/abcd-institute.

COMMUNITY WEALTHBUILDING

Community wealth building (CWB) is a people-centric approach to local economic development, which redirects wealth back into the local economy, and places control and benefits into the hands of local people.

Initially developed by US-based **Ted Howard** and **Gar Alperovitz** of the **Democracy Collaborative** in the mid 2000s, the approach is now also used and promoted in the UK by the **Center for Local Economic Strategies** (CLES).

Based on Ted Howard's remarks to an *Alternative Models of Ownership* conference, the Democracy Collaborative presents us with the 8 basic principles[48] behind community wealth building:

Labor matters more than capital: *We need a local economy in which people matter more than just maximizing profits. For instance, when a crisis hits, we need to act to preserve jobs rather than bailout the corporate bottom line. We can't let capital alone call the shots if we really want to build community wealth.*

Local, broad-based ownership: *A thriving local economy requires local ownership, where the control & economic advantages of that ownership are spread broadly (for instance through cooperative, community, or employee ownership). With concentrated and absentee ownership, the economy works to extract wealth on behalf of those at the top.*

Active democratic ownership and participation: *The neoliberal model sees communities as isolated individuals, engaged in civic life only as passive consumers. To build real community wealth, we need to rebuild the fabric of active*

---

[48] https://democracycollaborative.org/learn/blogpost/community-wealth-building-eight-basic-principles
Ted, we apologize for using your words verbatim, but we felt it was the best way to get your message across!

community, with opportunities for real participation and collective decision making at all levels of the economy.

Multipliers: *When a purchase is made locally, that money stays in the community longer, because local businesses are more likely to spend locally. This translates into greater local prosperity, greater community stability, and a tighter-knit network of local people and businesses – all key to building community wealth.*

Localizing investment: *There are vast pools of capital in the investment portfolios of local anchors, in personal and institutional bank deposits, and in our pension funds and retirement plans – imagine what's possible if these investments were put to work locally building community wealth, rather than fueling Wall Street and The City's extractive casino economy?*

Collaboration: *Building community wealth isn't just about more money locally – it's about the power that comes from building lasting relationships of mutual support. Fostering effective collaboration between anchors, local government, and neighborhood residents isn't just a matter of convenience or capacity, it's intrinsic to the project of community wealth building.*

Place really matters: *Don't expect wealth to trickle down. Without an intentional place-based strategy to make sure local assets work to build local wealth, there's nothing stopping wealth from leaving your community. And you need an intentional strategy to make sure that locally the hardest hit parts of your community are first in line for new opportunities: inequities won't undo themselves.*

Community wealth is where the next system begins: *This isn't about one or two good projects, or a small corner of a procurement budget getting earmarked for local vendors while everything else remains business as usual. It's about taking the* *first steps towards truly transforming our economy so that it works for the many, not the few.*

Community wealth-building is based on 5 core principles[49]:

- **progressive procurement** – developing local supply chains of businesses to support local employment and keep wealth within communities
- **fair employment and just labor markets** – Using anchor institutions to improve prospects of local people
- **shared ownership of the local economy** – supporting and growing business models that are more financially generative for the local economy
- **socially just use of land and property** – developing the function and ownership of local assets held by anchor organizations, so local communities benefit from financial and social gain
- **making financial power work for local places** – increase flows of investment within local economies by harnessing and recirculating the wealth that exists

Anchor organizations are large employers with a strong local presence in an area. They can exert sizable influence through their commissioning and purchasing of goods and services, through their workforce and employment capacity, and by creative use of their facilities and land assets. Positive use of these aspects can affect social, economic and environmental change in an area.

Anchor institutions are place-based organizations which have an influence on a community because they: 1) employ the local population, 2) spend on local goods and services, 3) own

---

49 "Community wealth building" Scottish Government

https://www.gov.scot/policies/cities-regions/community-wealth-building/

See also a list of case studies: https://www.inclusivegrowth.scot/community-wealth-building-case-studies/

or control local real estate assets, and 4) are invested in the future of the community. They are generally non-profit or social enterprises, but there is good reason to encourage *local businesses* to consider themselves as anchor institutions as well. Anchor institutions are central to the concept of **community wealth building** as a result of the scale of the jobs they provide, the scale of spend through procurement, their land and assets, and the fact that they are unlikely to leave that place.[50]

Anchor institutions have the economic potential to leverage their assets and revenues to promote local private sector development through[51]:

- Directing a greater percentage of their purchasing power toward local vendors based in the community.
- Hiring a greater percentage of their workforce locally.
- Providing workforce training for people needing assistance in the community.
- Incubating the development of new businesses, including social enterprise among nonprofits.
- Serving as an advisor or network builder.
- Leveraging real estate development to promote local retail, employer-assisted housing, and community land trusts.
- Using pension and endowment funds to invest in local job creation strategies and to provide community venture capital for nonprofits, entrepreneurs, and employee-owned firms.

The impact of anchor institutions is amplified by **cooperation** *between* them to maximize the benefits they bring to the community.

---

[50] *Community wealth building through anchor institutions*, a report by Centre for Local Economic Strategies (CLES) February 2017 https://cles.org.uk/publications/community-wealth-building-through-anchor-institutions/
[51] The Democracy Collaborative https://community-wealth.org/strategies/panel/anchors/index.html

This **ecosystem of collaboration** forms the backbone of community wealth building. The diagram below is derived from the "**Preston Model**" named after the town in the U.K.[52], which in turn was derived from the "**Cleveland Model**" in the US[53].

The Cleveland Model is the story of community wealth-building based on the **power of cooperatives**. The Evergreen Cooperative Initiative was launched in 2008 by a group of Cleveland-based institutions, including the Cleveland Foundation, Cleveland Clinic, University Hospitals, Case Western Reserve University, and the municipal government. Its goal is to create living-wage jobs in six low-income neighborhoods, where the median household income is below $18,500, in an area called Greater University Circle.

The initiative seeks to create an economic breakthrough in Cleveland by focusing on economic inclusion and building a local economy from the ground up, rather than relying on a trickle-down strategy. Rather than using public subsidies to attract low-wage jobs, the Evergreen strategy aims to catalyze new businesses owned by their employees. Additionally, instead of focusing on workforce training for employment opportunities that are typically unavailable to low-skill and low-income workers, the Evergreen Initiative first creates the jobs and then recruits and trains local residents to fill them.

The backdrop: Cleveland was among the Rust Belt cities that suffered from deindustrialization. Ohio lost 396,000 manufacturing jobs from 1990 to 2016, reducing the proportion of manufacturing jobs from 22.7% to 12.7% of all Ohioan jobs. Worker-owned cooperatives were viewed as an appealing economic development strategy, as they allow workers to

---

[52] "In 2011 Preston hit rock bottom. Then it took back control" by Aditya Chakraborty, *The Guardian*, January 31, 2018 https://www.theguardian.com/commentisfree/2018/jan/31/preston-hit-rock-bottom-took-back-control
[53] https://community-wealth.org/content/cleveland-model-how-evergreen-cooperatives-are-building-community-wealth

control their own jobs and prevent offshoring. Additionally, cooperatives offered higher wages and remain competitive without spending money on extractive corporate profits and overhead.

Recently, when the COVID-19 pandemic caused economic shutdowns, the small businesses belonging to the Evergreen Cooperative Initiative experienced growth. These businesses, which operate as independent worker-owned cooperatives under the Evergreen umbrella organization, not only earned profits but also distributed them to their employees, many of whom are also co-owners.

The vision is simple[54]:

Neighborhood by neighborhood, Evergreen Cooperatives Corporation is creating economic breakthroughs in Cleveland–and through its Business Services consulting arm, well beyond. Evergreen catalyzes local, sustainable companies that offer their employee-owners opportunities for personal, financial and career success. This strategic community wealth-building creates meaningful jobs, keeps precious financial resources within the Greater University Circle neighborhood and sows the seeds for rebuilding the local economy. Sustainable companies and meaningful jobs – together they can stabilize, revitalize and transform communities and individuals.

The Cleveland Model has made its way across the Atlantic to the UK. "Protecting community-owned land and assets from extractive, gentrifying developers is as crucial to maintaining local democracy as opposing the outsourcing of council services," explains Councillor **Matthew Brown**, leader of **Preston City Council** and senior fellow for community wealth building with **The Democracy Collaborative**[55].

---

[54] https://www.evgoh.com/mission-vision/

[55] *Preston Is Putting Socialist Policies into Practice* by Matthew Brown *Tribune Magazine,* January 20, 2022 https://tribunemag.co.uk/2022/01/community-wealth-building-preston-trade-unions-labour-party Learn more about the Democracy Collaborative at www.democracycollaborative.org

The Democracy Collaborative is creating an alternative to the traditional local economic development paradigm, which uses public resources to attract corporations and is designed to extract wealth and real estate capital in ways that displace communities.

Multiple cities in the US, the United Kingdom, and elsewhere are now institutionalizing this Community wealth-building paradigm in their planning and work, showing how economic growth can be rooted in communities for the primary benefit of workers and residents.

COMMUNITY WEALTHBUILDING

A FRAMEWORK FOR LOCAL REGENERATION

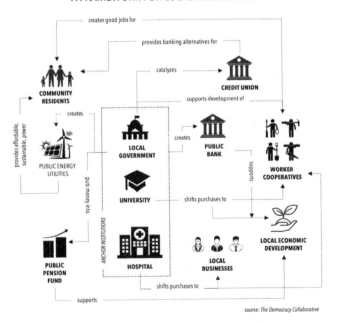

source: *The Democracy Collaborative*

A place-based regeneration strategy inventories the entire range of organizations in a community and helps bring them together to create a collaborative economy – focused on community wellbeing.

In our view, anchor institutions can also work well with much smaller for-profit and non-profit organizations to build community wealth. But *anchor institutions don't have to be local anymore.*

BASE OF THE PYRAMID + GREEN LEAP

A lot has changed since the publication of **C.K. Prahalad** and **Stuart Hart**'s article[56] *The Fortune at the Bottom of the Pyramid*. The BOP protocol provided the first articulation of how business could profitably serve the needs of the four billion poor in the developing world.

Fast forward to the "Green Leap." Here's **Stuart Hart** from his *Voice of the Planet* blog[57]:

*In the past decade, two exciting new commercial developments have burst onto the global scene. One revolves around the commercialization of **new green technology**; the other around better serving and **including the poor at the base of the income pyramid.***

*Both are exciting, but the problem is that they have **evolved as separate communities**. The green techies say, "Just give us the venture capital, and we'll invent the clean tech of tomorrow," as if it will then spring magically into reality.*

Proponents of the base of the pyramid approach seek to address poverty and inequity in developing countries through a new form of enterprise. They say, "How do we innovate business models, extend distribution, and become embedded in the

---

[56] "The fortune at the bottom of the pyramid" by C.K. Prahalad and Stuart L. Hart, *strategy + business*, January 10, 2002 https://www.strategy-business.com/article/11518

[57] Is it time to take the "Green Leap"? by Stuart Hart March 27, 2011
http://stuartlhart.com/blog/2011/03/is-it-time-to-take-the-green-leap.html

community to build viable businesses from the ground up?" But such "pro-poor" business advocates often lose sight of the environment, as if all this new economic activity will automatically create a sustainable form of development at the base of the pyramid. Tragically, that way of thinking could take us all over the cliff, if we end up with 6.7 billion people consuming like Americans.

The challenge of our time, therefore, is to figure out how to bring these two worlds together to enable a global "Green Leap." *Indeed, emerging clean technologies, including distributed generation of renewable energy, biofuels, point-of-use water purification, biomaterials, wireless information technology, and sustainable agriculture hold the keys to solving many of the world's global environmental and social challenges.*

Hart's view is that we should get our most promising technologists and entrepreneurs out of the US (and the rest of the developed world markets) and into the rural villages, urban slums, and shantytowns of the world where 4 billion plus people currently reside. It is here that the Green Leap will take place, he says.

But what if we were to add one more consideration? Prahalad and Hart were encouraging global multi-nationals to jump on the BOP bandwagon. Hart explains the Green Leap is already taking place in the developing world.

But it could just as easily take place in the developed world – in the **inner cities** or **failing suburbs** of US cities. And if you forget about multi-nationals and replace them with **entrepreneurial small businesses** and **co-operatives**, we suddenly have a very viable model for community-based eco-regeneration in the West. This is precisely what

Michael Gordon and **Christian Sarkar** proposed in their 2012 book *Inclusivity: Will America Find Its Soul Again?*

In 2021, the Federal Bank of St. Louis and the Aspen Institute co-published *The Future of Building Wealth: Brief Essays on the Best Ideas to Build Wealth — for Everyone*[58] The book asks: What does property ownership mean in the 21st century, and how can our nation broaden it for those who own little? It also reminds us of the following:

...public policy has played an outsized role in determining who is incentivized to build wealth — and who is not. Most notably, of course, is our nation's lamentable history of taking land from Native peoples and then giving or subsidizing land and other assets to overwhelmingly white people while legally or effectively barring Black and other people of color from accumulating wealth — a fact that best explains the majority of the racial wealth gap today, as the St. Louis Fed and other research have shown. Similarly, historical obstacles to women owning property well into the 20th century help explain the gender wealth gap today.

The book also informs us:

1. In the decades leading to the 2020s, the US has experienced historic levels of income and wealth inequality.
2. The bottom 50% of the population holds less than 1% of the nation's wealth, a low point not seen since the 1920s.
3. Wealth inequality exists on racial, gender, sexual orientation, generational and geographic lines.
4. There has been no increase in wealth held by Black households over the past seventy years.

---

[58] *The Future of Building Wealth: Brief Essays on the Best Ideas to Build Wealth–for Everyone* Editors: Ray Boshara, Federal Reserve Bank of St. Louis and Ida Rademacher, The Aspen Institute, 2021 https://www.aspeninstitute.org/wp-content/uploads/2021/10/the-future-of-building-wealth.pdf

Statistics like this help us understand that the "bottom of the pyramid" exists in the US as well as the developing world. It's time for regeneration.

MISSION-BASED CHANGE

Mariana Mazzucato is Professor in the Economics of Innovation and Public Value at University College London (UCL), where she is Founding Director of the Institute for Innovation & Public Purpose (IIPP). Her seminal work on public value and mission-based research and innovation drives EU-based policy for public value creation.[59]

Mazzucato's inspiration is the missions of the past — like the Apollo Program — and her goal is to apply those lessons to the more complex challenges of today. According to her theory, a "key lesson is that missions must be bold, activating innovation across sectors, across actors and across disciplines. They must also enable bottom-up solutions and experimentation."

For Mazzucato, *mission-oriented policies can be defined as systemic public policies that draw on frontier knowledge to attain specific goals or "big science deployed to meet big problems"*[60]

Is this even possible? Are our institutions up to the task? The difference between a technical challenge like the Apollo mission or even the Manhattan Project and a socio-

---

[59] See: "A problem-solving approach to fuel innovation-led growth" by Mariana Mazzucato © *European Union* February 2018 https://www.ucl.ac.uk/bartlett/public-purpose/sites/public-purpose/files/mission-oriented_ri_in_the_eu_mazzucato_2018.pdf

and "Governing Missions in the European Union" by Mariana Mazzucato © *European Union* June 2019 https://ec.europa.eu/info/sites/default/files/research_and_innovation/contact/documents/ec_rtd_mazzucato-report-issue2_072019.pdf

[60] Ergas, H. (1987) 'Does technology policy matter?', in Guile, B.R. and Brooks H. (eds.) Technology and global industry: Companies and nations in the world economy, Washington DC: National Academies Press, pp. 191-245 *(Mazucatto's attribution)*

political project like "100 Carbon Neutral Cities by 2030"[61] is stark: how do we get bureaucratic government agencies to work with the agility and focus of a scientific mission?

Mazucatto provides 5 criteria for missions:

- Bold, inspirational with wide societal relevance
- A clear direction: targeted, measurable and time-bound
- Ambitious but realistic research & innovation actions
- Cross-disciplinary, cross-sector and cross–actor innovation
- Multiple, bottom-up solutions

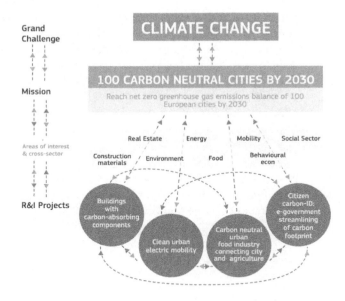

[61] See: 100 Climate-Neutral and Smart Cities by 2030: Implementation Plan (internal working document of the European Commission)

https://ec.europa.eu/info/sites/default/files/research_and_innovation/funding/documents/cities_mission_implementation_plan.pdf

Her aim – *that missions are both a means of setting economic growth in the direction of where we want to be as a society and a vehicle we can use to get there.* [62]

Unfortunately, big science can't solve big problems without **big changes**.

The problem with this approach is that the challenges we must face are true wicked problems, and state and government bureaucracies find it difficult to embrace "**regenerative innovation**."

What do we mean by regenerative innovation? It is *outcome-driven innovation*[63] applied to **regeneration projects**.

We can start as **Tony Ulwick** suggests, with the outcome, and then innovate to meet that outcome: **if we know what target to hit, the chances of hitting it increase dramatically.**

Let's explain. *What would it look like if we treated climate change as an actual emergency?* This is a question posed by **Jason Hickel** in *Current Affairs*[64]. His answer is based on the outcomes we *must* achieve:

*The single most important intervention is the one that so far, no government has been willing to touch: **cap fossil fuel use** and scale it down, on a binding annual schedule, until the industry is mostly*

---

[62] "A problem-solving approach to fuel innovation-led growth" by Mariana Mazzucato *European Union* February 2018 https://www.ucl.ac.uk/bartlett/public-purpose/sites/public-purpose/files/mission-oriented_ri_in_the_eu_mazzucato_2018.pdf

[63] "Outcome-Driven Innovation: JTBD Theory in Practice" by Anthony Ulwick *JTBD + Outcome-Driven Innovation*, June 22, 2017 https://jobs-to-be-done.com/outcome-driven-innovation-odi-is-jobs-to-be-done-theory-in-practice-2944c6ebc40e

[64] "What Would It Look Like If We Treated Climate Change as an Actual Emergency?" by Jason Hickel, *Current Affairs*, 15 November 2021 https://www.currentaffairs.org/2021/11/what-would-it-look-like-if-we-treated-climate-change-as-an-actual-emergency/

dismantled by the middle of the century. That's it. This is the only fail-safe way to stop climate breakdown.

So, what will achieve this outcome?

Hickel breaks it down.[65] We must:

1. Nationalize the fossil fuel industry and the energy companies, bringing them under public control, just like any other essential service or utility.
2. Protect people by establishing a firm social foundation—a social guarantee.
3. Tax the rich out of existence.
4. Enable massive public mobilization to achieve our ecological goals.
5. Commit to climate reparations.

He's not joking.

He explains[66]:

It will require an extraordinary struggle against those who benefit so prodigiously from the status quo — as has every movement that has ever changed the world, from the Civil Rights movement to the anti-colonial movement. It requires doing the hard work of community organizing, building wall-to-wall solidarities strong enough to hold up against political attacks. It requires forging alliances between the environmentalist movement and the labor movement, and across national borders, sufficient to pull off coordinated strike action.

This is what a **true mission-based change** looks like. Like the Apollo project, it's an "impossible mission." And yet, we believe it this is precisely what Mazzucato means by "mission."

---

[65] Ibid.
[66] Ibid.

Do we have the leadership we need to achieve this mission? It's far easier to make "net-zero by 2030/40/50" pledges.

ASK: *How does a mission driven by a top-down administrative structure (like the EU) engage the local-community in anything but a superficial level?*

ASK: *How does my government prove it's on the side of the people and not fossil fuel companies? (Yes, that's a leading question!)*

RESILIENT CITIES

When **Jane Jacobs** received a Rockefeller Foundation grant in 1958 to continue her research on how a city should function, she produced *The Death and Life of Great American Cities*, a seminal book which changed urban planning forever. Her advocacy of **mixed-use design** and **walkable streets** was the first acknowledgement of building community resilience through urban planning.

What is resilience? City resilience describes the capacity of cities to function, so that the people living and working in cities – particularly the poor and vulnerable – survive and thrive no matter what stresses or shocks they encounter.[67]

According to the U.S Census Bureau[68], "**Community resilience** is the capacity of individuals and households within a community to absorb, endure, and recover from the impacts of a disaster."

---

[67] Rockefeller Foundation (2013)

Resilience is a term that emerged from the field of ecology in the 1970s, to describe the capacity of a system to maintain or recover functionality in the event of disruption or disturbance. It is applicable to cities because they are complex systems that are constantly adapting to changing circumstances. The notion of a resilient city becomes conceptually relevant when chronic stresses or sudden shocks threaten widespread disruption or the collapse of physical or social systems. The conceptual limitation of resilience is that it does not necessarily account for the power dynamics that are inherent in the way cities function and cope with disruptions. (City Resilience Index, Arup and Rockefeller Foundation)

[68] *COMMUNITY RESILIENCE ESTIMATES Quick Guide*, U.S. Census Bureau, Department of Commerce, Dec 16, 2020, https://www2.census.gov/data/experimental-data-products/community-resilience-estimates/2020/technical-document.pdf

Thus, a city's resilience depends on *all its assets*, along with its leaders, its institutions, and its communities.

Let us also agree before we go much further that while **resilience is *not* regeneration**, it is still the "front-end of the battle."

Making Cities Resilient 2030 (MCR2030) is a cross-stakeholder initiative for improving local resilience through advocacy, sharing knowledge and experiences, establishing mutually reinforcing city-to-city learning networks, injecting technical expertise, connecting multiple layers of government and building partnerships. MCR2030 has developed a checklist[69] of "Ten Essentials for Making Cities Resilient." They are:

1. Organize for disaster resilience. Put in place an organizational structure with strong leadership and clarity of coordination and responsibilities. Establish Disaster Risk Reduction as a key consideration throughout the City Vision or Strategic Plan.

2. Identify, understand, and use current and future risk scenarios. Maintain up-to-date data on hazards and vulnerabilities. Prepare risk assessments based on participatory processes and use these as the basis for urban development of the city and its long-term goals

3. Strengthen financial capacity for resilience. Prepare a financial plan by understanding and assessing the significant economic impacts of disasters. Identify and develop financial mechanisms to support resilience activities.

---

[69] "The Ten Essentials for Making Cities Resilient Checklist" https://mcr2030.undrr.org/sites/default/files/inline-files/10%20Essentials%20%28from%20LG%20handbook%29_1.pdf

4. Pursue resilient urban development and design. Carry out risk-informed urban planning and development based on up-to-date risk assessments with particular focus on vulnerable populations. Apply and enforce realistic, risk compliant building regulations.

5. Safeguard natural buffers to enhance the protective functions offered by natural ecosystems. Identify, protect and monitor natural ecosystems within and outside the city geography and enhance their use for risk reduction.

6. Strengthen institutional capacity for resilience. Understand institutional capacity for risk reduction including those of governmental organizations; private sector; academia, professional and civil society organizations, to help detect and strengthen gaps in resilience capacity.

7. Understand and strengthen societal capacity for resilience. Identify and strengthen social connectedness and culture of mutual help through community and government initiatives and multimedia channels of communication.

8. Increase infrastructure resilience. Develop a strategy for the protection, and update the maintenance of critical infrastructure. Develop risk mitigating infrastructure where needed.

9. Ensure effective preparedness and disaster response. Create and regularly update preparedness plans, connect with early warning systems and increase emergency and management capacities.

10. Expedite recovery and build back better. Establish post-disaster recovery, rehabilitation, and reconstruction strategies that are aligned with long-term planning and providing an improved city environment.

There are numerous organizations and associations working on making the world's cities more resilient. Among them:

- **The Resilient Cities Network:** the world's largest city-led urban resilience network bringing together Its focus is on three priorities to be delivered through programs of collective action with member cities through a holistic resilience approach. It continues to pursue a **resilient recovery** to reinforce equity, to promote private-public partnerships, and foster stronger local economies. Also, cities need to be prepared to further build **climate resilience**, not only to protect citizens from water-related challenges but also to strengthen the capacity of communities to cope with the effects of climate change. The third priority is the promotion of **circular economies** through indigenous and technological solutions to rapidly and sensibly enhance waste management and food systems. The network consists of member cities and Chief Resilience Officers from the 100 Resilient Cities program, sharing a common lens for holistic urban resilience and with thousands of projects in implementation.

100 Resilient Cities (100RC) was pioneered by The Rockefeller Foundation in 2013, as part of its Global Centennial Initiative. In over five years of deep engagement with city leaders, communities, and the private sector, this dynamic network enabled transformational change in cities through support of resilience plans and early implementation of projects. A substantial investment from The Rockefeller Foundation enabled cities to hire a **Chief Resilience Officer**, develop a resilience strategy, access pro-bono services from private sector and NGO partners, and share and receive ideas, innovation and knowledge

through the global network of Chief Resilience Officers (CROs).

NB: Resilience *and* regeneration intersect in the person of **Judith Rodin**, who transformed two global institutions: The Rockefeller Foundation *and* the University of Pennsylvania. Rodin was *the* visionary behind "100 Resilient Cities" when she was the President of the Rockefeller Foundation, and previously in the community-renewal projects[70] in West Philadelphia, as president at Penn. Rodin literally wrote the books on impact investing and resilience: *The Power of Impact Investing: Putting Markets to Work for Profit and Global Good* (Wharton Digital Press, 2014) and *The Resilience Dividend: Being Strong in a World Where Things Go Wrong* (Public Affairs 2014). *resilientcitiesnetwork.org*

- **ICLEI – Local Governments for Sustainability**, is a global network of more than 2500 local and regional governments committed to sustainable urban development. Active in 125+ countries, they influence sustainability policy and drive local action for low emission, nature-based, equitable, resilient and circular development.[71] *iclei.org*

- **United Cities and Local Governments** (UCLG) is the largest organization of local and regional governments in the world. It is wholly committed to the full realization and renewal of local democracy, so as to empower local and regional governments to play their role in the future of humanity. The organization's *The Localization of the Global Agendas: How local action is transforming territories and communities*[72] puts special emphasis on building coalitions, defending the commons, and placing local level public

---

[70] See: https://collaborativehistory.gse.upenn.edu/stories/west-philadelphia-initiatives

[71] See: https://iclei.org/wp-content/uploads/2022/05/ICLEI_in_the_Urban_Era_2021-3.pdf

[72] https://www.uclg.org/sites/default/files/goldv_en.pdf

service delivery at the heart of the investments needed to realize the development agenda. The organization calls for all spheres of government and all stakeholders to embolden their ambitions and support the development of a 'whole-of-society' approach through localization. A critical part of the agenda is decentralization and the localization of the UN SDGs. *www.uclg.org*

- **C40 Cities:** a global network of mayors taking urgent action to confront the climate crisis. *c40.org*

From these organizations, we find that local strategies and plans for resilience can be a starting point for regeneration. Furthermore, these distributed strategies are centrally coordinated through these associations.

This is the foundation of a **"cosmo-local"** approach. **Arup** and the Rockefeller Foundation jointly created a framework for city resilience which has four main dimensions and 12 drivers that together illustrate what makes a resilient city.

The four main dimensions are:

- **Health and wellbeing:** Systems that ensure the health and wellbeing of people living and working in the city.

- **Economy and society:** The social and financial systems that enable urban populations to live peacefully, and act collectively.

- **Infrastructure and Environment:** Built and natural systems that provide critical services, protect and connect urban citizens.

- **Leadership and strategy:** The need for informed, inclusive, integrated and iterative decision making in our cities.

Using the City Resilience Index[73], *your* city can map its profile and measure progress, learning from other cities and towns.

The city of **Athens**, for example, has created a Resilience Strategy for 2030,[74] created in collaboration with 140 organizations and 900 citizens participating in 40 workshops, conferences or public events. The Athens Resilience Strategy offers a set of new integrated ways to prepare and protect the city's most vulnerable from future shocks and stresses that the city will face.

Boosting the city's resilience means creating new as well as revitalizing existing open and green public spaces. This is vital for a densely built and populated city like Athens, threatened by both intense heat (climate change) and earthquakes. The city needs to become more forward thinking and proactive, turning its challenges into resources (vacant buildings, newly arrived refugee and migrant populations, energy and waste). Around such resources it will build capacity and start to develop economies that, together with tourism and the creative sector, will generate the city's future. Finally, the city will strengthen its government, through becoming more transparent and accountable, opening streams of communication, creating a digital agenda and innovation strategy.

Eleni Myrivili, the **Chief Resilience Officer (CRO)** for the city explains: "Our resilience strategy is the first strategy that equips our city with new ways of thinking and dealing with the chronic stresses and the acute shocks that we are likely to experience in the future."

How did Athens survive the recent socio-economic crisis? Myrivili says: "We built strong collaboration mechanisms

---

[73] https://www.cityresilienceindex.org/#/city-profiles
[74] See: https://resilientcitiesnetwork.org/downloadable_resources/Network/Athens-Resilience-Strategy-English.pdf

among the public, private and civic sectors. This is an increasingly important aspect of city governance and it is absolutely crucial in forging city resilience."

The city recognized the need to create a **platform** to include all of the CSOs and NGOs dealing with health and social services, in order to better communicate to the municipal departments which outside partners are available to assist with citizen needs. Thus, the city launched the **Social Integration Initiative** (SII) that now has more than 160 registered organizations offering health and social services. The civil employees refer to the platform in order to determine which services are most appropriate to meet the needs of the beneficiaries in case the city does not meet these needs.

The resilience strategy work[75] began with a **diagnostic assessment** that identified the following **shocks** and **stresses** as the most important for Athens:

- **Earthquakes** Over 30% of buildings in the City of Athens were constructed before the first building code for earthquake protection, a serious vulnerability in a country with the 6th highest seismic activity level in the world.

- **Climate Change related Shocks (Heat waves, flash floods, poor air quality)** Climate change scenarios indicate that extreme heat events are expected to typify the city's future. Between 2021 and 2050, average summer temperatures in Athens are projected to increase by 2°C; between 2071 and 2100 the projected increase goes up to 4°C. The city is already observing a gradual increase in the length and level of high temperatures as well as the frequency and intensity of heat waves and other related phenomena such as flash floods and bad air quality.

---

[75] The team consists of Kostas Georgiou, Anthi Christou, Mairy Sarantari, and CRO Eleni Myrivili.

- **Civil Unrest** Demonstrations take place in Athens almost on a daily basis, and are organized by labor unions, political parties, anti-authoritarian groups, student groups, and other collectivities. These demonstrations vary in size and intensity but they always take place in the city center. People expressed fear of the city being engulfed in violence.

- **Cybercrime**
  Cybercrime in Greece is a rising challenge. The City of Athens is at the center of many operational decision-making procedures while also hosting several critical infrastructures and public utility networks. It is therefore a high-risk target for cyber-attacks.

- **Depressed Macroeconomic Conditions** Since 2009, Greece has been in recession, with depressed macroeconomic conditions and severe cuts in social and public services. High unemployment has been the worst of its consequences.

- **Aging Infrastructure** Many buildings in Athens are of very poor quality, have unsafe structural elements, and are not energy efficient. They do not comply with the regulatory guidelines for the Greek Building Code and their increasing energy demands add to the city's greenhouse gas emissions and energy poverty rates.

- **Migration** By the end of 2016 about 60.000 newcomers – refugees and immigrants - were recorded as living in Greece. Around 20.000 of them are currently living in Athens: half of them are Syrians while others come from Afghanistan, Palestine, Iran and Kurdistan.

- **Mistrust**
  During 2016, the Greek Ombudsman issued a report analyzing the widely spread feeling of mistrust between citizens and public services. This is only a small aspect of

the large phenomenon of mistrust that Athenians have towards all levels of government, administrative or elected. This is the outcome of centuries of political partisanship and mismanagement of resources, corruption and clientelism, lack of transparency and accountability.

Myrivili views **trust** as an important priority: "an open city is a city that is accountable, a city that can win back the trust of its people. *For Athens to be resilient it needs to build trust.* One of the main stresses that keep weakening the ability of the city to move forward, as well as the cohesion of Athenian society, is **mistrust**. The city is in the process of becoming more open and transparent through opening channels of communication, its data and its procedures."

The resilience team has mapped[76] its resilience plans painstakingly to *integrate* resilience planning with all the other ongoing initiatives in the city. The city of Athens wants to be: (1) an Open city (2) a Green city, (3) a Proactive city, and (4) a Vibrant city.

NOTE: for more information on city resilience plans around the world, see: https://resilientcitiesnetwork.org/network/

Furthermore, **Athens** is one of the Hub Cities for the MCR2030 with a focus on **heat resilience**.

What is required to move from resilience to regeneration? We believe the shift is **hyper-localization**, that is, getting community members engaged, neighborhood by neighborhood.

As we looked for this connection between resilience and local communities, we learned about the efforts of **Sylvester**

---

[76] See: https://resilientcitiesnetwork.org/downloadable_resources/Network/Athens-Resilience-Strategy-English.pdf (pp. 44-45)

Turner, the Mayor of the City of Houston[77]. Not only is he the chairman of the **Resilient Cities Network**, but he promotes a concept called **"complete communities"** - which is exactly what it sounds like, a neighborhood level engagement process for local communities.

COMPLETE COMMUNITIES

Complete Communities is an initiative from the **City of Houston** focused on bridging the gap between equity and opportunity. Made up of ten historically under-resourced neighborhoods which together are home to one in six Houstonians, Complete Communities exists to ensure all residents can achieve success without barriers to opportunity. Launched in April 2017 as a city-wide initiative to revitalize Houston's most under-resourced Neighborhoods, the mission of Complete Communities is to create a more equitable and prosperous city for all Houstonians by working with **local stakeholders** and **cross-sector partners** to improve designated neighborhoods.

We view this as the crucial link to community wealth-building absent from "sustainability" and "circular-economy" initiatives, a key ingredient to community regeneration.

The focus[78] of Complete Communities is on "equitable development" with a community-based mission, as explained by **Mayor Turner**:

Every Houstonian should know their neighborhood matters. Our mission is to build one complete city from recovery to resilience by championing the voices of residents that have been ignored for far too long and offering every Houston resident the foundational resources needed to thrive. We work across private, public, and nonprofit sectors to collectively overcome economic, environmental, and equity

---

[77] Christian Sarkar, one of the authors of this book, has called Houston "home" since 1980.

[78] See: https://www.houstoncc.org/about_the_initiative/index.php

challenges to transform Houston's legacy into one everyone can be proud of.

The mayor's interest in rebuilding underserved and under-resourced neighborhoods led to the creation of Houston's Complete Communities program in April 2017, which includes the following residential areas[79]: Acres Homes, Alief Westwood, Fort Bend Houston, Gulfton, Kashmere Gardens, Magnolia Park, Near Northside, Second Ward, Sunny Side, and Third Ward.

So, what is a **Complete Community?** A complete community is a connected community that is committed to civic engagement, building strong civic organizations, and nurturing new leaders. The concept is defined as follows:

A **sustainable** community with . . .
> Strong community partners
> Civic engagement
> Community buy-in

An **affordable** community with . . .
> Diversity of income
> No concentrated poverty
> A strong base of homeowners
> Quality rental units
> Energy efficient homes

A **healthy** community with . . .
> A quality grocery store
> Access to quality health care
> Parks
> Urban gardens or farms

---

[79] FYI: Beyoncé grew up in the 3rd Ward.

A **safe** community with . . .
>Low crime
>Low rates of automobile crashes
>No unsafe environmental hazards
>Safe places for residents to walk, run, bicycle, and recreate

An **economically strong** community with . . .
>Opportunities for upward mobility
>Quality and diverse retail
>Quality jobs within or easily accessible from the community
>Thriving small businesses
>Strong city tax revenues to pay for municipal services

A community with **quality schools** including . . .
>Highly rated elementary, middle and high schools
>Easy access to high quality and affordable early childcare
>Access to quality vocational schools, community colleges

A community with **good infrastructure** including . . .
>Complete streets including sidewalks, bike paths, and accessible transit stops
>Utility infrastructure
>Proper lighting

A **connected** community with . . .
>Access to broadband internet connectivity
>Quality public transit or other affordable transportation options
>Good roads connecting to other major job centers and central business districts
>Strong community organizations that connect

residents with each other and to others throughout the city

A **beautiful** and interesting community with . . .
Street trees
Public art
Public spaces
Preservation of historic neighborhoods

A **resilient** community with . . .
Flood protection
Good drainage
Community and public services

Each neighborhood has a **Complete Communities Action Plan** which outlines the vision, policies, goals and projects that have been identified by community stakeholders over a six-month planning process. Each plan includes initiatives in areas such as:

- Civic Engagement
- Economy and Jobs
- Education
- Health
- Housing
- Mobility and Infrastructure
- Neighborhood Character, Parks and Community Amenities
- Safety

Most importantly, the plans provide public metrics[80] which help track progress and build a community feedback loop.

---

[80] See: https://cms7files.revize.com/ldrhoustoncctx/Our%20Communities/third-ward-complete-communities-action-plan.pdf (p.11) For a complete list of community plans, visit:
https://houstoncc.org/our_communities/index.php

The program also establishes a Complete Communities University, including leadership training with classes designed to strengthen the existing skills of community leaders as they work to implement goals, actions and project aspirations laid out in the plans.

Courses include: Fundraising, Running Effective Meetings, Mediation & Conflict Resolution, Community Outreach, Department of Neighborhoods, importance of the Census and, Neighborhood Safety.

NOTE: The "Complete Communities" approach works well with the "Pyramid of Community Value" and Jobs to be Done approach we introduced at the beginning of the chapter.

CITY AS COMMONS

What if we viewed the **city as a commons** – an infrastructure we shared for mutual benefit? This is the thesis of **Shiela Foster** and **Christian Iaione** in their ground-breaking research at LabGov.

Here's how they describe[81] their goals:

*The new city governance model we propose — what we call "urban co-governance" — the city (as **public authority**) acts as a facilitator of the emerging co-management structures throughout its territory and enables **city inhabitants** to actively take part in the regeneration of their habitat, improve their lifestyle, and develop the community they belong to. In this way, LabGov practices and advocates for the transition from urban commons intervention to a more just and **democratic governance of the city as commons**.*

The **Co-City** – as they dub the city as commons – is governed by 5 design principles: Collective Governance, the Enabling

---

[81] http://labgov.city/city-as-a-commons/

State, Social and Economic Pooling, Experimentalism, and Technological justice.

The concept[82] of the Co-City situates the city as an infrastructure, enabling sharing and collaboration, participatory decision-making, and peer-to-peer production, supported by open data and guided by principles of distributive justice.

The Co-City Protocol is constituted of three elements: principles, the processes, and tools. The protocol is designed to create the most favorable environment for innovation through **urban commoning**, by adopting the conceptual pillars of the urban commons: sharing, collaboration, and polycentrism. The key is to transform the entire city or some parts of it into a laboratory by creating the proper legal and political ecosystem for the installation of shared, collaborative, polycentric urban governance schemes.

How do local communities become key actors in the production, delivery, and management of urban assets or local resources? The LabGov research reveals how common initiatives take new forms, like community land trusts, co-housing, neighborhood cooperatives, community-shared broadband and energy networks, and new local offices focused on citizen science and civic imagination.

The protocol was first applied and implemented in 2014 in the Italian cities of Bologna (the Co-Bologna project[83]) and Mantua (the Co-Mantova project), followed by Battipaglia (Co-Battipaglia), Reggio Emilia (Co-Reggio Emilia), Toscana (Collaborative Tuscany) and Roma (Co-Rome).

---

[82] See: "The Co-Cities Protocol" http://labgov.city/wp-content/uploads/sites/19/Protocol-.pdf
[83] https://co-bologna.it/

Details of the results and methods are available in their book: *Co-Cities: Innovative Transitions toward Just and Self-Sustaining Communities (Urban and Industrial Environments)* by Sheila Foster and Christian Iaione. (*MIT Press*, December 2022)

COMMUNITY AS A PLATFORM

Too often we operate under the mistaken assumption that private or state digital platforms are the only solutions available for digital community enablement. Extending the "city-as-a-commons" view to the digital realm creates a new and exciting possibility for public value creation: "community-as-a-platform."

As top-down, country-based platforms continue to grow, Sangeet Paul Choudary points out that control over the trade in goods and services shifts from countries to digital platforms.[84] He explains the ramifications:

Public and private actors in China are working in close cooperation — in a country-level platform strategy — to create digital infrastructure that aligns with the BRI, to promote standards that drive the adoption of such infrastructure, and to strengthen China's points of control in the digital economy. This strategy extends across four key themes: trade, payments, smart cities, and social credit. If successful, this strategy could fundamentally shift trade and financial flows toward a China-centric economic order and could even reshape political systems in participating countries.

The weakness of this platform strategy is that it is grounded on the same fallacy that John McKnight warned us about: it is a **top-down**, needs-based transaction system which **fails to build local trust**. And *that* is an opportunity for **community-based platforms.** Local ownership or municipal ownership of community platforms allows for greater flexibility and local

---

[84] *China's country-as-platform strategy for global influence*, Sangeet Paul Choudary, Brookings Institute, November 19, 2020 https://www.brookings.edu/techstream/chinas-country-as-platform-strategy-for-global-influence/

empowerment. The opportunity is a bottom-up platform which is built *by* communities, *for* communities.

© Christian Sarkar , Enrico Foglia, and Philip Kotler 2022

The growing importance of the groups like the **Platform Cooperativism Consortium** are creating a space for community collaboration. Platform cooperatives are businesses that use a website, mobile app, or protocol to sell goods or services. They rely on democratic decision-making and shared ownership of the platform by workers and users.[85] Their tool library is a place for co-ops to find and share digital tools with each other. They are justifiably upset with "platform capitalism" because they view the Internet slipping out of ordinary users' control. Their point-of-view:

The power held by principal platform owners like Uber, Amazon, and Facebook has allowed them to reorganize life and work to their benefit and that of their shareholders. "Free" services often come at the cost of our valuable personal information, with little recourse for users who value their privacy.

---

[85] Platform Cooperativism Consortium https://platform.coop

The paid work that people execute on digital platforms like Uber or Freelancer allows owners to challenge hard-won gains by 20th-century labor struggles: workers are reclassified as "independent contractors" and thus denied rights such as minimum wage protections, unemployment benefits, and collective bargaining. Platform executives argue that they are merely technology (not labor) companies; that they are intermediaries who have no responsibility for the workers who use their sites. The plush pockets of venture capitalists behind "sharing economy" apps allow them to lobby governments around the world to make room for their "innovative" practices, despite well-substantiated adverse long-term effects on workers, users, the environment and communities. At the same time, in the gaps and hollows of the digital economy, a new model follows a significantly different ethical and financial logic.

Bottom line? Digital platforms *can* be owned and managed differently.

Is it any wonder that we are beginning to see a new wave of startups and businesses striving to do good, to create a *platform around purpose*? For example:

- **Up & Go** offers professional home services like house cleaning, (and soon childcare and dog walking) by those who are looking for assistance with laborers from local worker-owned cooperatives. Unlike extractive home-services platforms which take up to 30% of workers' income, Up & Go charges only the 5% it needs to maintain the platform.

- **Fairbnb.coop** is a platform for vacation-rentals which gives back 50% of its revenues to support local community projects of your choice such as social housing for residents, community gardens and more.

- **MiData** is a Swiss "health data cooperative," creating a data-exchange which will securely host member-users' medical records. MiData aims to out-compete private, for-profit data brokers and ultimately return the control and monetization of personal data to those who generate it.

• **Gratipay** provides a free subscription-based patronage infrastructure for developers of open-source ventures, by enabling credit-card transactions at-cost, subtracting only the processing fees from users' subscriptions

• **MyCelia**'s goal is to empower a fair, sustainable and vibrant music industry ecosystem involving all online music interaction services. They seek to unlock the huge potential for creators and their music related metadata so an entirely new commercial marketplace may flourish, while ensuring all involved are paid and acknowledged fully, and to see that commercial, ethical and technical standards are set to exponentially increase innovation for the music services of the future.

All of these businesses are developing ecosystems and platforms built around connecting customers with the job to be done, for less, or for free. They are seeking to build a more equitable, common platform for value exchanges. What happens when this bottom-up approach goes nationwide?

The result is what Istakapaza CEO **Alok Sinha** calls "Community as a Platform" – a **community-based** approach that is being developed in India to include all sectors: public, private, and plural.[86]

---

[86] Interview with Alok Sinha, CEO, Istakapaza.com *Disclosure: Christian Sarkar is on Istakapaza's advisory board.*

COMMUNITY AS A PLATFORM

PRIVATE **SECTOR**	PUBLIC **SECTOR**		PLURAL **SECTOR**
INDUSTRY PLATFORMS Agriculture Mining Forestry Fishing Quarrying Packaging & Processing or Raw Material Manufacturing Processing Construction Energy Retail & Wholesale Transportation & Distribution Restaurants Media Tourism Insurance, Banking & Healthcare Legal Culture Scientific research Education Information Technology	*CITIZEN SERVICES* Education Energy Health Transportation Social Security Direct Services *FUNCTIONS* Defense Law Enforcement Intelligence International Affairs Corrections		*PHILANTHROPIC SERVICES* Environment & Conservation Donor/Recipient Traceability Foundation ecosystem *CO-OPS + COLLABORATIVE CAPITALISM* Smart contracts Business formation on the fly Value sharing *LOCAL COMMUNITIES* Entrepreneurial and startups Capacity building and training Local NGOs Regional access Global access
	SUPPORT SERVICES Supply Chain Management HR Management Financial Management Digital Enablement	*TRANSPARENCY* Immutable Records Citizen Protection Blockchain: Smart Contracts Encryption	*HYBRID BUSINESS MODELS* Collaborative revenue Local Growth Public value creation Societal value creation

© Christian Sarkar and Philip Kotler 2021

"Our goal is start by building deep vertically-integrated platforms that empower not just the big industry players but small startups and local entrepreneurs in a seamless experience," explains Sinha. "The strategy is one of inclusivity and local empowerment in Tier I, 2 and 3 cities across India. We say that no one owns the ecosystem, we are all participants. We begin with the local community, but it scales to the country-level. So, it can turn into Country-as-a-Platform."

This is a step in the direction of citizen-owned public platforms. What if there was a non-profit version of Facebook? What if your local post-office was a public platform for banking, for e-commerce, for community digital enablement?

Of special note is **Dark Matter Labs**, a not-for-profit which designs and builds the underlying infrastructure to support the new civic economy, exploring how ownership, legal systems, governance, accountancy and insurance might begin to change.

Co-founder Indy Johar says[87]:

...we are witnessing a failure to understand and accelerate the possibility & growth offered by new technology. How can smart outcome driven legislation unleash product and service innovation; how can real-time compliance reduce risk but facilitate greater innovation; what does real-time data driven regulation mean our historic economies from Freight to Real-Estate; how does smart regulation open up the unprecedented capacity for contingent, contextual and connected regulation and public interest Governance. To place this opportunity most literally – what would happen for example, if we no longer planned cities zonally through static and analogue means but instead re-imagined "planning" through real-time data driven outcomes, pricing & impacts – this is increasingly a possibility, a reality which has the capacity to drive the total reinvention of our cities in ways as yet only imagined in architectural manifestos. What is clear, is we need to shift from regulating the ghost of the industrial economy to the reality of network economy if we are unlock its benefits and mediate its impacts and potential damage.

Johar believes we need a "boring revolution" – the development and experimentation with new civic infrastructures to manage our emergent future.

Johar again[88]:

In our current systems, we have effectively outsourced societal decision making and theories of value to centralised capital production of banks. The exceptional power bestowed on commercial banks to issue credit fundamentally determines which activities and sectors of society receive funding and thus their viability. In a regenerative future, this dynamic will need to be reimagined.

---

[87] https://provocations.darkmatterlabs.org/the-necessity-of-a-boring-revolution-a71b1ae6f956
[88] https://provocations.darkmatterlabs.org/financing-city-transitions-a-public-civic-deep-code-innovation-challenge-9f2ef55b4bda

ECOSYSTEMATIC

Our final approach to regeneration is based on the idea that we can view **community assets as ecosystems**, under the following categories:

- **Nature:** the natural assets surrounding the community
- **Culture**: music, art, theater, literature, music, dance, and other forms of expression
- **Social**: the talents and skills of individuals and groups or associations
- **Economic**: the financial resources and pools available
- **Education**: the public educational system
- **Infrastructure**: the essential, public infrastructure of the community including utilities and services like electricity, trash pickup, drinking water, sewage processing, roads, etc.
- **Agriculture**: starting with soil health, the local practices of cultivation and care for the local farmer
- **Environment**: protecting the natural world from human impact
- **Technology**: the digital divide is a threat to democracy
- **Politics**: access and equal voting rights for all
- **Law**: ending unjust incarceration and exploitative prison labor

Each ecosystem category has its own agents, terrain, flows, vehicles, interactions, and value. Growing community ecosystems is about connecting people's capacities so they can participate in meaningful ways that add **value** to themselves and the larger **local community**.

community level

ECOSYSTEMATIC VIEW

What are the **JOBS-to-be-Done?**
Whose **AGENDA** is being served?

purpose

→ TIME

terrain	agents	stocks + flows	vehicles	interactions	value
space	roles	assets	transport	relationships	meaning
WHERE	*WHO*	*WHAT*	*HOW*	*HOW*	*WHY*
physical	creator	people	individuals	creating	public	survival
geographical	consumer	assets	families	consuming	private	essentials
natural landscape	producer	information	associations	hoarding	plural	livelihood
architecture	attacker	ideas	business	sharing	hybrid	belonging
urban layout	defender	knowledge	institutions	taking	commons	loving
commercial	co-opter	energy	NGOs	giving		caring
residential	collaborator	objects	coops	consuming		
social	partner	products	government	exchanging		
public	teacher	services	administration	helping		
private	helper	culture	emergency	fighting		
commons	observer	trust		governing		

© Christian Sarkar Philip Kotler 2018

An **ecosystematic view** of the community allows us to interpret and **make sense** of the interactions of daily *life as a theater*.

- The space or **terrain** is defined as **place** – the actual physical and structural configuration of the territory.
- The **agents** are the roles of the participants or **actors** in the ecosystem **theater.**
- The **stocks** and **flows** are the assets and the movement of those assets over time: into, within, and out of the community theater or ecosystem.
- The **vehicles** are the agents of **transport** for interactions.
- The **interactions** are the actions taken by the various agents – they create **relationships** between the agents.
- **Value** is assigned to the interactions by the agents and by the community (we will explore this further through the concept of the "community value pyramid").
- **Purpose** is the **governing intent** of the interactions in the ecosystem.

An ecosystematic approach allows us to understand the trajectory of local community asset development and its impact over time.

The evolution of community ecosystems is largely based on the **interactions** and **relationships** within the community. As the community gains agency, creates and builds activities to further its interests, the ecosystem grows with it – creating an expanding network of engagement.

The entire ecosystem can be viewed, again, through a negative lens – an **ecosystem of problems**, or conversely – through a positive lens – as an **ecosystem of opportunities**.

COMMUNITY "NEEDS" VIEWED AS AN ECOSYSTEM

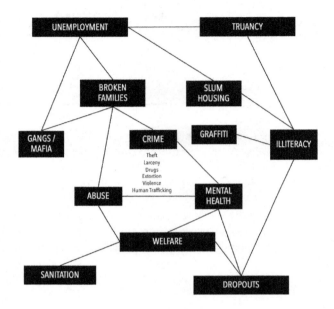

adapted from: John Kretzmann and John McKnight
Building Communities from the Inside Out: A Path Toward Finding and Mobilizing a Community's Assets (1993)

Community regeneration includes "**community development**" which is best described as a process where community members come together to take **collective action** and generate solutions to **common problems**. The key here is true community-leadership, *consent*, and active participation.

COMMUNITY "ASSETS" VIEWED AS AN ECOSYSTEM

adapted from: John Kretzmann and John McKnight
Building Communities from the Inside Out: A Path Toward Finding and Mobilizing a Community's Assets (1993)

Each category or asset – if it exists in the community – exists in an extended ecosystem with its attendant relationships and agents. These community-based ecosystems or parts of the ecosystem can also be viewed as a **commons** – through a process of **commoning**. Commoning implies that "commoners share and govern commons, establishing practices and relations in line with the political principles of building common wealth."[89]

---

[89] "Defining and discussing the notion of commoning" Alessio Kolioulis, The Bartlett Development Planning Unit, University College London, GOLD VI Working Paper Series #14 April 2022
https://gold.uclg.org/sites/default/files/14_defining_and_discussing_the_notion_of_commoning_by_alessio _kolioulis_the_bartlett_development_planning_unit_university_college_london.pdf

Emerging commoning projects are often not in direct opposition to the state but seek instead active collaboration with governmental actors. Indeed, commoning practices and instruments have shifted towards a more democratic approach and are increasingly co-produced by groups and communities in collaboration with state institutions such as municipalities and local governments.[90]

We are on the cusp of a new paradigm: a regenerative economy which could be built from the community upwards – *cosmolocal*, instead of global.[91]

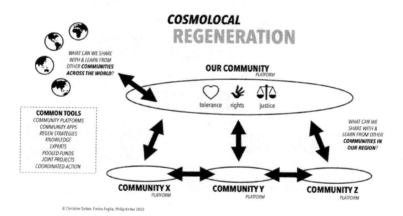

© Christian Sarkar, Enrico Foglia, Philip Kotler 2022

Regeneration is thus a continuous process of local ecosystem development – growing and nurturing the agents or actors in the community. Lest we forget, now is a good time to note that a key measure of regeneration is the wellbeing of the community, which includes **local wealth building.** Without *local* **value creation**, we're **not regenerative**.

---

[90] "The CO-City: Sharing, Collaborating, Cooperating, and Commoning in the City" by Christian Iaione, *The American Journal of Economics and Sociology* Vol. 75, No. 2, Questioning the Commons: Power, Equity, and the Meaning of Ownership (MARCH, 2016), pp. 415-455
[91] See: https://wiki.p2pfoundation.net/Cosmo-Localism and this classic: *The Cosmolocal Reader* https://clreader.net

CULTURAL REGENERATION

Cultural regeneration is a process that seeks to protect, repair, invest, and transform cultural resources and heritage in a particular region or community. It often involves cultural institutions, organizations, and individuals working together to promote cultural tourism, arts and crafts, heritage conservation, and community engagement.

As we mentioned earlier, Palermo's Leoluca Orlando used cultural regeneration as a powerful force to regenerate the city, to create cultural connections with citizens by reopening cultural institutions - the opera-house, for example.

Artists and creatives are community value creators – they play a vital role in community renewal by contributing to the social, economic, and cultural fabric of their communities:

Creative Placemaking: Artists can use their skills and creativity to transform underutilized public spaces into vibrant community gathering places, such as creating murals, sculptures, or interactive installations. This process of creative placemaking can attract new visitors and help build a sense of community pride and ownership.

Economic Development: Art-based businesses can be a catalyst for economic development in a community, by providing jobs, attracting tourists, and contributing to the local economy. Additionally, artists can help revitalize struggling neighborhoods by opening studios, galleries, and performance spaces.

Cultural Preservation: Artists can help preserve and celebrate a community's cultural heritage through their work. This can include traditional art forms such as dance, music, and storytelling, as well as contemporary art that reflects the community's current identity.

Social Engagement: Art can be a powerful tool for bringing people together and fostering social connections. Artists can use their work to promote dialogue and understanding across diverse communities, and to address social issues such as inequality, injustice, and environmental sustainability.

Creatives have the ability to inspire and engage communities, spark creativity and innovation, and contribute to a community's sense of identity and pride. By leveraging their talents and skills, community leaders can unleash the forces of cultural regeneration to promote positive change.

*"San Benedetto" – mural by **Igor Scalisi Palminteri**
in Ballarò, Palermo, Sicily*

Street art can elevate the neighborhood. **Igor Scalisi Palminteri,** a celebrated muralist in Palermo, Sicily, explains[92]:

---

[92] https://www.igorscalisipalminteri.it

"My work has shifted from my studio to the streets almost by accident, assuming the features of Neo-muralism. What I do is only the result of my choices, from my encounter with the Capuchin friars to the years spent at the Academy of Fine Arts and my work with children, painting the first walls. My roots are in the streets. My artistic vision has a social approach, I am attracted to fragile environments. My works always focus on what happens around a wall, which is never made of bricks alone, but people too."

Another form of cultural regeneration can be driven by private citizens who share their private art collections with the public through museums and other exhibits.

This is the case with Palermo's **Palazzo Butera**, an institution we will discover later in this book.

Collaborations between modern designers and traditional artisans can create new channels for community wealth-building. This is the case with **made/in** and **White Champa** – both run by designers. We'll learn more about them in next chapter.

Finally, technologies such as 3D-printing open up new possibilities for reinterpreting master sculptures as officially licensed *artclones* – available to museum visitors and cultural tourists. Again, we uncovered an innovative startup in Palermo: **artficial**, the world-leader in artclone production.[93]

The following table outlines the different dimensions of cultural regeneration:

---

[93] Learn more about artclones via the *Artclone Review*: www.artclonereview.com

CULTURAL REGENERATION PATHWAYS	DEFINITION	EXAMPLES
Heritage Conservation	Preservation and restoration of cultural heritage assets such as historic buildings, monuments, and artifacts	Restoration of ancient ruins, museums, and cultural sites
Cultural Fusion	Extension of cultural identity and work by combining elements of modern art with traditional techniques and styles	Collaboration between designers and technology with traditional art forms (textiles, artclones, fashion, etc.)
Community Engagement	Involving and empowering local communities in cultural regeneration projects, and fostering a sense of ownership and participation	Community-led festivals, workshops, and cultural events
Economic Development	Using cultural resources to generate economic activity, such as tourism and creative industries	Cultural tourism, arts and crafts markets, and creative industries hubs
Identity and Representation	Emphasizing the unique cultural identity and representation of a region or community	Celebrating cultural traditions, music, dance, and cuisine
Education and Learning	Providing opportunities for learning and education about local culture and heritage	School visits to museums, cultural heritage sites, and educational workshops

Here are some examples of **cultural regeneration projects** communities can initiate and promote:

1. **Arts initiatives:** Projects that support local artists and promote artistic expression can contribute to cultural regeneration. For example, a community may create public art installations or provide funding for local artists to create new works.

2. **Community festivals:** Festivals that celebrate local traditions and culture can bring people together and foster a sense of community. For example, a city may host an

annual cultural festival that showcases local food, music, dance, and crafts.

3. **Historic preservation:** Preserving historic buildings, monuments, and landmarks can help to maintain a community's cultural identity and promote a sense of pride in the community's heritage. For example, a town may restore an old theater or courthouse and turn it into a cultural center.

4. **Cultural education programs:** Programs that provide opportunities for people to learn about different cultures can promote cultural understanding and appreciation. For example, a community may offer language classes, cooking classes, or traditional music and dance lessons.

5. **Indigenous land and language reclamation**: Projects that support Indigenous communities in reclaiming their land and language can promote cultural revitalization. For example, a tribe may work to reclaim ancestral lands, or a language revitalization program may be established to preserve and promote an endangered Indigenous language.

6. **Environmental restoration and traditional ecological knowledge preservation:** Projects that link cultural practices to environmental sustainability can create a space for cultural regeneration while addressing issues of climate change. For example, projects could include traditional ecological knowledge mapping or restoration of traditional farming practices.

Cultural regeneration projects are most effective when they involve broad community participation and are informed by the cultural traditions and practices of the community. By promoting cultural understanding and preserving cultural heritage, these projects can contribute to a more vibrant and resilient community.

Visit www.regenemarketing.org for more information.

3. THE REGENERATIVE ORGANIZATION

Six of the top ten longest running family-run enterprises in the world are Italian. Some of them are purpose-built to create community value.

The oldest is **Fonderie Pontificie Marinelli** (founded in 1000 AD) – and is still in operation in Agnone, a small Italian town of 5,200 inhabitants in the province of Isernia in Molise. The product? Bells. Granted the honor of using the Papal Coat of Arms in 1924 by Pope Pio XI, the world's oldest foundry still makes bells using the ancient technique known as "lost-wax casting" and its bells are used across the globe, from New York to Beijing, Jerusalem, and South American.

What is it that makes Italian companies resilient? Is it the family-owned aspect? The vision of the founder? Is it the cultural and socio-political landscape of the Italian city-states?

These are questions we were trying to answer, as part of a series of research initiatives with the **Regenerative Marketing Institute**. Our goal was to better understand the traditional *and* contemporary factors for business longevity and resilience, and to develop a practical framework for regeneration. In the course of our work, we entered into an exploration of what defines a regenerative business.

Our research findings from Italy suggest the following positive characteristics for these small champions:

- **The Founding Mission:** the business has kept its founding spirit alive, often rejuvenated by the current leadership
- **Leading with Trust:** the company is built on long-term trust-based architectures and business models

- **Commitment to Community:** the enterprise has deep local roots and is designed to improve community wellbeing
- **Imagination-driven Innovation:** the business builds unique, differentiated products
- **Time-Equity:** the institution invests in building customer and community intimacy and puts in the **time** to create deep connections. Building customer intimacy is not a technology. It is an investment in time spent building and nurturing future profits.
- **Cultural Traditions:** the company balances traditions and "family" values with competitive pressures
- **Collaboration Platforms:** the company builds a community-centric platform for creating community value
- **Multi-generational Loyalty:** employees and their families have a life-long relationship with the business, often over multiple generations
- **Customer Focus:** customer relationships are built on *deep trust*, not exploitation
- **Local Funding:** Financial support from local based banks and financial institutions tightly connected with the local community so that access to the credit is easier thanks to long-term personal relationships.
- **Local Circular Economy**: supplier, partners, consultants are chosen among local community creating a common vision where the success of the company is shared with community stakeholders
- **Local Sustainability**: great attention to local environmental practices where most of the time the founders and his/her family reside
- **Company size**: growth is not a priority, but stability and quality is. Most of the companies are "mid-sized" at best.

Now, with **climate change** becoming a major driver of change, we see regeneration integrated into business strategy. Some of these companies are quick to change course and adapt to the new requirement of deep-decarbonization and ethical supply chains.

Some of the shortcomings of these companies include:

- **Finance:** lack of access to big institutional/international investors interested in long-view investments
- **Digitalization:** many, though not all, are lagging in their implementation of digital strategies
- **Gender inequality:** the glass ceiling is real and an obstacle to company performance
- **Branding:** weak marketing and branding acumen is often combined with an inability to see what is required to expand beyond existing markets

The traditional "go-to-market" approach we've used for the past 100 years is about building a product and taking it to market based on a customer value-proposition. Because the business is built on the volume of its transactions, the business does not focus on long-term community relationships. In fact, it is often at odds with community aspirations, and must play "nice" by being a good corporate citizen – via CSR and public relations.

But what happens when you redesign your organization to be regenerative? *It becomes an anchor in the community, a proponent of the Common Good.*

WHAT IS A REGENERATIVE ORGANIZATION?

If you go back and ask the founder of an organization – why did you start this business (or institution) they won't say "so we can grow year over year by 23.5%," or "so we can leverage synergies." They're going to say that they could not stop themselves – the idea in their heads just had to become reality.

A regenerative organization **creates value** for the **organization** *and* the **community** simultaneously. In the previous chapter we examined the various dimensions of community value. Regenerative organizations **create organizational and community value** *and* **support Nature** – leading to a better quality of life in the local community.

REGENERATION
AN ORGANIZATIONAL PERSPECTIVE

© Christian Sarkar, Enrico Foglia, and Philip Kotler, 2021

We also need to understand the difference between a sustainable and a regenerative organization. The following table outlines the key differences:

Attributes	Sustainable Organizations	Regenerative Organizations
Vision	Minimizing negative impact on environment and society	Maximizing positive impact on environment and society
Goal	To maintain a balance between economic growth, environmental protection, and social responsibility	To regenerate the Common Good by restoring ecosystems and social systems while fostering economic stability
Mindset	Reducing harm	Regenerating the Common Good
Approach	Mitigation and reduction of negative impact	Creation and amplification of positive impact *(protect, restore, invest, transform)*
Innovation	Incremental improvements in sustainability practices	Disruptive and innovative solutions to promote regeneration
Resource/Asset Use	Efficient use and reduction of resource consumption	Regeneration of common resources *(protect, restore, invest, transform)*
Community	Collaboration and engagement with stakeholders	Co-creation and empowerment of local communities
Profit	Profit is necessary for sustainability, but not the only goal	Profit is a means to achieve a regenerative outcome
Success Metrics	Reduction in negative environmental and social impacts	Increase in positive environmental and social impacts, as well as a stable local economy
Examples	Recycling, reducing carbon footprint, socially responsible investing	Common Good projects: Regenerative agriculture, circular economy, community wealth-building, natural ecosystem restoration, worksharing, etc.

While sustainable and regenerative organizations may share some similarities, the key difference is the mindset and approach towards advancing the Common Good. Regenerative business seeks to go beyond just minimizing negative impact and aims to promote the Common Good, actively restore and regenerate natural and social systems while also delivering a *steady-state* economy.

NOTE: If your organization views regeneration merely as a cost, you have already lost.

ZERO DISTANCE TO REALITY

How close are is your organization to the customer? This is a popular idea today – the idea of **"zero distance"** to the customer.[94]

In 2015, Professor **Dennis Campbell** published "Zero Distance to Users" as a Harvard Business School case. He taught the case in his "High Performance Organization and Cultural Design" class. From the case, the principles of Zero Distance are as follows:

- Having a management philosophy that allows the organization to proactively react to newly identified user needs
- An organizational design and processes that eliminate organizational barriers that separate employees from end users
- The use of user-focused and independent teams that can move fast and smoothly within the organization
- End-to-end accountability for the experience of end users is taken by the company and/or independent teams
- The systematic collection, storage and use of end user data in order to increase value for end users
- Commitment to the ecosystem principles of openness, equality, co-creation and co-sharing.

The very structure of the corporation creates alienation – a distancing from the world around us. Zero-Distance leads to

---

[94] See: https://business-ecosystem-alliance.org/zero-distance-award/

reconnection and regeneration. To understand "**zero distance to reality**," here are 8 indicators of **separation**:

(1) distance to the **Planet**
(2) distance to **Democracy**
(3) distance to the **Customer**
(4) distance to the **Shareholder**
(5) distance to the **Community**
(6) distance to the **Employee**
(7) distance to the **Supplier**
and
(8) distance to **Capital**

THE ZERO DISTANCE CHALLENGE

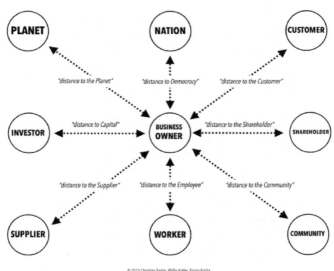

© 2023 Christian Sarkar, Philip Kotler, Enrico Foglia

How does your organization plan to close these gaps?

There has been a fatal breakdown in the distance between capital and reality. "The purpose of the business is to produce profitable solutions to the problems of people and planet, not profiting from producing problems," says **Colin Mayer**, a professor of management at the University of Oxford's Saïd Business School[95].

Mayer thinks that **capitalism is increasingly recognized as a *source* of rising levels of inequality, environmental degradation, social exclusion, political divisiveness, and mistrust.**

"There is a growing view that corporations are psychopathic in terms of the way in which they exploit at the expense of others," says Mayer.

This mistrust comes from the idea that the sole purpose of business is about producing profits, which has also been a substantial contribution to the failures of capitalism – he explains. This has to do with how profit is currently measured and includes the benefits generated "from cutting down ancient woodlands, polluting rivers, emitting CO_2 in high quantities, and employing people at very low wages in their supply chains," said Mayer.

"We are looking to redefine the notion of profit around what the purpose of a business can and should be," he adds. "Businesses should expect to help us solve problems for individuals, communities, societies, and the natural world."

"A profit should be earned net of the cost associated with rectifying, remedying, mitigating, offsetting, and compensating

---

[95] "Rethinking The Purpose of Business with Oxford Professor Colin Mayer" by Karl Moore *Forbes* May 22, 2022, https://www.forbes.com/sites/karlmoore/2022/03/22/rethinking-the-purpose-of-business-with-oxford-professor-colin-mayer/ SEE also: https://www.thebritishacademy.ac.uk/programmes/future-of-the-corporation/

for the damages that companies produce for people and the environment."

Add to this, **Henry Mintzberg** explanation to the **crisis underlying the crisis**[96]:

"Beneath the current economic crisis lies another crisis of far greater proportions: the *depreciation in companies of community* — people's sense of **belonging** to and **caring** for something larger than themselves."

BUILDING A TRULY REGENERATIVE ORGANIZATION

Peter Drucker warned us[97] that the corporation "is in trouble because it is seen increasingly by more and more people as deeply at odds with basic needs and basic values of society and community."

And:

"…an institution, like an individual, is not an island unto itself. It has to solve the basic problem of balancing the need for concentration and for self-limitation with concern for its environment and compassion for its community."

These were prophetic words. **The modern corporation is obsolete.** It has no connection to the needs of society.

Here's why:

1. **Obsolete business models:** current business models are designed to be

ORGANIZATION
should it exist at all?
could we shift to a better organizational structure?

PEOPLE
can we make employees true partners?

PRODUCT
should it exist at all?

redesign for
- longevity
- modularity
- repairability
- modularity
- repurposing
- ethical supply chain

SUPPLY CHAIN
- decarbonize?
- eliminate waste?
- protect Nature
- Common Good

COMMUNITY VALUE
- business model
- ecosystem building
- infrastructure
- community wealth-building

---

[96] Rebuilding Companies as Communities by Henry Mintzberg, *Harvard Business Review*, July-August 2009, https://hbr.org/2009/07/rebuilding-companies-as-communities
[97] *The Concept of the Corporation*, Peter Drucker, 1946

exploitative and extractive. They are not prepared to be regenerative – protect and nurture Nature, and build community wealth.

2. **Narrow focus:** corporations prioritize shareholder interests over those of employees, customers, and the community, leading to social and environmental degradation.

3. **Short-term thinking:** Companies are often driven by quarterly earnings and short-term financial goals, rather than long-term sustainability and social responsibility.

4. **Inadequate governance:** The governance structures of corporations often lack transparency and accountability, and fail to align the interests of top management with those of shareholders, let alone other stakeholders like the community.

5. **Ideological paralysis:** Some corporations are slow to adapt to changes in mindset or technology. This makes them vulnerable to disruption by more agile and forward-thinking competitors. If your executive group is comprised of mainly former accountants and former sales people, your organization in trouble.

This suggests that the corporation needs to change and evolve to better serve the needs of all stakeholders and ensure long-term success in a rapidly changing world.

But what about purpose?

What would your organization look like if it was serious about championing the Common Good?

The first step is to look at your business purpose – does it serve the Common Good? If you're truly interested in serving the Common Good, what might your policies look like with regards to executive pay, worker relations, the community, stock buybacks?

See what we mean? **The traditional corporate structure was *not* designed to be regenerative.** So, your organization really *does* have to change.

In his book *The Vanishing American Corporation: Navigating the Hazards of a New Economy*, Professor **Gerald Davis** explains[98]:

…public corporations – companies that sell shares to the public, rather than being privately owned – are in retreat in the United States. The number of American companies listed on the stock market has dropped by more than half in the past 15 years, as departures outnumber initial public offerings (IPOs) almost every year. Some of this is due to economic crises and industry consolidation, but most of it is caused by the increasing obsolescence of the corporate form.

Professor Davis sees two possible scenarios developing:

*The first is ubiquitous Uberization, in which jobs are completely decomposed into tasks that are staffed on demand. This is the pathway to the "precariat," with rampant markets and pervasive economic uncertainty. The second is the **revival of communities** as the locus of economic activity. We have the raw materials for a revival of **localism** enhanced by global connections: a **"cosmopolitan locavorism"** that builds on the components of the old corporate economy to create a more democratic and equitable economy.[99]*

The decline of the corporation opens up opportunities for *new forms of economic organization*, concludes Professor Davis.

---

[98] *The Vanishing American Corporation: Navigating the Hazards of a New Economy* by Gerald Davis, Berrett-Koehler Publishers, Inc., 2016

[99] Ibid. "Cosmolocal locavorism" seems to be the same as "cosmolocalism" as presented in the previous chapter.

These forms of organization will be more local, more democratic, and more sustainable and regenerative.

What might these new structures look like?

THE SEARCH FOR REGENERATIVE ORGANIZATIONAL STRUCTURE

Here are several forms we can propose as alternatives to the traditional corporation:

Cooperatives: an autonomous association of persons united voluntarily to meet their common economic, social and cultural needs and aspirations through a jointly-owned and democratically-controlled enterprise.[100]

Benefit corporations: Benefit corporations are *for-profit* companies that are legally required to consider the impact of their decisions on society, the environment, and other stakeholders, in addition to their financial performance. There is mounting criticism that the B-corp is simply *another form of greenwashing* – based on the lack of transparency and lack of accountability[101].

Social enterprises: Social enterprises are businesses that prioritize social or environmental goals, and use commercial strategies to achieve them.

Employee-owned firms: Employee-owned firms are companies in which employees own a significant portion of the stock and have a say in how the company is run.

Partnership structures: Partnership structures, such as limited liability partnerships (LLPs) and limited partnerships

---

[100] https://www.ica.coop/en/cooperatives/cooperative-identity/

[101] Nespresso's recent Certification as a B Corp has raised concerns that there is currently no way for the B Impact Assessment (BIA) or certification process to measure or hold Nespresso to self-imposed commitments. "The B Corp Standard is at Risk" 6/15/2022 https://fairworldproject.org/the-b-corp-standard-is-at-risk/

(LPs), allow for more flexible ownership and governance arrangements than traditional corporations.

Community Development Corporations: Community Development Corporations (CDCs)[102] are nonprofit, community-based organizations focused on revitalizing the areas in which they are located, typically low-income, underserved neighborhoods that have experienced significant disinvestment. While they are most commonly celebrated for developing affordable housing, they are usually involved in a range of initiatives critical to community health such as economic development, sanitation, streetscaping, and neighborhood planning projects, and oftentimes even provide education and social services to neighborhood residents.

Community Interest Companies (CIC): a special type of limited company which exists to benefit the community rather than private shareholders (existing in the UK)[103]. Formed to help companies that did not have charitable status and found it difficult to ensure that their assets were protected for public benefit. CICs are more lightly regulated than charities but do not have the benefit of charitable status, even if their activities are entirely charitable in nature.

While there's a lot of attention showered on the **B-Corp**, it is the **cooperative movement** which is building momentum across the world.

Why?

Because **the traditional corporation is *not* a democracy.** In the US, for example, the anti-union ideology of business does not create an environment of trust. It destroys the idea that your organization is a community.

---

[102] https://community-wealth.org/strategies/panel/cdcs/index.html

[103] https://www.communitycompanies.co.uk/community-interest-companies-cic

A business is a community of employees serving a community of customers.

The incomparable **Charles Handy** explains[104]:

A good business is a community with a purpose. Communities are things you belong to, not things you can own. They have members, members who have certain rights, including the right to vote or express their views on major issues. It is ironic that those countries that boast most stridently of their democratic principles derive their wealth from institutions that are defiantly undemocratic, with all serious power held by outsiders and power inside wielded by a dictatorship or, at best, an oligarchy.

This is a contradiction which cannot be ignored anymore. **We cannot pretend to embrace democracy while building institutions led by dictators.** It is the reason why billionaires are not exactly the best choice of leaders for the common good[105].

Charles Handy, again[106]:

Trust, too, is fragile. Like a piece of china, once cracked it is never quite the same. And people's trust in business, and those who lead it, is today cracking.

And:

The employees of a company are treated, by the law and the accounts, as the property of the owners and are recorded as costs, not

---

[104] "What's a Business For?" by Charles Handy, *Harvard Business Review*, December 2002
https://hbr.org/2002/12/whats-a-business-for
[105] "Why Can't Billionaires Advance the Common Good?" by Philip Kotler and Christian Sarkar,
FIXcapitalism.com, December 6, 2020 http://fixcapitalism.com/why-cant-billionaires-advance-the-common-good/
[106] "What's a Business For?" by Charles Handy, *Harvard Business Review*, December 2002
https://hbr.org/2002/12/whats-a-business-for

assets. This is demeaning, at the very least. Costs are things to be minimized, assets things to be cherished and grown.

THE COOPERATIVE MOVEMENT

Could it be that the healthiest and happiest companies in the world are democracies? **Rachel Gertz** thinks so[107]. She's the CEO and of a digital project management training company called Louder Than Ten. Her take:

In a cooperative, workers own and manage the company. Unlike a traditional structure, where decision-making is at the top level, every worker has one equal vote on all company matters.

And:

Co-ops aren't necessarily anti-profit. It's just that they're controlled by the workers. They grow sustainably and ethically, providing a living wage for their members and giving back to their communities when they can. Co-ops reject the idea that people are labor. They know that people own labor.

Gertz converted her traditional company to a coop and sold it to the employees.

She recommends The Sustainable Economies Law Center's "Legal Guide to Cooperative Conversions."[108]

The **International Cooperative Alliance** has adopted *seven cooperative principles*[109] - guidelines by which cooperatives put their values into practice. They make the case for an alternative way to run and nurture a business that is diametrically opposite to the prevailing viewing that your *employees are the enemy!*

---

[107] "How We Converted to a Cooperative—and How You Can, Too" by Rachel Gertz *Yes!* May 10, 2022
https://www.yesmagazine.org/opinion/2022/05/10/company-converted-to-a-cooperative
[108] https://www.co-oplaw.org/knowledge-base/legal-guide-cooperative-conversions/
[109] https://www.ica.coop/en/cooperatives/cooperative-identity/

1. Voluntary and Open Membership

Cooperatives are voluntary organizations, open to all persons able to use their services and willing to accept the responsibilities of membership, without gender, social, racial, political or religious discrimination.

2. Democratic Member Control

Cooperatives are democratic organizations controlled by their members, who actively participate in setting their policies and making decisions.

Men and women serving as elected representatives are accountable to the membership. In primary cooperatives members have equal voting rights (one member, one vote) and cooperatives at other levels are also organized in a democratic manner.

3. Member Economic Participation

Members contribute equitably to, and democratically control, the capital of their cooperative. At least part of that capital is usually the common property of the cooperative. Members usually receive limited compensation, if any, on capital subscribed as a condition of membership.

Members allocate surpluses for any or all of the following purposes: developing their cooperative, possibly by setting up reserves, part of which at least would be indivisible; benefiting members in proportion to their transactions with the cooperative; and supporting other activities approved by the membership.

4. Autonomy and Independence

Cooperatives are autonomous, self-help organizations controlled by their members. If they enter into agreements with other organizations, including governments, or raise capital from external sources, they do so on terms that ensure democratic control by their members and maintain their cooperative autonomy.

5. Education, Training, and Information

Cooperatives provide education and training for their members, elected representatives, managers, and employees so they can contribute effectively to the development of their co-operatives. They inform the general public - particularly young people and opinion leaders - about the nature and benefits of co-operation.

6. Cooperation among Cooperatives

Cooperatives serve their members most effectively and strengthen the cooperative movement by working together through local, national, regional and international structures.
\

7. Concern for Community

Cooperatives work for the sustainable development of their communities through policies approved by their members.

REGENERATIVE BUSINESS MODELS

Regenerative businesses must – by definition – build **community wealth** *and* **regenerate the Common Good.**

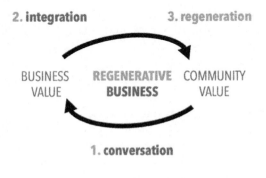

© Christian Sarkar, Enrico Foglia, and Philip Kotler 2021

What is unique about the regenerative business model is the idea that **community value creation** is *equally important* as **business value creation**. The process is based on a continuous **dialogue** between the business and the community, followed by an **integration of purpose**, which in turn leads to **community regeneration**.

Thus, a regenerative business is also in the business of building **local trust.**

The regenerative business has two recipients of value – the **customer** and the **beneficiary**. It uses its profits to create value for the community it serves. Its purpose is not profit-making, but community regeneration. Its strength is the creation of deep community relationships which make it more resilient in times of crisis. The currency is trust.

Our regenerative business model is a "double loop" model with a customer and a beneficiary.

Based on **Alex Osterwalder**'s business model canvas, we're interested in creating both business value and community value simultaneously. Earlier we mentioned that business schools don't teach us how to create community value. They're still focused on value extraction, value optimization, value creation – for one stakeholder – the owners and investors. This **"double-loop" regenerative business model**[110]is an attempt to remedy this shortcoming.

The value-proposition has a dual aspect:

1. What value do we create for the customer?
2. What value do we create for the community?

REGENERATIVE
"DOUBLE LOOP" **BUSINESS MODEL**

Developed by: Christian Sarkar, Enrico Foglia, and Philip Kotler 2021   *adaptation of Alex Osterwalder's Business Model Canvas (Strategyzer)*

---

[110] A more detailed version of this "double-loop" regenerative business model canvas is available at www.regenmarketing.org

In our work, we often use an abbreviated version of the "double loop" regenerative business model:

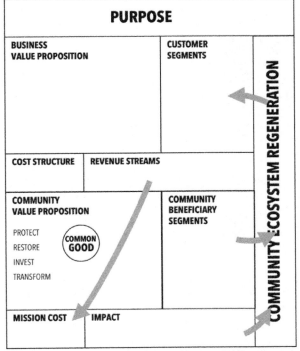

adaptation of Alex Osterwalder's Business Model Canvas (Strategyzer)

Customer touchpoints are well known and studied as part of creating the customer journey. But what about community and societal touchpoints?

Across every activity in its value chain and across all **community touchpoints,** the regenerative business identifies the **state of the Common Good,** and what is required *for* regeneration.

ORGANIZATIONAL REGENERATION
of **THE COMMON GOOD**

	PROTECT	REPAIR	PROTECT	TRANSFORM
SOCIAL				
ECONOMICS				
NATURE				
WORK				
CULTURE				
MEDIA				
LAW				
TECHNOLOGY				
POLITICS				

© Christian Sarkar, Enrico Foglia, and Philip Kotler, 2022

The stories we present in this book show us that business can do both. Even non-profits can become more regenerative by actually tackling the root causes of the problem or suffering they are trying to alleviate.

Finally, the regenerative business model is about **regenerating the community ecosystem** – in service to the Common Good. Here are three specific ways to nurture and build community ecosystems:

1) Worksharing
2) Collaborative Projects
3) Community Partnerships and Entrepreneurship

WORKSHARING

A new trend of reciprocal and remote working is gaining traction in certain parts of the world. In Italy, for example, there is an innovative approach to distributed worksharing we call "**southsharing**."

An example of this approach is the opening of a south office in Palermo by **BIP**, the Italian consulting firm. The brainchild of chairman **Nino Lo Bianco**, the south office hired locals, sent native Palermitans living in the North back to their city of choice, engaged in remote work for Northern clients, and begin creating business opportunities in the South.

This establishes a *regional* **"wealthsharing strategy"** which seeks to create new synergies in the South, including skills and capacity building with university students in Palermo. The jobs are in sectors like cyber security, digital transformation, innovation, and sustainability.

How does southsharing differ from its cousin - outsourcing? It is *not* based on cost. The employees in southworking areas are *paid the same* as the employees in the north.

How do companies build a platform for work-sharing across enterprise boundaries? The "gig-economy" is part of this shift, but working conditions[111] are not exactly praise-worthy.

Occupations on web-based, digital labor platforms can be roughly divided into 'microtasks' and 'macrotasks.' Microtasks are short and often of a clerical nature, such as copywriting, content access, product categorization, verifying and validating data, content moderation (the removal of pornography or violent images before they are uploaded on social media accounts), text or audio transcription, and filling out surveys. Prices are set by the client or platform without negotiation, and clients pay a fee. 'Macrotasks' are longer-term projects that typically require specialized skills, such as IT programming or graphic design. Most macrotask platforms are designed so that workers set up individual profiles indicating their expertise and rate, with the final price for their work set via a bargaining process with the client. Clients can pay per project or hourly; if hourly, the platform may facilitate the monitoring of the work through surveillance software. Most macrotask platforms charge the worker a fee, typically ranging from 5% to 20% of the project cost.

---

[111] "Working conditions on digital labour platforms: Opportunities, challenges, and the quest for decent work" by Janine Berg, Marianne Furrer, Ellie Harmon, Uma Rani, Michael "Six" Silberman 20 September 2019 https://voxeu.org/article/working-conditions-digital-labour-platforms

The problem is that "even workers who perform valuable labor for successful companies often do so for low wages and without the protections of a regulated employment relationship." There's an urgent need for "an international governance system to set minimum standards as well as develop the infrastructure necessary for facilitating payments to social security systems." But, to date, our digital platforms have largely escaped workplace regulations, and many don't even pay their fair-share of taxes[112].

COLLABORATIVE PROJECTS

If we are serious about solving problems, we must learn to collaborate across organizational boundaries. Why is it too much to ask that governments, NGOs and development institutions, and businesses work together with the communities involved to build integrated solutions?

REGENERATIVE **PROJECT**
COLLABORATION

*How do we **share** roles, priorities and activities?*

PUBLIC   PRIVATE   PLURAL

community assets

ESSENTIALS

FOOD SECURITY
WATER
HOUSING
EMPLOYMENT
HEALTHCARE
EDUCATION
SKILLS TRAINING
DIGITAL INCLUSION
HUMAN RIGHTS
ENERGY

DESIGN ▶ **FINANCE** ▶ **BUILD & OPERATE** ▶ **MAINTAIN** ▶ **UPGRADE**

Because of the interrelated nature of the problems that drive the cycle of poverty, the only way to solve these problems is to employ an integrated development model which attacks several challenges at once: clean water, food, health, education, employment, and housing.

---

[112] See: "Amazon Avoids More Than $5 Billion in Corporate Income Taxes, Reports 6 Percent Tax Rate on $35 ITEP.ORG February , 2022 Billion of US Income" https://itep.org/amazon-avoids-more-than-5-billion-in-corporate-income-taxes-reports-6-percent-tax-rate-on-35-billion-of-us-income/

Housing, for example, is a *delivery mechanism* for healthcare. This can be achieved using *"whole village development"* an approach proven by the **Solar Electric Light Fund** (SELF.org) in sub-Saharan Africa. A house is of little value without supporting infrastructure. SELF's model includes water, food, health, education, and enterprise:

	WATER	**FOOD**	**HEALTH**	**EDUCATION**	**ENTERPRISE**
Description	Solar energy powers purification pumps and filters delivering clean water to communities	Solar energy powers water pumps which enable drip irrigation for critical crops	Solar energy powers health clinics allowing key equipment, lighting, vaccine refrigeration	Solar energy powers schools to enable computer and Internet access	Solar energy powers local entrepreneurial and community activities
Process	SELF provides assessment, training, installation and follow-up	SELF provides assessment, training, installation and follow-up	SELF partners with a local health organization (Partners In Health)	SELF provides assessment, training, installation and follow-up	SELF provides assessment, training, installation, follow-up, and micro-lending
Governance	local community	local community	local community	local community	local community
Examples	Nigeria, India	Benin	Haiti, Lesotho, Tanzania	South Africa	Nigeria

For over 30 years, SELF has worked to deliver solar power to rural villages in Africa, Asia, and Latin America by facilitating a new generation of "whole village" solar electrification projects. In many of the countries in which SELF works, there is no other organization undertaking a similar, independent role in providing power to villages without existing resources.

Interestingly, SELF spun off a for-profit company in India in 1995 – SELCO, India. SELF and SELCO achieved international recognition as the first company to concentrate on the marketing and servicing of SHS in rural India. Under the management of H. Harish Hande, SELCO became a force of change in its own right. Today, SELCO is an umbrella of organizations, each tasked to address gaps in the energy access ecosystem:

SELCO India: Runs grassroots operations which market, sell, install, and service decentralized energy products like home solar systems. SELCO Solar Light is a registered private limited company.

SELCO FOUNDATION: An open-source innovation research lab for replicable social innovations across areas: livelihoods[113], education, and health. SELCO Foundation is a registered non-profit organization.

SELCO'S INCUBATION PROGRAM: Nurtures and catalyzes the clean energy enterprises that deploy and maintain sustainable solutions for underserved communities. SELCO's Incubation program is housed within SELCO Foundation.

SELCO FUND: An impact fund that seeks to deploy patient capital such as equity or debt to last mile energy access enterprises. SELCO Fund is registered as a Social Venture Fund under SEBI.

In an integrated development model, the NGO understands local community problems intimately, the government is responsive to the needs of the community through sound policy, land use arrangements and transparency, and businesses work with both to serve the poor as a customer, partner, employee and supplier. Activities and plans are coordinated, even synchronized. A local economy is born, driven by inclusive business practices.

Let's look at how a hybrid or collaborative business model might be designed to deliver "**housing-as-a-service**" We start

---

[113] *175 Sustainable Energy Driven Applications* SELCO FOUNDATION
https://drive.google.com/file/d/1VMHq7Sus6jDR2MrPikeYclZ8z0kuDbxd/view

with a template which shows all the participants and the major process milestones in the service delivery process and adapt it to housing:

Different phases can be managed by different players. For example, a **hybrid business model** might include a configuration as follows:

	DESIGN	**FINANCE**	**BUILD**	**OPERATE**	**UPGRADE**
COMMUNITY	X	X	X	X	X
NGO	X		X	X	X
BUSINESS	X	X	X		X
GOVERNMENT	X			X	X

In the **Design** phase, the community works with all parties to develop a solution that works for them.

In the **Finance** phase, community members finance their houses with a lending bank that is capped on a low-profit scheme (under the watchful eye of a government panel).

In the **Build** phase, the community works with businesses to build the houses they designed in the previous phase. The NGO may subsidize land ownership and cost of construction.

The **Operate** phase may include jobs for the community and training services from an NGO. The government may inspect and require periodical safety inspections.

And finally, when the time comes to **Upgrade**, all players come to the table to develop the next solution.

Since infrastructure projects are implemented in phases, they can also be managed in phases. Governments, businesses and NGOs can collaborate to provide basic services for a community at an affordable cost. **Imagine if this were to happen across all 638,000 villages in India.**

And why should we stop at housing? All **public services** could be designed, built, financed, maintained, and upgraded using this hybrid business model concept.

The hybrid/collaborative-business model allows the community to be involved in each service as a consumer *and* as an employee or owner. A common enough idea is that building low-cost housing can help create an ecosystem of house builders and suppliers – often members of the community being served. The idea is to transfer that thinking across all the integrated services provided. The hybrid business model can pay for the ongoing employment of community workers for sanitation, energy, education, health, housing, of course, but even something like entertainment, where the community itself becomes the entrepreneur, charging a micro-fee for movies or soccer games shown in the village community center, for example.

COMMUNITY PARTNERSHIPS AND ENTREPRENEURSHIP

Moladi, a South African pioneer in affordable housing, proposes a **smart village** based on community partnerships.

Founded in 1986 by South African social entrepreneur **Hennie Botes**, the company aims to replace the classic brick-and-mortar construction with an easier method: using lightweight, removable and re-usable plastic formwork that are filled with a patented fast setting aerated mortar to cast entire houses on-site[114]. The process is deliberately designed to be labor intensive and mostly uses local supplies (apart from the reusable formwork and a special additive (MoladiChem) to

---

[114] https://www.futureofconstruction.org/case/moladi/ See also moladi.com

boost local employment and local production without requiring prior construction experience.

Dubbed the "future of construction in the developing world" by the **World Economic Forum**, the company was designed to address six key challenges of low-cost housing projects in developing countries:

1) lack of sufficient funds,
2) shortage of skilled laborers,
3) lack of resources
4) workflow control
5) time constraints, and
6) wastage.

Moladi proposes to help governments create **worker-owned cooperatives** to install and maintain their houses, thus building a community-based ecosystem of entrepreneurship and skills training.

We can't begin to talk about community regeneration without acknowledging the ground-breaking humanitarian work of the late **Dr. Paul Farmer** of **Partners In Health (PIH)**.

Dr. Farmer's untimely passing at a relatively young age – at a time when the world needs him more than ever – came as a wicked shock to all of us who have stood in awe at the life and work of this great soul (pictured with the late Bishop Desmond Tutu).

As co-founder and chief strategist of PIH, Paul Farmer was responsible, along with his colleagues, for pioneering innovative community-based treatment strategies that demonstrate the delivery of high-quality health care in resource-poor settings.[115]

PIH, for those who might not know, is a mission-driven healthcare organization. Here is how they position themselves:

Our mission is to provide a preferential option for the poor in health care. By establishing long-term relationships with sister organizations based in settings of poverty, Partners In Health strives to achieve two overarching goals: to bring the benefits of modern medical science to those most in need of them and to serve as an antidote to despair.

We draw on the resources of the world's leading medical and academic institutions and on the lived experience of the world's poorest and sickest communities. At its root, our mission is both medical and moral. It is based on solidarity, rather than charity alone.

When our patients are ill and have no access to care, our team of health professionals, scholars, and activists will do whatever it takes to make them well — just as we would do if a member of our own families or we ourselves were ill.

PIH is also recognized around the world for its innovative approach to healthcare in the poorest communities – from Haiti – where the young Farmer started his mission, to Rwanda – the place of his unfortunate passing. PIH's model of healthcare delivery is based on "5 S's":

- **Staff:** well trained, qualified staff in sufficient quantity to respond to need
- **Stuff:** ensuring the tools and resources needed for care delivery and administration
- **Space:** safe, appropriate spaces with capacity to serve patients
- **Systems:** leadership and governance, information, financing, and

---

[115] https://www.pih.org/article/remembering-dr-paul-farmer

- **Social support:** providing basic necessities and resources needed to ensure effective care

Over the years, PIH's biggest innovation is the concept of the **"community healthcare worker"** (CHW) – whose job is to "offer compassionate care to those who need it most."

In PIH's *accompaniment* model of care, patients build a **trusting relationship** with a CHW who will accompany them in solidarity through their journey back to health – with stunning outcomes.

In a test for the treatment of tuberculosis, for example, a 100% clinical cure was observed in all patients receiving **full support** (free care plus a range of socioeconomic supports), versus only 56% cure and 10% mortality in patients receiving **free care** alone.[116] The overwhelming evidence of **community worker** effectiveness cannot be disputed.[117]

The second innovation of PIH's healthcare delivery model is the adoption of a **human rights approach** – which is more effective than a traditional healthcare approach, because it includes services that address social and economic determinants of health as well.

At PIH-supported sites, patient care is supplemented for those most in need—through providing education, housing, food, clean water, job training, and/or other special services or training opportunities. Thus, "healthcare" extends beyond the medical and addresses the whole patient. From providing food to cash transfers to transportation to housing, PIH stays true to their mission to do *whatever it takes* to ensure health is a human right for all.

This ecosystematic view is also evident in their vision for educating the next generation of doctors and nurses. PIH's

---

[116] "Community health and equity of outcomes: the Partners In Health experience" by Daniel Palazuelos, Paul E Farmer, Joia Mukherjee, *Lancet*, May 2018 https://doi.org/10.1016/S2214-109X(18)30073-1

[117] https://www.pih.org/pages/evidence-of-community-health-worker-effectiveness

University Hospital in Mirebalais (Haiti) and their University of Global Health Equity in Butaro (Rwanda) demonstrate the medical industry does not have to follow the exorbitant and unaffordable approach it has taken in the USA, for example.

Since 2020, PIH has also participated in the **People's Vaccine movement**, a worldwide coalition of organizations campaigning to scale vaccine manufacturing to the levels needed to rapidly meet global needs.

REGENERATIVE
BUSINESS MODEL

ORGANIZATION: *Partners In Health (www.pih.org)*

adaptation of Alex Osterwalder's Business Model Canvas (Strategyzer)

In terms of the supply chain, PIH's Medical Informatics team designed OpenBoxes, an open-source software for tracking the movement, consumption, and storage of supplies, so that global colleagues can follow orders heading to health facilities around the world.

At the heart of PIH's success is trust – **the patient never walks alone.** And, in the community, they are viewed as a trusted partner and friend.

The success of PIH is precisely because it **rejects** neoliberalism's economic ideology, which demands that interventions be cheap above all else.[118]

"The idea that some lives matter less is the root of all that is wrong with the world," said Paul Farmer, and this speaks to Farmer's commitment to social justice and his belief that every human life has equal value and worth.

It reflects his tireless work to address global health inequities and ensure that the most marginalized communities have access to quality healthcare.

Another example of community partnership comes to us from the fashion industry which is not known for its sustainability, let alone regeneration. **White Champa** and **made/in** are both example of regenerative principles applied to the world of fashion.[119]

It starts with the idea that handcraft is no longer on the periphery of the fashion world. Enlightened fashion consumers now see craft elements as a desirable commodity in contemporary fashion.

Anjana Das and **Nicole Hardt**, the designers behind **made/in**, explain: "In the accelerating trajectory of twentieth-century fashion, textile handcrafts were increasingly pushed to the margins of fashion. The patient, painstaking and ecologically harmonious methods of crafting by hand were

---

[118] "Community health and equity of outcomes: the Partners In Health experience" by Daniel Palazuelos, Paul E Farmer, Joia Mukherjee, *Lancet*, May 2018 https://doi.org/10.1016/S2214-109X(18)30073-1

[119] See: whitechampa.com and made-in.org

subordinated to the rules of efficiency, speed and pricing. Textile handcrafts – once treasured for their excellence, beauty and cultural significance – became increasingly relegated to the space of "handicrafts" bazaars, a place for tourists to browse them in search of bargain souvenirs from exotic locations."

What does this mean?

"Fortunately, recent social trends of ethical consumption and the "slow fashion" movement are giving textile handcrafts a chance to recapture the attention of a wider audience," says Das.

"We started the made/in project to build on this awareness. Our goal in documenting the reality of textile handcraft today – without nostalgia or sentimentality – is to outline a vision for the future of crafts in the fashion world. For we feel strongly that crafts have great potential to capture the new as well as the old, integrating tradition and excellence with the demands of our times. The possibilities for aesthetic and technical innovation within handcraft are immensely exciting, and we want to share that excitement – just as we want to stress the potential for increasing the social and economic empowerment of craftspeople while fostering ecological responsibility."

The project's initial focus is on products made in India and Germany, but the concerns are strikingly similar in artisanal communities all over the world.

The central question is whether textile handcraft can remain relevant as part of a more thoughtful and sustainable fashion industry? Or will the human creativity and skills needed for textile handcrafts become a relic of the past?

Das' research and her own experience of over 20 years provides an answer:

"We believe that the answer lies in integrating the wealth of traditional craft knowledge with new technologies and digital innovation. With aesthetic and technical ingenuity and collaborative energy, craftspeople and designers can together breathe new life into textile handcraft and ensure that it has appropriate monetary value... We see immense value – and potential – in *fostering transparent, egalitarian and authentic collaborations between artisans and designers.*"

For Das, there are six principles[120] which are interwoven:

1. Excellence, 2. Social empowerment, 3. Economic empowerment, 4. Innovation, 5. Culture and beauty, and 6. Ecological responsibility

REGENERATIVE
"*DOUBLE LOOP*" **BUSINESS MODEL**

ORGANIZATION: made/in   **COMMUNITY**: artisan communities in India

PURPOSE Integrate traditional craft with technological innovation to create products which are appealing and regenerative

BUSINESS VALUE PROPOSITION

Creation of a line with a relevant global aesthetic in textile handcrafts, Community of like-minded clients who value sustainability and equality between designers, artist and artisans

CUSTOMER SEGMENTS

Global customers interested in the intersection of art and design in conjunction with excellence in craft

COST STRUCTURE
Labor costs, production/material costs, leased space, marketing costs

REVENUE STREAMS

COMMUNITY VALUE PROPOSITION

Recognition of artisan excellence, reduced waste through on demand production, Egalitarian communication between global North and global south, fair pay for all involved, protection of creative intellectual property rights

COMMUNITY BENEFICIARY SEGMENTS

Craft communities, global awareness for textile handcraft

MISSION COST
Same as running cost

IMPACT
regenerative products and local wealth-building

Developed by: Christian Sarkar, Enrico Foglia, and Philip Kotler 2021

COMMUNITY ECOSYSTEM REGENERATION

adaptation of Alex Osterwalder's Business Model Canvas (Strategyzer)

---

[120] https://made-in.org/about/manifesto

ECOSYSTEM BUILDING FOR THE COMMON GOOD

One example of community ecosystem building is the work of **Eroi Normali** (normal heroes), an Italian think tank and agency which works to promote the virtues of local thinking as an incubator of civic thought and public utility projects. An independent and autonomous non-profit, it looks for innovative solutions to regional problems – to bring back economic vitality and regenerate the livelihoods and enterprises in local villages.

Massimiliano Molese – the founder – explains: "we're promoting a new way of seeing and being, favoring love and respect for the local ecosystem over the consumerism and the fascination for what's global." He's promoting a **"THINK LOCAL"** initiative across Italy,  but particularly in the state of **Campania**. The concept is simple: use a QR code to connect various regional institutions – public and private, to create a series of connected community projects in a local network:

- **Panels and Webinars:** workshops and talks between companies, professionals, entrepreneurs, politicians, academics and representatives of the main institutions involved that will discuss ideas on the topic of THINK LOCAL. The meetings create space to connect, interact and share insights in order to generate new, meaningful ideas and projects and develop lifelong relationships and partnerships.
- **Street Advertising:** local street art to advertise the THINK LOCAL initiatives in the local area.
- **Industry4Tourism:** Private companies display a special QR code linked to a shared web page that illustrates the beauties of the region where they are based. Each product becomes a virtual card to engage a potential tourist around the world.

- **Poetry Readings:** public readings held right outside a local library, by an evocative building or under the shade of a historical monument to create local connections.
- **Street Art:** bringing art - colors and forms - to the old and empty walls of local neighborhoods, villages, and cities. To offer these spaces to artists so that they can move and inspire through the universal language of creation.
- **Local Maps:** a local map of an "unconventional tour" to guide visitors and locals on a journey of discovery of artistic, gastronomic, cultural, commercial and social aspects of the local community.
- **Limited Edition Products**: the design of limited-edition products to be gifted or sold during the THINK LOCAL campaign. Money raised through these products contributes to the redevelopment of green areas or can be used to fund new activities.
- **Treasure Hunts:** a scavenger hunt for young people and adults to take them to all the landmarks of the city; participants are invited to share their experiences on social media
- **VIP Ambassadors:** artists, singers, actors and actresses, the most influential people that were born in a certain neighborhood are invited to take the lead and to become ambassadors of their place of origin.

"It's about regenerating wonder in your local area," says Molese, who is already planning THINK LOCAL campaigns across not just Italy, but the EU and the world.

TOWARDS A REGENERATIVE VALUE CHAIN

A regenerative organization assesses its own *value chains* looking for potential violations of human rights, reducing carbon footprints, and improving community engagement to help drive results across *all 9 Domains* of the Common Good.

Is this too much to ask?

What does a regenerative value chain look like?

TRADITIONAL VALUE CHAIN	**REGENERATIVE VALUE CHAIN**
Linear, one-way process focused on producing goods and services for profit.	Cyclical, multi-dimensional process focused on creating value for all stakeholders while *promoting the Common Good* and regenerating natural, social, and financial capital.
Extraction of resources and production processes often contribute to environmental degradation and social inequality.	Focus on regenerative practices that restore and regenerate natural ecosystems and promote social equity – whilst focusing on the *9 Dimensions of the Common Good.*
Limited engagement with stakeholders beyond customers and shareholders.	Collaboration across the value chain to co-create and co-design solutions that benefit all parties – but particularly focused on local community impact.
Limited focus on employee well-being and development beyond basic legal requirements.	Emphasis on employee well-being and development, including training, education, and opportunities for growth and advancement.
Limited attention to long-term sustainability and resilience of the business.	Focus on creating a regenerative business model that is resilient in the long term, including through diversification of revenue streams and consideration of potential future challenges.
Measuring success primarily in terms of financial performance and shareholder returns.	Measuring success through a triple-bottom-line approach that considers social, environmental, and financial performance, and emphasizes the importance of creating community value.

This is not a traditional approach by any means. But it is an approach whose time has come.

If we look to maximize the positive impacts across the value chain for *all* 9 Domains of the Common Good, we will evaluate community impact in terms of the following domains: Social,

Economics, Nature, Work, Culture, Media, Law, Technology, and Politics.

Along each step of the value-chain we ask: what is the job to be done with respect for these 9 Domains? What should we protect/repair/invest/transform?

What can we commit to by way of collaboration with local communities to make a difference?

VALUE CHAIN REGENERATION

REGENERATIVE PRODUCTS, SERVICES, AND EXPERIENCES

The regenerative organization continuously questions its continued existence: "if we were to get into the industry today, would we still be doing what we do today? Or would we do something different?" This was the "paranoid" mindset of Andy Grove when he reinvented Intel.

What will make your organization regenerative?

Would you still build the same products? What about your services, and the experiences you provide?

In 1967, Philip Kotler introduced us to the 5 product levels based on perceived levels of **customer-value**:

1. **Core benefits:** the benefit the customer is really buying, for example: food to satisfy hunger and provide nutrition

2. **Basic product:** the generic product – a category like fish or chicken

3. **Expected product:** meeting customer expectations for the product category – the taste and flavor of the fish and chicken

4. **Augmented product:** exceeding customer expectations – gourmet or special recipes like butter chicken

5. **Potential product:** new transformational opportunities for the future – meatless fish and chicken, anyone?

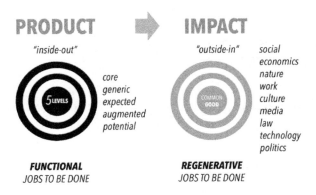

PRODUCT REDESIGN
for REGENERATION

PRODUCT ➡ **IMPACT**

"inside-out"

5 LEVELS

core
generic
expected
augmented
potential

FUNCTIONAL
JOBS TO BE DONE

"outside-in"

COMMON GOOD

social
economics
nature
work
culture
media
law
technology
politics

REGENERATIVE
JOBS TO BE DONE

© 2023 Christian Sarkar, Philip Kotler, and Enrico Foglia

This product-centric view, an *inside-out* view of product impact, has served us well for over half a century, but now, the new imperative is *outside-in*: examining the **impact** of the product on the world. Go beyond "unmet needs" to product impact.

Community Impact: Do your products, services, and experiences **create community value?** How do you impact the **9 Dimensions of the Common Good?** Companies that analyze their impact of the Common Good and find ways to move from negative to positive impact are the companies that customers will follow. Studies show[121] that over the past five years, products making ESG-related claims accounted for 56 percent of all growth—about 18 percent more than would have been expected given their standing at the beginning of the five-year period.

Similarly, service design will have to take into account not just the **dimensions of service quality** but also the impact of your services on the community and the Common Good. Thus, we still must work on the 5 dimensions of service quality[122]:

1. **Reliability:** the ability to perform the promised service dependably and accurately

2. **Assurance:** the knowledge and courtesy of employees and their ability to convey trust and confidence

3. **Tangibles:** the appearance of physical facilities, equipment, personnel and communication materials

4. **Empathy:** the provision of caring, individualized attention to customers

---

[121] "Consumers care about sustainability–and back it up with their wallets" Feb 6, 2023 *McKinsey Insights,* https://www.mckinsey.com/industries/consumer-packaged-goods/our-insights/consumers-care-about-sustainability-and-back-it-up-with-their-wallets#/

[122] Based on Parasuraman, A, Ziethaml, V. and Berry, L.L., "SERVQUAL: A Multiple- Item Scale for Measuring Consumer Perceptions of Service Quality' *Journal of Retailing,* Vol. 62, no. 1, 1988, p. 22, 25 and 29

5.   **Responsiveness:** the willingness to help customers and to provide prompt service

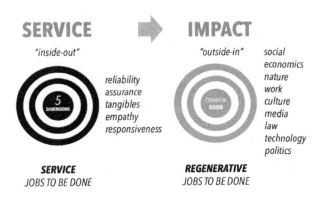

SERVICE REDESIGN
for REGENERATION

SERVICE ➡ **IMPACT**

"inside-out"

reliability
assurance
tangibles
empathy
responsiveness

"outside-in"

social
economics
nature
work
culture
media
law
technology
politics

SERVICE
JOBS TO BE DONE

REGENERATIVE
JOBS TO BE DONE

© 2023 Christian Sarkar, Philip Kotler, and Enrico Foglia

What about **experience design**?

The *5 Es of experience design* are engage, entertain, educate, enrich, and empower. All experiences will still follow the 5 Es, but every action and interaction will have to take into account how your experience design impacts the Common Good. This is *not* an accounting or finance function – and is why it requires a new form of leadership.

For example, everyone knows Disneyland and Disneyworld were childhood experiences for a majority of middle-class kids all across America. But what happens when Abigail Disney, the granddaughter of Walt Disney, accuses Disney of poor working conditions[123], after meeting with Disneyland employees to better understand their work-grievances?

And how does it help **Starbucks'** reputation if its heavy-handed **union-busting** tactics pit managers against workers in a bid to keep Starbucks union-free? Howard Schultz got his inspiration for the **"third place"** from the coffee-houses in Italy. Maybe he should have learned about employment rights as well[124]. By choosing to fight unionization, Starbucks has created an existential crisis for itself.

Why? *Because the "third place" should be community space.*

Ray Oldenburg[125], a sociologist, believed in a balanced existence of three kingdoms: home, workplace, and a "third place" for social interaction. The third place is a relaxed environment where people form spontaneous relationships and socialize, crucial for building strong communities, empathy, and a sense of belonging. Oldenburg observed the decline of third places in suburban areas in post-war America, but third places can be any cheap public gathering places such as cafes, parks, community centers, etc., which serve as the living room of a community.

Oldenburg viewed third places as the heart of a community's social vitality. The idea is based on the Common Good. Starbucks is waging war on its founding philosophy because it did not create a "fourth place" – a

seat for employees on the board[126] – a practice which is not

---

[123] "USA: Disney criticised for alleged poor working conditions in Disneyland resort" Business & Human Rights Resource Centre, 19 July, 2019 https://www.business-humanrights.org/en/latest-news/usa-disney-criticised-for-alleged-poor-working-conditions-in-disneyland-resort/

[124] https://sbworkersunited.org *disclosure: one of the authors is related to someone working at this organization*

[125] Project for Public Spaces, https://www.pps.org/article/roldenburg

[126] 17 European Member States and Norway have enacted legal provisions allowing for employee representation, with voting rights, on the supervisory board and/or board of directors of companies headquartered on their national territory.

uncommon in Europe. In fact, it turns out that the Starbucks board is stacked with anti-worker executives[127]. The ideology of the board of directors could well destroy the company.

Does anyone remember Kinko's – the copy place? After the FedEx buyout, it's office services and supplies business crashed. FedEx failed to see that Kinko's wasn't just another office supplies store, but was in fact a community – a meeting place – a third place. Destroy that third place, and you kill your business.

This brings us to the topic of **public space**. A public space is an area or place that is accessible to the general public, usually without any cost or restriction, and is owned and maintained by the government or other public entities. Examples include parks, plazas, streets, sidewalks, and public buildings.

What is the impact of public space on the community?

A community in decline must begin by reclaiming its public space. This is what Palermo's Leoluca Orlando had to contend with as he struggled to regenerate Palermo.

What causes public spaces to decline? Several factors:

Absence of Public Trust: Public spaces which don't serve the public can be hijacked by private interests and neighborhood bosses to undermine public trust.

Lack of maintenance: Public spaces require regular maintenance, such as cleaning, repairing, and updating amenities, to keep them safe and attractive for users. Without proper maintenance, public spaces can quickly become dirty, unsafe, and unappealing.

---

[127] "The Union Busters on Starbucks' Board of Directors" by Derek Seidman, November 23, 2021
https://inthesetimes.com/article/union-busters-starbucks-labor-buffalo

Underfunding: Public spaces require adequate funding to maintain and improve them. A lack of funding can result in deferred maintenance, reduced services, and limited amenities, which can contribute to their decline.

Poor design: Public spaces that are poorly designed may not be well-suited for their intended use or may not meet the needs and preferences of the community. This can result in low usage and poor user experiences, which can contribute to their decline.

Safety concerns: Public spaces that are perceived as unsafe or have high rates of crime can discourage people from using them, which can contribute to their decline. This can be exacerbated by factors such as poor lighting, lack of surveillance, and inadequate police presence.

Social issues: Public spaces can be negatively impacted by social issues such as homelessness, drug use, and vandalism, which can create a perception of disorder and contribute to their decline.

Addressing these factors requires collaboration between government agencies, community groups, non-profits, and private entities.

Conversely, when public space is reclaimed and maintained, as we see in the case of Palermo, we see the following benefits:

Promoting social interaction: Public spaces provide opportunities for people to gather, interact, and socialize with others from diverse backgrounds. This can help build social connections, reduce social isolation, and foster a sense of community.

Encouraging physical activity: Public spaces can provide opportunities for physical activity such as walking, jogging, cycling, and sports. This can promote physical health, reduce obesity, and improve overall well-being.

Enhancing environmental quality: Public spaces such as parks and green spaces can help improve air quality, reduce noise pollution, and mitigate the effects of climate change by providing shade and absorbing carbon dioxide.

Boosting local economies: Public spaces can help attract visitors and tourists, support local businesses, and generate economic activity in surrounding areas.

Fostering creativity and cultural expression: Public spaces can serve as venues for cultural events, public art installations, and other forms of creative expression, which can help foster creativity, spark innovation, and enhance cultural identity.

Thus, public spaces can provide a range of benefits that contribute to individual and community well-being, social cohesion, economic development, and environmental sustainability.

Anton Cebalo writes that the decline of public space demolished America's social fabric[128]:

"The decline of American third places had an impact on the collective dreams of the entire country. This is because community spaces are inherently proto-political spaces as well — areas where common ideas are lived through and acted upon. By congregating and talking, individuals gain a sense of agency. Without it, their society lives off the borrowed language

---

[128] "Midcentury Planners Demolished America's Social Fabric" by Anton Cebalo *Palladium* March 29, 2023 https://www.palladiummag.com/2023/03/29/midcentury-planners-demolished-americas-social-fabric/

of a democratic sensibility that no longer exists as part of everyday life."

REGENERATIVE STARTUPS: ZEBRAS, NOT UNICORNS

In 2017, four women - Astrid Scholz, Mara Zepeda, Jennifer Brandel, and Aniyia Williams began the **Zebra movement**. The women decided that they'd **had enough of competing with unicorns and chasing the current VC model**.

They took a stand[129]:

The current technology and venture capital structure is broken. It rewards quantity over quality, consumption over creation, quick exits over sustainable growth, and shareholder profit over shared prosperity. It chases after unicorn companies bent on 'disruption' rather than supporting businesses that repair, cultivate, and connect.

Why zebras?

- To state the obvious: unlike unicorns, zebras are real.
- Zebra companies are both black and white: they are profitable and improve society. They won't sacrifice one for the other.
- Zebras are also mutualistic: by banding together in groups, they protect and preserve one another. Their individual input results in stronger collective output.
- Zebra companies are built with peerless stamina and capital efficiency, as long as conditions allow them to survive.

The capital system is failing society in part because it is failing zebra companies: profitable businesses that solve real, meaningful problems and in the process repair existing social systems.

---

[129] "Sex and Startups" by Jennifer Brandel, Mara Zepeda, Astrid Scholz, and Aniyia Williams
https://medium.com/@sexandstartups/sex-startups-53f2f63ded49#.6xc7ss1ew

Their view was in turn inspired by Rebecca Solnit who writes[130] about "the tyranny of the quantifiable." In such a system, Solnit writes, "what can be measured almost always takes precedence over what cannot: private profit over public good; speed and efficiency over enjoyment and quality." This she attributes partly to the failure of language to communicate the value of "slipperier things," things that "cannot be named or described."

Their central thesis is that **the business model is *the* message**[131]:

"...developing alternative business models to the startup status quo has become a central moral challenge of our time. These alternative models will balance profit and purpose, champion democracy, and put a premium on sharing power and resources. Companies that create a more just and responsible society will hear, help, and heal the customers and communities they serve."

The case studies that follow highlight organizations which are doing just this – building a double-loop regenerative business model to serve both **customers** *and* **community**. Most of the companies were started with small seed investments from founders or public-sector grants – not the VCs (who can't conceive of funding zebras!)

Learn more about the Zebra movement at Zebras Unite – a coop for zebras!

VISIT: zebrasunite.coop

---

[130] https://www.newyorker.com/books/page-turner/woolfs-darkness-embracing-the-inexplicable
[131] https://medium.com/zebras-unite/where-unicorns-fear-to-tread-building-businesses-that-are-better-for-the-world-35190e632c9e

A WARNING: REGENWASHING - THE NEW GREENWASHING

Raz Godelnik warns us that "regeneration is used by companies to obscure the fact that they are mainly involved in degenerative business and are either afraid or too comfortable to change their business model in transformative ways."[132]

For example, did you know, for example, that Wal-Mart claims to be a **"regenerative business"**?

From their website, we learn[133]:

Regenerating means restoring, renewing and replenishing in addition to conserving. It means decarbonizing operations and eliminating waste along the product chain. It means encouraging the adoption of regenerative practices in agriculture, forest management and fisheries – while advancing prosperity and equity for customers, associates and people across our product supply chains. And, working with our suppliers, customers, NGOs and others, we hope to play a part in transforming the world's supply chains to be regenerative.

Wait a minute.

Remember **the Wal-Mart Effect**? It's a term used to refer to the economic impact felt by local businesses when a large company like Wal-Mart opens a location in the area. The Wal-Mart Effect usually manifests itself by *forcing smaller retail firms out of business and reducing wages for competitors' employees.*

Wal-Mart is *not* a regenerative company – not at least how we define one in this book. Sorry.

---

[132] "The myth of the regenerative business model" by Raz Godelnick, November 30, 2022 *Medium*
https://razgo.medium.com/the-myth-of-the-regenerative-business-model-2ed20c6ede54
[133] https://corporate.walmart.com/newsroom/2020/09/21/walmarts-regenerative-approach-going-beyond-sustainability

As we just showed, regeneration is already being used as a *narrative of distraction,* precisely at a time when the world needs *collective action* to solve its most urgent problems.

The term **regenerative agriculture** has likewise been co-opted[134]:

Large food corporations, such as ADM, Cargill, Danone and Nestlé, are pursuing regenerative agriculture programs as part of their climate initiatives. Other corporate-led spaces such as the Food and Land Use Coalition and the World Economic Forum (WEF) support similar programs. All of those focus on encouraging farmers to tweak their agricultural practices in ways that are said to reduce the use of chemical fertilizers and/or build back carbon in soils. But the corporations are not putting up much of their own money into these programs. Danone's annual contribution is equal to one day of sales. Nestlé's much publicized support to regenerative agriculture is a paltry 1.5% of what it pays its shareholders in dividends every year. Farmers will have to cover the costs for implementing these new practices, which corporations use as a justification to maintain their emissions.

Agribusiness corporations are also using regenerative agriculture to market themselves to financial investors. Financial companies buying up farmland, for instance, advertise that their massive, industrial farms will be "regenerative" to attract money from pension funds. The Brazilian soybean farming company SLC Agrícola is responsible for massive deforestation but it recently raised US$95 million on financial markets to buy new fuel-efficient tractors, "green fertilizers", and various digital technologies as part of its regenerative agriculture program.

If we can't trust the words we use, what sense is there in anything at all?

---

[134] An agribusiness greenwashing glossary *Local Futures*, September 2022, https://www.localfutures.org/an-agribusiness-greenwashing-glossary/

REBUILDING/DESTROYING TRUST

Steve Case tells us there are four ways[135] a company can become a "pillar" of its local community:

1. *validate* a city's identity — it needs to establish that its success is the area's success
2. *represent* its home to other places around the country and the globe
3. *create wealth* that the whole community can feel
4. *reinvest* in its home

Case is on the right track – he is correct about all four points, but he *does not go far enough*. We must also ask if the business builds or nurtures community assets – advancing **the common good**.

What about the business which does *not* support the community, but by its actions demonstrates that it is not engaged in wellbeing? What does it look like when a business **extracts value** from the local community for the sake of profit and profit maximization alone?

The **Cluetrain Manifesto**, one of the earliest guides to the Internet, is still valid. It turns out that **markets** *are* **conversations**[136] after all. And here are a few more of the *95 Theses*:

- To speak with a human voice, **companies must** *share the concerns* **of their communities.**
- But first, they must **belong** to a community.
- Companies must ask themselves where their corporate cultures end.

---

[135] "How a Company Becomes a Pillar of Its Local Community" by Steve Case, *Harvard Business Review*, Oct 3, 2022 https://hbr.org/2022/10/how-a-company-becomes-a-pillar-of-its-local-community

[136] The first thesis of the Cluetrain Manifesto – "1. Markets are conversations."
https://www.cluetrain.com/#manifesto (RIP, Christopher Locke)

- If their cultures end *before the community begins*, they will have **no market**.
- Human communities are based on discourse — on human speech about human concerns.
- The community of discourse is the market.
- *Companies that do not belong to a community of discourse will die.*

Thus, a regenerative organization – business, non-profit, or government agency – is in the business of **building local trust.**

Trust – a so-called intangible value – is the critical component of *collaboration*. In communities (and cultures) with low-trust, the following cultural behaviors are observed[137]:

- Facts are manipulated or distorted
- Information and knowledge are withheld and hoarded
- People spin the truth to their advantage
- Getting the credit is very important
- New ideas are openly resisted and stifled
- Mistakes are covered up or covered over
- Most people are involved in a blame game, badmouthing others
- There is an abundance of "gossip" and "rumor" talk
- There are numerous "meetings after the meetings"
- There are many "undiscussables"
- People tend to over-promise and under-deliver
- There are a lot of violated expectations for which people make many excuses
- People pretend bad things aren't happening or are in denial
- The energy level is low

---

[137] *Interview: Stephen M. R. Covey on "The Speed of Trust"* (2007 interview by Christian Sarkar) https://christiansarkar.com/2008/02/my-interview-with-stephen-m-r/

- People often feel unproductive tension–sometimes even fear

Why are these attributes present in a community? In your business?

Regenerative organizations, on the other hand, engender **deep trust**. It begins (and ends) with the company's relationship with the local community. In fact, the business may even be community-owned. Trust can be measured. It can be built. It can be strengthened. This is the central challenge for institutions today.

Does deep-trust scale community-wide? Nothing happens without *trust*. The reasons are usually historical, based on past conflicts. They lead to a critical problem: the *inability* to collaborate. Thus, the primary job of a community leader is building trust. This is what we were thinking as we learned from the people we met. Individually they were quite impressive, but collectively there was a clear lack of collaboration.

For **businesses** we ask: *is there a genuine concern for people, purposes and the community as a whole or is profit your sole motive?* The businesses that are operating "by themselves, for themselves" are not good community partners, and are often non-participants in the planning or support of community projects.

This mindset can sometimes be traced back to the mindset of the founder, and cannot be changed without a "conversion" process for the founder and/or senior executive team. What must be done to help them engage and participate in community regeneration?

All institutions must learn how to come together and nurture a **community ecosystem** to *promote the Common Good*.

A MATURITY MODEL FOR REGENERATION

There is no simple way to classify "regeneration-maturity" so we created a hypothetical 5-level maturity model for regeneration.

Perhaps you will recognize the level that your organization occupies. The conventional approach to regeneration is to see it as **sustainability** *plus*.

So, it's a more *conscious capitalism* – one that reduces its carbon footprint though the supply chain (except for Scope 3 emissions) and pledges "net-zero by 2030/40/50 (pick one)."

It also says "beyond sustainability, we will help our employees and suppliers improve their livelihoods" by increasing their wages and benefits to just over industry standards in the communities they work in.

Unions are not encouraged or tolerated.

The organization lobbies politicians to reduce taxes, regulations, and penalties for emissions and waste disposal.

Sound familiar?

Under this approach, even Wal-Mart is classified as "regenerative."

Absurd, isn't it?

So - what might a maturity model for a regenerative organization look like?

And how does it compare to the maturity models for CSR or a "sustainable" business?

LEVEL	Traditional Business (CSR)	Sustainable Business	Regenerative Business
Stage 1: **Awareness**	Limited awareness of sustainability issues; CSR and rampant greenwashing	Awareness of sustainability issues, but mainly focused on compliance and risk management	Deep understanding of sustainability issues and potential for positive impact on society, environment, and the Common Good.
Stage 2: **Efficiency**	Efforts to improve efficiency and reduce waste, primarily to reduce costs.	Systematic approach to resource efficiency, incorporating renewable energy and sustainable materials. Circular economy is an aspirational goal.	Whole economy approach that eliminates waste, regenerates natural systems, and builds local community wealth.
Stage 3: **Responsibility**	Limited engagement with stakeholders beyond compliance requirements	Active engagement with stakeholders, including employees, suppliers, and customers, to promote sustainability	Collaborative approach to co-create community value with neighborhoods, NGOS, non-profits, civic associations, and other businesses
Stage 4: **Innovation**	Limited innovation focused on incremental improvements	Innovation focused on sustainable products, services, and business models	Regenerative innovation creates new systems and paradigms that benefit the local community, society and environment
Stage 5: **Regeneration**	Minimal consideration of natural systems and ecosystem services	Efforts to protect and restore natural systems, and create net positive impact on environment and society	Intentional efforts to regenerate natural and social systems and create thriving ecosystems; Common Good projects are the norm.

STAGE 5 REGENERATION: TOTAL REGENERATION

Let's dig deeper into what that Stage 5 - Total Regeneration might look like:

A Stage 5 regenerative organization does not work by itself, but brings together *other* organizations and institutions – along with all the stakeholders **to build community trust focused on the Common Good.**

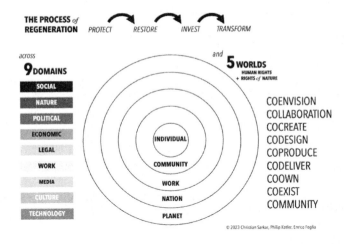

© 2023 Christian Sarkar, Philip Kotler, Enrico Foglia

What exactly does that mean? Here's our COMMON GOOD questionnaire and rating scale:

On a scale of 1-10:
1-4 = strongly disagree (DEGENERATIVE)
5-6 = neutral (NEUTRAL)
7-10 = strongly agree (REGENERATIVE)

To get an accurate reading, it's best that each Common Good Domain is tracked at three levels: local, national, and worldwide.

SOCIAL

- Are we committed to equality – race, gender, sexual orientation, religion, etc.?
- Do we respect and support Human Rights?
- Do we protect the privacy rights of all?
- Are we working to improve access and quality to public goods and services like healthcare, education, safety, food security, for all members of society?
- Do we support immigration reform and amnesty?
- Do we prohibit forced labor - in the form of prison labor, indentured labor, bonded labor, human trafficking, around the world?
- Do we work to create a better social climate for the communities we work with? Society at large?
- Do we work to improve the standard of living?
- Do we support propped public health policies for all?
- Do we stand for just immigration policies?
- Do we stand against polarization and divisive agendas?
- Do we support consumer protection agencies and watchdog groups?
- Does senior management demonstrate high standards of personal propriety?

ECONOMICS

- Do we support policies that fight income inequality?
- Do we support just trade policies?

- Do we partner and encourage local small businesses and entrepreneurs?
- Do we support public interests like affordable transportation and housing?
- Do we support public investments in infrastructure and education?
- Do we pay our fair share of taxes to local, national, and global authorities?
- Do we avoid tax shelters and financial manipulation to escape our tax responsibilities?
- Do our employees (including part-timers) get paid enough to afford a living?
- Do we support the development and protection of local community interests?
- Do we balance our economic interests and the economic health of the public?

NATURE

- Do we stand against ecocide – the destruction of entire ecosystems?
- Do we embed sustainability into all our activities and future plans?
- Do we support the Rights of Nature?
- Do we advocate and promote conservation and protection of our public lands?
- Have we redesigned our supply chain around a circular economy?
- Are we aware of the impact of biotech and its ramifications on the environment?
- Do we take environmental impact studies seriously?
- Do we have an action plan to eliminate water and air pollution?
- Do we get our energy from clean, renewable sources?

- Are we leading our industry in environmental stewardship?
- Do we take a stand against unnecessary development and exploitation of natural resources?
- Do we encourage public awareness and education?

WORK

- Do we provide our employees with a living wage?
- Do we provide our employees the opportunity to form unions?
- Do we put our employees' workers' voices at the heart of our business model?
- What is the ratio of CEO Pay to our frontline employees?
- Do we avoid exploiting our labor or the labor of our suppliers?
- Do we promote equal pay for equal work?
- Do our employees have a voice? Representation on the board?
- Do we provide training and safety for all employees and part-time workers?
- Do we practice work safety? Are employee concerns dealt with transparently?
- Do we encourage a democratic workplace?
- Do we respect workers' rights?
- Are integrity concerns openly and freely discussed in the workplace and is it safe to report suspected violations of integrity?
- Do we allow our employees to become co-owners?

CULTURE

- Do we engage with and support local cultural organizations in the community?
- Do we provide funding or resources to cultural organizations or events in the area?
- Do we take steps to preserve or promote local culture or traditions?
- Do we prioritize hiring and supporting local talent, including artists and performers?
- Do we collaborate with other businesses or organizations to support cultural regeneration?
- Have we taken steps to promote diversity and inclusivity within our business and the surrounding community?
- Do we actively seek out opportunities to showcase local culture, such as through art installations or public events?
- Do we measure the impact of our efforts to support cultural regeneration?
- Do we have any plans for future initiatives or collaborations that will support cultural regeneration in the area?
- Do we face any challenges or obstacles in supporting cultural regeneration, and have we worked to overcome them?

MEDIA

- Do we support the free press?
- Do we believe the media should have the right to report freely on business activities?
- Are we against taking legal action against a media organization or journalist for reporting on our business?

- Do we financially support media organizations or journalism initiatives that promote free and independent journalism?
- Do we respond positively to media criticism or negative coverage of our business?
- Do we ever promote open communications and avoid trying to influence or pressure journalists to report a certain way or to avoid reporting on certain issues?
- Do we believe that the public has the right to access information about our business, including financial information and business practices?
- Can we say we don't attempt to restrict or limit access to information about your business?
- Do we support anti-corruption reporting?
- Do we support the principles of open journalism?

LAW

- Do we support the rule of law?
- Do we respect employment and labor laws?
- Do we seek just business practices that avoid corruption and improper influence?
- Do we seek and encourage laws to promote workplace safety?
- Do we seek and stand for reasonable financial regulations that protect the rights of consumers?
- Do we work for just laws for all members of the community?
- Do we respect property laws and encourage public engagement and transparency?
- Do we respect and promote Human Rights?
- Do we have an agenda for promoting integrity?
- Does senior management participate in the development of the necessary legal and institutional frameworks for a just society?

TECHNOLOGY

- Do we prioritize the use of environmentally sustainable technology?
- Do we take serious steps to reduce our carbon footprint by changing our product strategy?
- Do we incorporate renewable energy sources into our operations?
- Do we invest in research and development for innovative and sustainable technologies?
- Do we support and promote the use of technology to benefit the local community and address societal challenges?
- Do we prioritize data privacy and security for our customers and users?
- Do we address issues related to algorithmic bias and fairness in our use of technology?
- Do we support the development of open-source and community-driven technology and public value platforms?
- Do we ensure the ethical use of technology and strive to prevent harmful effects on individuals or the community?
- Do we contribute to technology education and digital literacy initiatives in the community?

POLITICS

- Do we support Democracy?
- Do we promote a transparent and open government that allows for the meaningful participation of all stakeholders in the development and implementation of public policies?
- Do we support voter rights?

- Do we encourage our employees to vote, by giving them the time to do so?
- Do we oppose gerrymandering?
- Are we paying our fair share of taxes?
- Do we support campaign finance reform?
- Are we transparent with our lobbying activities?
- Do our lobbying efforts align with stakeholder values?
- Do we support fair trade?
- Do we support competition in our industry?
- Are we supporting long term policies in technology?
- Do we welcome just regulations? Do we support privacy and data security?
- Are we supporting a healthy and transparent foreign policy?
- Do we oppose public policies that give us an unfair advantage?
- Do we seek a level playing field without special consideration?
- Do we avoid corruption and seek to remove it from all levels of society and government?
- Do we promote a transparent and open government that allows for the meaningful participation of all stakeholders in the development and implementation of public policies?
- Do we support a government for the Common Good?

Score your organization – and work to understand the impact your activities have on the Common Good. Make it a part of your business strategy and operations.

Can your company even contemplate this way of being?

Or do you need to *change the type of organization* you are?

What about leadership?

Do we trust our leaders to do the right thing?

4. REGENERATIVE LEADERSHIP

By now it should be obvious to the public that our leaders are (for the most part) not interested in serving the Common Good. They are engaged in an ancient form of misleadership – maximizing value for themselves and their sponsors. If there is one attribute which separates the regenerative leader from the traditional leader, it is their *focus on the Common Good*.

LEADERSHIP *for* THE COMMON GOOD

	TRADITIONAL LEADERSHIP	REGENERATIVE LEADERSHIP
FOCUS	Short-term, results-oriented	Long-term, values-driven
GOALS	Maximize profits, shareholder value – primacy of private interests over public interests	Balance social, environmental, and economic outcomes – with a focus on the Common Good
DECISION-MAKING	Top-down, hierarchical – based on fear and authority	Collaborative, inclusive – based on openness and consensus
RELATIONSHIPS	Transactional, power-based	Transformational, partnership-based
COMMUNICATION	Command and control; devaluation of the free-press	Transparent, empathetic; support of the free-press
INNOVATION	Incremental, efficiency-focused	Disruptive, creativity-focused
IMPACT	Self-serving, narrow	Positive, holistic
SUSTAINABILITY	Exploitative	Regenerative
ADAPTABILITY	Reactive	Proactive

© Christian Sarkar, Philip Kotler, and Enrico Foglia 2022

The second sign of the regenerative leader is that they nurture and grow *other* regenerative leaders. They are always teaching, always helping, and most of all, they are connected to the truth – maintaining what we call "zero-distance" to reality. The regenerative leader is not motivated by money or rewards but is always working for the next generation, and the ones that come after. The regenerative leader is inclusive, and works to bring everyone along – *no one is left behind.* They are nearly **ego-free** (remember that graphic about ego-system vs. eco-system?)!

The regenerative leader is not often recognized in society, but is instead recognized by the people who are involved in *doing* the work – the artisans, crafts people, the creatives, and the manual laborers who earn their daily bread. This is not the case with most executives in business. In fact, traditional businesses may actually shun the regenerative leader. Only now, in times of crisis, are we beginning to understand the importance of leadership for the Common Good. Our survival as a species depends on it.

Politicians are no different. They too lead with surveys and polls. Or worse – simply as executors for the elites that sponsor them.

CAN POLITICS BE REGENERATIVE?

This is an existential question for today's politics. If you look at the US today, we see that our politicians can't even stand up to the NRA, let alone address climate collapse. Instead, they distract us with culture wars and fake controversy – banning books, and literally canceling democracy via gerrymandering and voter suppression.

Interestingly, we found a regenerative politician in Sicily! A family-oriented professional, **Cettina Martorana** initially didn't want to run for office in the Sicilian regional elections of 2022. Her kids challenged her with a question – "How come you tell us to do what's right but you aren't taking that advice when you are asked to run?" The result? Martorana ran as a candidate in the regional elections. Her political philosophy is based on regeneration, she says. What exactly does that mean? And, can politics truly be regenerative? We tracked her down for this interview. *Note: it was Martorana who was instrumental in inviting us to accept the challenge of the Palermo Rigenerativa project.*

How did you decide to run for office and what makes your campaign different?

Unfortunately, our political world is not in sync with reality – especially when it comes to the concerns people have with the impact of fires, floods, draught, and the unbearable temperatures that are coming. Instead, we see a dismissal of climate science and an intentional obfuscation of facts to slow the adoption of legislation to fight climate change.

We've created a psychological climate of eco-anxiety for the young. I know this because I have three children.

*When the candidate running for president of the Sicilian Assembly asked me to run on her ticket, I refused at first, but my children and my husband both convinced me to run. My campaign is about **regeneration**, and I believe it is truly the only way forward.*

What do you mean by regeneration?

My understanding of regeneration is based on what we learned from COVID. As you know, COVID destroyed our tourist economy in Sicily. Now, with Sicilian families in trouble and our planet in danger, we cannot simply go through another cynical cycle of politics. What this means that we must rethink the very idea of "left" versus "right" and come together to solve problems.

We have to act. For our children and our children's children.

Last year, when I was councilor for economic actives of the Municipality of Palermo, the Mayor and I invited the Regenerative Marketing Institute to Palermo; we wanted to learn about different approaches to community regeneration which went beyond the sustainability and circular-economy paradigms which sound good on paper, but achieve little in terms of actually stopping our climate crisis.

*We also learned that the climate crisis is also an economic crisis and a social crisis. In a **permacrisis world**, we cannot focus on one issue at the expense of another. The real shift is what we do to move from an economy of exploitation and extraction to a regenerative economy. Nature must become a priority. Or we will no longer have an island to live on.*

We must ask ourselves – is politics making our world better or worse? Our communities? Our future…

If the answer is no, then we must make the shift to regeneration.

Can you give us some details?

*We use a metaphor based on the **olive tree** – which is a familiar one for us in the Mediterranean:*

ALBERO DELLA RIGENERAZIONE

NATURA

SERVIZI
AGRICOLTURA
ISTITUZIONI
TRASPORTO
INDUSTRIA
NO PROFIT
ENERGIA
CHIESA
ATTIVITÀ COMMERCIALI
EVENTI
UNIVERSITÀ
EDUCAZIONE
ARTE E CULTURA
TURISMO
FAMIGLIA
LAVORO
TOLLERANZA
GIUSTIZIA
DIRITTI

CETTINA MARTORANA
cettinamartorana.it

*What we call the **"tree of regeneration"** is simply an olive tree which connects the community together, from the foundation or roots – based on tolerance, rights, and justice, to the three fruits we hold dear: family, honest work, and nature. Our communities are connected – and how we treat the weak is a measure of our strength.*

How would we act if we were truly serious about doing something about the climate crisis? Would we keep doing what we've been doing? Paying lip-service to the Planet and little else?

Why did you use comics in your campaign?

How do we get young people to listen to our vision? By including them in the vision-making process. But first we must explain what we stand for in a way that attracts attention, and our comics did that for sure.

cettinamartorana.it

How did you come up with all the answers?

That's it. We don't have the answers. But we Sicilians do have a spirit to solve problems. That's why Sicily has survived for over the centuries.

I'm not saying the left has all the answers either. But in Italy, the parties on the right were until recently telling their constituents to cut the South loose – that we didn't belong to Italy. And now they've shifted from south-bashing to immigrant-bashing. The reality is we need to all work on finding solutions, not polarizing people with hate.

Our vision is not division. **It's regeneration.**

To young we say: bring us your ideas. We hear you!

###

Martorana did *not* win her election, but she ran the world's first campaign (that we know of) which was based on a clearly articulated regenerative political strategy – seeking solutions and consensus, not polarization and power.

She's an example of a regenerative leader – a new archetype of leadership the world demands today

The world desperately needs more.

THE REGENERATIVE EFFECT

Leaders lead. And the first job of leadership is truth-telling. Anything less is misleadership.

In traditional debates, we have been taught that a message is convincing because of the three elements of persuasion: *ethos*, *pathos*, and *logos* (we'll dismiss kairos). But now, in a post-truth age, in a time of "fake news" and "alternative facts," we add one more critical element: the spirit of the messenger themselves – *thumos*, the messenger's enthusiasm and passion for the message.

Why is this dangerous? Because bombast and attention-seeking behavior is mistaken for leadership – the truth be damned. Our media – owned by power elites and funded by corporate dinosaurs – cannot bring themselves to report the truth.

The President of Ireland, **Michael D. Higgins** explains:[138]

"Many economists remain stuck in an inexorable *growth narrative*, or at best a *'green growth' narrative*. A fixation on a narrowly defined efficiency, productivity, perpetual growth has resulted in a discipline that has become blinkered to the ecological challenge – the ecological catastrophe – we now face. That narrow focus constitutes an empty economics which has lost touch with everything meaningful, a social science which no longer is connected, or even attempts to be connected, with the social issues and objectives for which it was developed over centuries. It is incapable of offering solutions to glaring inadequacies of provision as to public needs, devoid of vision."

Leadership experts **James Kouzes** and **Barry Posner** tell us that there are there are ten "fundamental truths about leadership and becoming effective leaders:[139]

1. You Make a Difference

2. Credibility Is the Foundation of Leadership

3. Values Drive Commitment

---

[138] "President condemns 'obsession' with economic growth" by Pat Leahy, *The Irish Times*, Apr 28 2023
https://www.irishtimes.com/politics/2023/04/28/president-condemns-obsession-with-economic-growth/
[139] *The Truth About Leadership: The No-fads, Heart-of-the-matter Facts You Need To Know.* James M. Kouzes and Barry Z. Posner, Jossey-Bass. 2010..

4. Focusing on the Future Sets Leaders Apart

5. You Can't Do It Alone

6. Trust Rules

7. Challenge Is the Crucible for Greatness

8. You Either Lead by Example or You Don't Lead at All

9. The Best Leaders Are the Best Learners

10. Leadership Is an Affair of the Heart

To these factors, we add:

11. A Profound Commitment to Community, Nature, and the Common Good

12. The Regenerative Effect

What is the **Regenerative Effect**? It's the opposite of the toxic leadership we see everywhere.

The regenerative effect is the metaphorical "green thumb" of the gardener – everything they touch or get involved with – does better. They protect, repair, invest, and transform all aspects of community life – from Nature on down. The regenerative effect nurtures and grows an ecosystem of regenerative leaders – and creates a boundaryless community, both inside and outside the organization or group they lead.

The traditional CEO is not a regenerative leader (sorry Jack Welch). The work of leadership has never been more clear: it is to bridge the gap — across all boundaries — and to create a way forward for the **Common Good**.

The **pyramid of love** below reminds us that it is possible to resolve conflicts and escalate peace.

THE PYRAMID *of* LOVE

PEACE
the act or intent
to extend kindness
and compassion to all
people, cultures, and nature

JUSTICE
life, dignity, safety
non aggression, non violence,
courtesy, fairness, and truthfulness

INCLUSION
economic inclusion, political inclusion
educational inclusion, employment inclusion
social and housing inclusion and integration
digital inclusion and privacy, criminal justice equality

ACTS OF GOODWILL
friendliness, empathy, appreciation, recognition, benevolence
social inclusion, respect, uplifting humor/jokes

IMPARTIAL ATTITUDES
acknowledging the individual, respectful remarks, celebration of differences,
inclusive language, micro-solidarity, tolerance and dignity
questioning biases by seeking out diverse views and people
questioning negative information or misinformation, seeking common ground

© 2021 Christian Sarkar and Philip Kotler

Says **David Hinds** of Steel Pulse: *"Where there is no love, there can be no justice; and where there is no justice, there will never be peace."*

That about sums it up. *Extending the pyramid of love externally, into the community – that's another way to view the regenerative effect.*

Finally, the narrative of the regenerative leader is *not* based on hope. Rather, it is based on **truth**. What is the job to be done now for the Common Good? Where do we as an organization play a role? What must be done?

NARRATIVE *of* REGENERATION

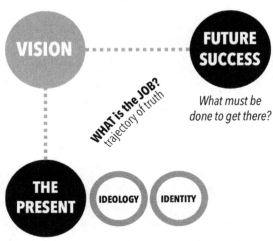

The narrative of regeneration finds ways to bridge the ideology and identity based narrative traps of the present and creates an inclusive pathway to the future – a future of regeneration of the Common Good.

Again, the narrative of regeneration is a narrative of leadership because it seeks to take us from what seems to be, if the doomers are correct, societal and ecological collapse, to a future of cosmo-local, community-based living.

Finally, the task of the regenerative leader is to **mobilize the community to act.** Not chat or talk, not hold conferences, but to *act*.

All of this brings us to the role of government. Shouldn't our governments be promoting the **Common Good**? Isn't that the definition of regenerative governance? Here's a list we compiled – does your government check the boxes?

REGENERATIVE **GOVERNMENT**

GOVERNMENT *for* THE COMMON GOOD
the citizen's checklist

- ❑ Provide **universal access** to **healthcare**
- ❑ Invest in **education** and **lifelong learning** opportunities
- ❑ Ensure access to safe and **affordable housing**
- ❑ Increase access to **nutritious food options** and **reduce food waste**
- ❑ Encourage **renewable energy development** and **phase out fossil fuel use**
- ❑ Promote **public transportation** and **bike-friendly infrastructure**
- ❑ Protect **natural resources** and promote **conservation** efforts
- ❑ Encourage **sustainable agriculture** and support **local food** systems
- ❑ Promote the use of **green infrastructure** and reduce reliance on gray infrastructure
- ❑ Ensure access to **safe drinking water** and **sanitation**
- ❑ Implement policies that **reduce income inequality** and **address poverty**
- ❑ Increase access to **high-speed internet** in **rural** and **underserved areas**
- ❑ Create programs to **support small businesses** and **entrepreneurship**
- ❑ Invest in **public spaces**, such as parks and community centers
- ❑ Support **arts** and **cultural programs** that enrich communities
- ❑ Promote policies to **end discrimination** and **racism** across all groups
- ❑ Ensure access to **affordable childcare** and **family support services**
- ❑ Increase access to **mental health** services and support
- ❑ Support programs to **reduce substance abuse** and **addiction**
- ❑ Promote **public safety** through **community policing** and **crime prevention** initiatives
- ❑ Implement policies to **reduce greenhouse gas emissions** and **mitigate climate change**
- ❑ Encourage the use of **alternative transportation options**, such as electric cars and bikes
- ❑ Promote **sustainable tourism practices** and responsible travel
- ❑ Invest in **public research** and development to **promote innovation**
- ❑ Increase **access to affordable** and **quality higher education**
- ❑ Promote **worker rights** and **fair labor** practices
- ❑ Encourage the use of **regenerative farming** practices
- ❑ Promote **social** and **environmental impact investing**
- ❑ Implement policies to **reduce waste** and **encourage recycling**
- ❑ Support **research and development** of **sustainable technologies**
- ❑ Increase **access** to **affordable** and **reliable public transportation**
- ❑ Encourage the use of **electric** and **hybrid vehicles**
- ❑ Provide incentives for **green building practices** and **energy-efficient homes**
- ❑ Increase access to **affordable** and **healthy food options** in low-income areas
- ❑ Encourage the use of **reusable products** and **reduce single-use plastics**
- ❑ Promote access to **public lands for recreation** and **conservation**
- ❑ Implement policies to **reduce deforestation** and **promote reforestation** efforts
- ❑ Support initiatives to **reduce air pollution** and improve **air quality**
- ❑ Invest in **renewable energy infrastructure** and **grid modernization**
- ❑ Encourage the **development of green jobs** and **sustainable industries**
- ❑ Promote the use of **green chemistry** and **sustainable materials**
- ❑ Support **community-based initiatives** that address local needs
- ❑ Increase **access to affordable healthcare** for all, regardless of income or background
- ❑ Promote **civic engagement** and **community involvement** in **decision-making** processes
- ❑ Ensure **transparency** and **accountability** in **government decision-making** and **operations**
- ❑ Invest in **public digital platforms** to create alternatives to existing digital monopolies
- ❑ **Break up large companies** with industry market share of more than 10 percent
- ❑ Promote **cooperatives** and alternative forms of **local business**
- ❑ Promote **community banking** and investments **in local startups**
- ❑ Reduce the gap between **executive pay** and **worker pay**
- ❑ Increase **taxes** on **luxury products** and **services**
- ❑ Increase **taxes** on the **hyper-rich** and **corporations**
- ❑ End **corporate personhood**
- ❑ Eliminate **waste** and redundancies in **government bureaucracy**
- ❑ Reduce **government spending** on **war** related activities
- ❑ Audit the **military**
- ❑ Eliminate **privatization** of government services
- ❑ Create **benchmarks for government** service performance

5. REGENERATIVE INNOVATION

Regenerative innovation. What is it and how does it work?

The late **Clay Christensen** described three kinds of innovation[140]:

Empowering Innovation: transforms complicated and costly products available to a few into simpler, cheaper products available to the many, thus creating jobs, because they require more and more people who can build, distribute, sell and service these products. Empowering investments also use capital — to expand capacity and to finance receivables and inventory.

Sustaining Innovation: replaces old products with new models, but creates few new jobs; such innovation has a neutral effect on economic activity and on capital.

Efficiency Innovation: reduces the cost of making and distributing existing products and services. Such innovations almost always reduce the net number of jobs, because they streamline processes, reduce capital investments, and eliminate waste.

Vijay Govindarajan and **Chris Trimble** added a fourth[141]:

Reverse innovation: the development of ideas (products, services, experiences) in an emerging market and coaxing them to flow uphill to Western markets.

---

[140] "A Capitalist's Dilemma, Whoever Wins on Tuesday" by Clayton Christensen, *New York Times*, November 3, 2012 https://www.nytimes.com/2012/11/04/business/a-capitalists-dilemma-whoever-becomes-president.html
[141] A Reverse Innovation Playbook" by Vijay Govindarajan *Harvard Business Review* April 2012 https://hbr.org/2012/04/a-reverse-innovation-playbook

Now we introduce a fifth kind of innovation: **regenerative innovation**.

Regenerative innovation is the *redesign of everything* – business model, products and services, experiences, the value chain, supplier and partner agreements, to *account for the Common Good*. It is *outcome-driven innovation*[142] applied to **regeneration projects**.

What does that look like? Here are a few ways to make innovation more regenerative:

Adopt regenerative design principles: Begin with a circular economy to minimize waste and pollution by keeping resources in use for as long as possible. Then add regenerative principles in terms of local wealth-building and "communityship." Regenerative design prioritizes environmental, social, and economic sustainability in the design process.

Use biomimicry: Biomimicry is the practice of emulating nature's strategies and designs to solve human problems. By drawing inspiration from nature, innovation can be made more regenerative by reducing waste and using renewable resources.

Implement life-cycle assessments: A life-cycle assessment is a comprehensive analysis of the environmental impacts of a product or service throughout its entire life cycle. By implementing life-cycle assessments, innovation can be made more regenerative by identifying and mitigating negative environmental impacts.

---

[142] "Outcome-Driven Innovation: JTBD Theory in Practice" by Anthony Ulwick *JTBD + Outcome-Driven Innovation*, June 22, 2017 https://jobs-to-be-done.com/outcome-driven-innovation-odi-is-jobs-to-be-done-theory-in-practice-2944c6ebc40e

Develop closed-loop systems: Closed-loop systems are designed to recycle and reuse waste products to create new products or services. By developing closed-loop systems, innovation can be made more regenerative by reducing waste and conserving resources.

Promote local regenerative agriculture: Regenerative agriculture is a farming approach that prioritizes soil health, biodiversity, and ecosystem services. By promoting regenerative agriculture, innovation can be made more regenerative by reducing environmental impacts and promoting sustainable food systems.

Utilize renewable energy sources: Renewable energy sources, such as solar and wind power, are essential for reducing greenhouse gas emissions and promoting energy independence. By utilizing renewable energy sources, innovation can be made more regenerative by reducing environmental impacts and promoting renewable energy infrastructure.

Encourage "Common Work": Collaboration between diverse stakeholders, such as government, industry, and civil society, is essential for promoting regenerative innovation. By encouraging collaboration, innovation can be made more regenerative by promoting inclusive decision-making and co-creation of solutions.

Prioritize social equity and the local community: Social equity must be prioritized in the innovation process to ensure that the benefits of innovation are shared equitably across society. By focusing on the needs of the local community, innovations can improve local conditions, and create community value beyond simply business value. By prioritizing social equity, innovation can be made more regenerative by promoting social and economic justice.

Foster a regenerative culture: Finally, to make innovation more regenerative, we need to foster a regenerative culture that values sustainability, collaboration, and social equity. By fostering a regenerative culture, innovation can be made more regenerative by promoting values and behaviors that support regenerative innovation.

"Everything, everywhere, all at once" — that's what United Nations (UN) Secretary General Antonio Gutierrez says is needed to stop **climate change's** worst effects on our world. So regenerative innovation is literally *design justice*.

The **Design Justice Network** gives us a few pointers.[143] Let's begin by understanding what is meant by the term "designing for justice."

Design justice rethinks design processes, centers people who are normally marginalized by design, and uses collaborative, creative practices to address the deepest challenges our communities face.

THE 10 PRINCIPLES OF DESIGN JUSTICE

1. We use design to **sustain, heal, and empower** our communities, as well as to seek liberation from exploitative and oppressive systems.
2. We **center the voices of those who are directly impacted** by the outcomes of the design process.
3. We **prioritize design's impact on the community** *(and planet)* over the intentions of the designer.
4. We view **change as emergent from an accountable, accessible, and collaborative process**, rather than as a point at the end of a process.*
5. We see the role of the **designer as a facilitator rather than an expert**.

---

[143] See: https://designjustice.org

6. We believe that **everyone is an expert based on their own lived experience**, and that we all have unique and brilliant contributions to bring to a design process.
7. We **share design knowledge and tools** with our communities.
8. We work towards **sustainable, community-led and - controlled** outcomes.
9. We work towards **non-exploitative solutions** that reconnect us to the earth and to each other.
10. Before seeking new design solutions, **we look for what is already working** at the community level. We honor and uplift traditional, indigenous, and local knowledge and practices.

These principles are a great starting point for any project and should be given far more visibility, not just in the world of design, but also the wider systems of our society – economic, social, political, environmental, etc.

THE 9 Cs of COMMON WORK

We also must stress the idea of **bringing community members and organizations together** to create joint-community value. This is what we call **"Common Work."**

A useful way to think of Common Work is to understand the 9Cs – and use them where applicable:

1. Co-envision
2. Collaboration
3. Cocreate
4. Codesign
5. Coproduce
6. Co-deliver
7. Co-own
8. Coexist
9. Community

CO-ENVISION: To envision in a regenerative way means to look beyond the present and imagine a future that is sustainable and flourishing for all. It involves co-creating a vision that takes into account the needs of the environment and all living beings, as well as social and economic considerations. This process requires collaboration and creativity, and a willingness to challenge conventional thinking and embrace innovative solutions.

COLLABORATION: Collaboration in a regenerative context means working together in a way that values the input and perspectives of all stakeholders. It involves creating an environment of mutual respect and trust, where diverse viewpoints are encouraged and differences are seen as strengths. Collaborative efforts should be guided by a shared vision and a commitment to co-create solutions that benefit all parties involved.

COCREATE: To co-create in a regenerative way means to work together to generate new ideas, products, or services that meet the needs of the present while preserving the capacity of future generations to meet their own needs. Co-creation is a collaborative process that involves active participation and engagement from all stakeholders, and is based on a shared understanding of the problem to be solved.

CODESIGN: Codesign in a regenerative context means designing products, services, or systems in collaboration with all stakeholders, with the goal of creating solutions that are sustainable and beneficial for all. It involves understanding the needs and perspectives of all users and incorporating them into the design process, as well as taking into account environmental, social, and economic considerations.

COPRODUCE: To coproduce in a regenerative way means to work together to produce goods, services, or knowledge in a way that is sustainable and beneficial for all. It involves sharing resources, knowledge, and expertise, and collaborating in a way that creates value for all parties involved. Coproduction requires a shared vision and a commitment to equitable distribution of benefits.

CO-DELIVER: Codelivery in a regenerative context means delivering goods or services in a way that is sustainable and beneficial for all. It involves collaborating with all stakeholders in the delivery process, from production to distribution, and ensuring that the delivery process takes into account environmental, social, and economic considerations. Codelivery requires a commitment to transparency, accountability, and continuous improvement.

CO-OWN: To co-own in a regenerative way means to share ownership and responsibility for the outcomes of collaborative efforts. It involves creating a sense of shared ownership and accountability, where all stakeholders have a voice and a stake in the success of the project. Co-ownership requires trust, transparency, and a willingness to work together to achieve shared goals.

COEXIST: To coexist in a regenerative context means to live and work together in a way that values diversity and promotes resilience. It involves creating an environment where all living beings can thrive, and where social and economic systems are designed to support the flourishing of all. Coexistence requires a commitment to mutual respect, empathy, and a recognition of the interconnectedness of all life.

COMMUNITY: A regenerative community is one that is built on a foundation of shared values, trust, and collaboration. It is a place where all members have a voice and a stake in the success of the community, and where resources are shared in a way that supports the well-being of all. A regenerative community is resilient, adaptable, and committed to continuous learning and improvement. It is a place where diversity is celebrated and where all members are empowered to contribute to the common good.

Thus, the boundaries of **regenerative innovation** must be in **alignment** with both business *and* community value creation.

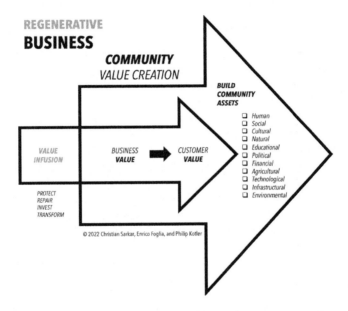

And since we're discussing design, let's examine the economy as well. The economy does not work for the Common Good. It works for a few.

Time's up.

6. A REGENERATIVE ECONOMY

The Wall Street narrative is – *the responsibility of business is to make a profit.* And the name of the economist **Milton Friedman** is usually brought up to defend this narrative.

Friedmanism is a myth. What **Milton Friedman**[144] actually said was "there is one and only one social responsibility of business — to use its resources and engage in activities designed to increase its profits so long as it *stays within the **rules of the game**, which is to say, engages in open and free competition *without deception or fraud.*"

Friedman assumed business was responsible, with business leaders who minded the rules of the game and who did not seek unlimited power. He envisioned competitive markets, not monopolies. And he was wrong, because he could not fathom the full extent of the corruption, both public and private. He also didn't appreciate the *long shadow of colonialism* – which still haunts the world and is the root cause of inequality, racism, gender inequality, and societal instability. The business world cannot continue operating in a historical vacuum.

When the US was founded, for example, the country's founders wisely restricted corporations exclusively to a business role. *Corporations were forbidden from attempting to influence elections, public policy, and other realms of civic society.*[145]

The wealthiest 10% of Americans hold 89% of stocks, worth $35.87 trillion.[146]

---

[144] *A Friedman doctrine – The Social Responsibility Of Business Is to Increase Its Profits,* by Milton Friedman, *New York Times,* September 13, 1970 https://www.nytimes.com/1970/09/13/archives/a-friedman-doctrine-the-social-responsibility-of-business-is-to.html

[145] "Our Hidden History of Corporations in the U.S." *Reclaim Democracy!*
https://reclaimdemocracy.org/corporate-accountability-history-corporations-us/

[146] "How Many Americans Own Stock?" Jack Caporal, *The Motley Fool* Nov 2, 2021

So, what happened? We ask the question which changed a young conservative's life[147]: **How did conventional economic theory and practice become a leading cause of—not the solution to—poverty, exclusion, and environmental system collapse?**

Today, the US political system does *not* serve the public. According to **Katherine Gehl** and **Michael Porter**[148]:

The starting point for understanding the problem is to recognize that our political system isn't broken. Washington is delivering exactly what it is currently designed to deliver. The real problem is that our political system is no longer designed to serve the public interest, and has been slowly reconfigured to benefit the private interests of gain-seeking organizations: our major political parties and their industry allies.

Ask: does *my* government work for the Common Good, the common interest? Or rather, does it favor the powerful – those with money and influence?

BROKEN ECONOMICS, BROKEN COMMUNITIES

Lynn Parramore, a senior research analyst at the **Institute of New Economic Thinking**, reminds us that Margaret Thatcher described the goal of our current neoliberal system as follows: *"Economics are the method: the object is to change the soul."* Parramore explains[149]:

---

https://www.fool.com/research/how-many-americans-own-stock/

[147] *When Corporations Rule the World* by David Korten, 1995

[148] "WHY COMPETITION IN THE POLITICS INDUSTRY IS FAILING AMERICA" by Katherine Gehl and Michael Porter https://www.hbs.edu/competitiveness/Documents/whycompetition-in-the-politics-industry-is-failing-america.pdf

[149] "Our Economic System is Making Us Mentally Ill" by Lynn Parramore *Institute of New Economic Thinking,* March 18, 2022 https://www.ineteconomics.org/perspectives/blog/our-economic-system-is-making-us-mentally-ill

Neoliberalism seeks to shift how human beings exist in the world, to change how we relate to each other and what we expect from life. Over time, we move from considering ourselves mutually responsible beings with a shared fate to isolated atoms liable solely for our own lives. Gradually, we shift from empowered citizens to people destined for servitude to arbitrary economic powers that lay well beyond our reach or understanding. Our humanity fades into an abstract realm of incomprehensible numbers and data, and we become little more than commodities, or even embodied externalities, in an invisible global economy ruled somehow by an invisible fist.

Unsurprisingly, this mode of existence produces maladies of mind, body, and spirit, elevating some of our most troublesome instincts as it denigrates many of the best.

The world is viewed through the **lens** *of* **selfish competition** – a societal sickness we've chosen to call "*Ayn Rand disease*." [150]

Rand's belief that those who rely on social welfare are "parasites," and those who hoard large amounts of private wealth are heroic supermen has become the guiding principle of Republican cruelty – starting with **Alan Greenspan** (a Rand acolyte) who, according to Gary Weiss, initiated the era of "Reaganomics" in the early 1980s by engineering "an increase in the most regressive tax on the poor and middle class."[151] For Greenspan, "Social Security was a system of altruism at its worst. Its beneficiaries were looters. Raising their taxes and cutting their benefits was no loss to society."

---

[150] Mark Twain called the sickness of the South *Sir Walter Scott disease*. Now, we see neoliberalism and Wall Street's obsession with profit at social and environmental cost, as *Ayn Rand disease* – a reductionist view based on greed, selfishness, exploitation, and private, unchecked power. Not only was Ayn Rand a horrible writer, Flannery O'Connor wrote: "She makes Mickey Spillane look like Dostoevsky." When reality impinged on Rand's life she ended up accepting both Social Security and Medicare to help her face her unfortunate health difficulties.

[151] *Ayn Rand Nation: The Hidden Struggle for America's Soul* by Gary Weiss, St. Martin's Press; Reprint edition (February 28, 2012)

The ultimate irony that Rand herself was collecting Social Security at the end of her life is conveniently overlooked by Randians. Rand taught "there is no such thing as the public interest," and that Social Security and Medicare steal from "creators" and redistribute their wealth. This was a "sublimely enticing argument for wealthy businessmen who had no interest whatever in the public interest…. Yet the taxpayers of America paid Rand's and Frank O'Connor's medical expenses."

Another irony: Rand was an atheist, and considered belief in God a "psychological weakness" and "an evil."[152] And yet the Republicans use religion and Rand *together* to create moral outrage whilst fighting the common good.

Other prominent public officials infected with Ayn Rand disease include Supreme Court Justice Clarence Thomas, elected representative Rand Paul, and Stephen Moore, former director of Fiscal Policy at the Cato Institute (yet another GOP "think tank" which advocates for individual liberty, tax cuts for the rich and the privatization of social security in the US).

And what happens when Ayn Rand contagion spreads to the workplace?

In 2008, then Sears CEO (hedge fund manager) **Eddie Lampert** actually restructured the company on Ayn Rand's principles of individualism and competition, thinking this would lead to greater profits.

Lynn Parramore describes what that was like:

Lampert broke the company into over 30 individual units, each with its own management, and each measured separately for profit and loss.[153]

---

[152] Ayn Rand collection, *YouTube* https://youtu.be/PJBLUQQ_a7g
[153] "Ayn Rand killed Sears" by Lynn Stuart Parramore *Salon*, July 18, 2013
https://www.salon.com/2013/07/18/ayn_rand_killed_sears_partner/

The result? Executives started undermining other units because they knew their bonuses were tied to individual unit performance. They began to focus solely on the economic performance of their unit at the expense of the overall Sears brand. Teamwork and purpose went out the window.

Here's Parramore again:

In a society dominated by this kind of thinking, you find yourself inculcated with a competitive mindset the minute you enter school. The simplest expression of your vitality, like singing, running, or jumping, is quickly nudged into a competitive framework. You can't just jump for joy; you have to be the number one jumper. The point is not the intrinsic reward of the activity but the thrill of beating someone else, or perhaps the negative relief of not being a loser. You are trained to categorize your fellows according to whether they win or lose, sensing that you should just give up on activities in where you don't "excel."

And most importantly, Ayn Rand disease creates a sense of displacement and insecurity:

You begin to understand that you don't have much agency in the world. Life feels precarious, and that is exactly what neoliberals intended because they believed that living in such a state was necessary to "discipline" people to accept their place in a world ruled by capitalists.

If you're from the United States, you might recognize this as one reason why we don't have Universal Healthcare. Or why our government is systematically destroying public infrastructure like our educational system.

We know the **local community can become the focus of meaningful change** – through *regeneration*. Instead of more centralization, we need decentralization – the **devolution of power** to local communities, and **deep democracy**.

The times call for new community-level capabilities required to make the shift to regeneration. And perhaps most importantly, the transition requires new forms of leadership – based on collaboration, local ecosystem development and education.

That doesn't mean we abandon global collaboration and coordination. It means we rethink and reconfigure our global ecosystems to create **value for *all*, not just the few**.

There is no shortage of criticism for our destructive economic model. More and more, the blind acceptance of *Ayn Rand disease* and its precepts – particularly how they are practiced in our markets – is being rejected by the next generation of thinkers.

For business, this means we must ask: *how does Brand Activism apply at the local-community level?*

David Korten calls it the "suicide economy[154]" – for three reasons:

1. **Counts Ecosystem Destruction for Financial Gain as Wealth Creation:** It values life only for its market value. And counts as wealth creation the depletion of Earth's capacity to support life in order to grow the financial assets of those who already have financial assets far beyond any need. This assures both the systematic depletion of Earth's capacity to support life and increasing control of what remains of that capacity by a tiny oligarchy.

---

[154] "The New Economy" by David Korten, *Next System Project*, August 10, 2016 https://davidkorten.org/wp-content/uploads/2019/01/NEXT_SYSTEM-Living_Earth_System_Model.pdf

2. **Drives a Growing Global Class Division between the Profligate and the Desperate:** It encourages and celebrates ever more excessive and wasteful consumption by the few while reducing the many to increasing desperation and exclusion from access to the essential means of living—including clean air to breath, water to drink, fertile soils to grow food, and a place to live.

3. **Limits Meaningful Participation in Rule Making to the Winners in a Rigged Game:** A corporate dominated, money-driven political system puts the power to make the rules in the hands of those who profit from environmental destruction and economic exclusion, thus creating a positive feedback loop reinforcing political choices that assure ultimate system collapse.

This "suicide economy" systematically **destroys** the foundations of its own—and our—existence, explains Korten.

According to Korten, the first "fatal" error of the suicide economy is the **choice of money rather than life** as the defining cultural value. The second? The **choice of global corporations rather than living communities** as the institutional locus of organization and power.

These two flawed choices have brought us to the brink. Korten spells it out[155]:

We embrace corporations as our source of money. We forget that nature is our source of life. From here, we easily buy into the fallacies of an economics that counts the destruction of life to make money as

---

[155] "The New Economy" by David Korten, *Next System Project*, August 10, 2016 https://davidkorten.org/new-economy-system-model/

wealth creation, and a politics that equates corporate rule with democracy.

In Korten's suicide economy, economists assure the public that maximizing corporate profits will maximize GDP growth and maximizing GDP growth will maximize benefits to all—because their mathematical models say so.

For Korten, this is merely an "intellectually and morally bankrupt ideology posing as a science."[156]

Michel Bauwens spells out the craziness of the current economic system[157]:

We must rethink the way our economic system works. I believe in "cosmo=localization": everything that is heavy should be local and everything that is light is global. Another way to name this would be to talk about 'subsidiarity in material production', i.e. to produce as close as possible to the place of need. This is important because transportation nearly has three times the environmental cost of production. We need to reorganise the world's industrial system with distributed manufacturing. Think about the coffee cups you get from your local Starbucks. They are made from petrol extracted in Saudi Arabia, which has taken nature one million years to produce (!), this is then shipped to China to be turned into those plastic covers, then reshipped across the world. Think of all the resources used for items with an average lifespan of 15 seconds for an espresso cup. There is such a waste in our current system, that we desperately need a transition. A transition towards decentralised, on-demand manufacturing which has access to common global knowledge, using only what we need, with biodegradable and modular constituents, rather than 'planned obsolescence'.

---

[156] Our term for this is *"Ayn Rand disease."*

[157] "Michel Bauwens on the Commons Transition" interview with Vicent Lassalle via
https://primer.commonstransition.org/4-more/michel-bauwens-on-the-commons-transition

I am not at all against globalization, quite the contrary. However, concerning physical goods we need to relocate production. It is absurd that a tennis ball used in a Wimbledon match has travelled 40'000km during its production.

The **Pope** too, describes the current paradigm in less than flattering terms. He calls it an "**economy of exclusion**" [158]:

Just as the commandment "Thou shalt not kill" sets a clear limit in order to safeguard the value of human life, today we also have to say "thou shalt not" to an economy of exclusion and inequality. Such an economy kills. How can it be that it is not a news item when an elderly homeless person dies of exposure, but it is news when the stock market loses two points? This is a case of exclusion. Can we continue to stand by when food is thrown away while people are starving? This is a case of inequality. Today everything comes under the laws of competition and the survival of the fittest, where the powerful feed upon the powerless. As a consequence, masses of people find themselves excluded and marginalized: without work, without possibilities, without any means of escape.

Human beings are themselves considered consumer goods to be used and then discarded. We have created a "throw away" culture which is now spreading. It is no longer simply about exploitation and oppression, but something new. Exclusion ultimately has to do with what it means to be a part of the society in which we live; those excluded are no longer society's underside or its fringes or its disenfranchised – they are no longer even a part of it. The excluded are not the "exploited" but the outcast, the "leftovers".

We need to understand that **the economy of exclusion, excludes not just the poor, but Nature as well.**

---

[158] *EVANGELII GAUDIUM*, #53 Pope Francis

https://www.vatican.va/content/francesco/en/apost_exhortations/documents/papa-francesco_esortazione-ap_20131124_evangelii-gaudium.html#No_to_an_economy_of_exclusion

Business schools are also to blame for this distortion, as are the media, the press, and the business gurus who continue to justify the primacy of "**shareholder value maximization**."

Even the late Jack Welch, the primary proponent of this approach, ended up calling it the **"dumbest idea in the world."**[159] Too bad he didn't believe that when he was CEO.

Every shortcoming — the financialization of the economic system, companies' short-term growth and profit objectives, insufficient investment in the infrastructure, neglect of the environment, and more — is linked, and each surmountable.

What are we to make of *the emphasis on **individualism and self-interest at the expense of community and the commons.*** There must be another way.

Once again, here's Lynn Parramore[160]:

Our common good is enhanced by political arrangements in which cooperative forms of participation and the needs of ordinary people are prioritized. This means pretty much doing the opposite of what neoliberals have championed. We acknowledge that governments can and must intervene in markets so that people are protected from abuse. We focus relentlessly on getting money out of politics and making voting something that everybody can do easily. We regulate business, enhance the power of working people, and ensure that the global economy is not just one big race to the bottom but a system in which the needs and rights of all inhabitants are considered.

Most of our institutions are not fit for the task ahead. They were built to create and deliver administrative control,

---

[159] "Welch condemns share price focus," by Francesco Guerrera, *Financial Times*, March 12, 2009 https://www.ft.com/content/294ff1f2-0f27-11de-ba10-0000779fd2ac#axzz1eiLpL2PZ

[160] "Our Economic System is Making Us Mentally Ill" by Lynn Parramore *Institute of New Economic Thinking*, March 18, 2022 https://www.ineteconomics.org/perspectives/blog/our-economic-system-is-making-us-mentally-ill

patterned on colonial command, unresponsive to the needs of the local community. By the way, this is also the framework for state and local administration – designed for rule, not service.

We must ask: *what is stopping us from doing the right thing?* What prevents us from investing in the common good?

Scott Russell Sanders explains[161]:

...we have been conditioned to accept a narrow view of wealth. The language of value in America is overwhelmingly economic. We encounter it in advertising, editorials, political speeches, corporate reports, business news, films and television shows. We hear of every up and down in stock markets and currency exchanges, profits and losses on balance sheets, fundraising totals for political parties, sales figures for holidays, multi-million-dollar trades in pro sports, box office yields of movies, auction prices for paintings. We rarely hear of any form of wealth except what can be measured in money. We are told that the Gross Domestic Product is the best gauge for how well the economy is doing, and therefore how America is doing; the higher the GDP the better. Yet this figure merely sums up the market value of all goods and services produced in a given period, and thus includes the dollars set in motion by traffic accidents, corruption trials, bank foreclosures, school shootings, Parkinson's disease, and every other social ill. As gauged by its effect on GDP, the opioid epidemic has been good for the economy, and so has the Iraq War.

At a recent *Financial Times* conference, titled - "Moral Money," **Stuart Kirk**, HSBC's Asset Management head of responsible investing, actually said: *"Who cares if Miami is six meters under water in 100 years?"*[162]

---

[161] "An Economy of False Profits" Scott Russell Sanders, *Notre Dame Magazine* Summer 2018
https://magazine.nd.edu/stories/an-economy-of-false-profits/

[162] HSBC AM global head of responsible investing: 'Who cares if Miami is six metres under water in 100 years?'
James Baxter-Derrington, *Investment Week*, 19 May, 2022
https://www.investmentweek.co.uk/news/4050010/hsbc-global-head-responsible-investing-cares-miami-metres-water-100

How did finance become so disconnected from the world? From society?

Kirk's thinking: *At a big bank like ours, what do people think the average loan length is? It is six years. What happens to the planet in year seven is actually irrelevant to our loan book. For coal, what happens in year seven is actually irrelevant.*

"Let's get back to making money out of the transition," he advised the "moral money" audience.

Ouch. Where did these guys lose the plot?

One recent answer is: **"Davos Man"** – a term coined by the political scientist **Samuel Huntington** and the subject of **Peter Goodman**'s *Davos Man: How the Billionaires Devoured the World.*

Who is the Davos Man? Those "so enriched by globalization and so native to its workings that they are effectively stateless, their interests and wealth flowing across borders, their estates and yachts sprinkled across continents, their arsenal of lobbyists and accountants straddling jurisdictions, eliminating loyalty to any particular nation."[163]

In an interview with Lewis Lapham[164], Goodman explains: *We see a systematic bottom-up transfer of wealth from all of us to a handful of people who are capable of employing lobbyists by the dozens, who have perverted the workings of our democracies in order to concentrate more and more wealth in their hands at the expense of everyone else. They have dismantled government programs and public infrastructure. They have transferred the proceeds to themselves. And in so doing they have not only ended up with most of the wealth, they have rendered our democratic societies dysfunctional.*

---

[163] *Davos Man: How the Billionaires Devoured the World* by Peter Goodman, *Custom House*, January 18, 2022
[164] "The Cosmic Lie" Lewis H. Lapham interviews Peter S. Goodman, *Lapham's Quarterly*, April 4, 2022
https://www.laphamsquarterly.org/roundtable/cosmic-lie

What's worse is that the "new" billionaires are not content to simply collect their cash and play with their toys.

Now, says Goodman, "that would have us believe that they are not only not the source of our problems in the world but they are the solution to our problems."[165]

And we are powerless to stop them. Or so it seems.

When did our leaders becomes so disconnected from reality?

ENCLOSING THE COMMONS: THE ROOTS *of* PRIVATIZATION

The roots of this **disconnect** go back in time – to the pre-colonial past in England. A famous "Scene of the Diggers" – an English Civil War Woodcut from 1649 proclaims: "England is not a Free People till the Poor that have no Land, have a free allowance to dig and labour the Commons..."

"England is not a free people, till the poor that have no land, have a free allowance to dig and labour the commons..."
Gerrard Winstanley, 1649

James Boyle, a law school professor at Duke, points us to a 17th century folk poem:

> The law locks up the man or woman
> Who steals the goose off the common
> But leaves the greater villain loose
> Who steals the common from the goose.

---

[165] "The Cosmic Lie" - Lewis H. Lapham interviews Peter S. Goodman, *Lapham's Quarterly*, April 4, 2022
https://www.laphamsquarterly.org/roundtable/cosmic-lie

The law demands that we atone
When we take things we do not own
But leaves the lords and ladies fine
Who takes things that are yours and mine.

The poor and wretched don't escape
If they conspire the law to break;
This must be so but they endure
Those who conspire to make the law.

The law locks up the man or woman
Who steals the goose from off the common
And geese will still a common lack
Till they go and steal it back.

He calls it "one of the pithiest condemnations of the English enclosure movement — the process of fencing off common land and turning it into private property. In a few lines, the poem manages to criticize double standards, expose the artificial and controversial nature of property rights, and take a slap at the legitimacy of state power. And it does it all with humor, without jargon, and in rhyming couplets."[166]

The enclosing of the commons never ended. Today, we are faced with the privatization of everything. Studies have shown that *none* of the world's top industries would be profitable if they paid for the natural capital they use.[167]

It's time to *rethink everything*.

---

[166] "Stealing the Common from the Goose" by Jay Walljasper January 2013
https://www.onthecommons.org/magazine/"stealing-common-goose"

[167] "None of the world's top industries would be profitable if they paid for the natural capital they use' *Grist* https://grist.org/business-technology/none-of-the-worlds-top-industries-would-be-profitable-if-they-paid-for-the-natural-capital-they-use/ SEE: http://naturalcapitalcoalition.org/wp-content/uploads/2016/07/Trucost-Nat-Cap-at-Risk-Final-Report-web.pdf

RETHINKING EVERYTHING

Times of crises call out for public leadership in service of the Common Good. Absent that leadership, businesses have a responsibility to not be silent, and more importantly, to act. In a Democracy, that means they will act in a transparent way to:

(1) ensure the public is given access to the truth, and protected from misinformation and "alternative facts."

(2) ensure elections will be fair and free (without the imposition of poll taxes, and other suppression techniques like gerrymandering and the use of dark money)

(3) promote policies for the Common Good, instead of tax-breaks that serve narrow, special interests.

Capitalism – dominant as it is – has run its course. The question we have to ask is: **why is capitalism not compatible with democracy?**

Robert Reich explains[168]:

Decades ago, America's wealthy backed a Republican establishment that believed in fiscal conservatism, anti-communism, and constitutional democracy. But today's billionaire class is pushing a radically anti-democratic agenda for America — backing Trump's lie that the 2020 election was stolen, calling for restrictions on voting, and even questioning the value of democracy.

Peter Thiel, the billionaire tech financier who is among those leading the charge, writes "I no longer believe that freedom and democracy are compatible."

---

[168] "What you need to know about the anti-democracy movement" by Robert Reich May 19, 2022
https://robertreich.substack.com/p/the-anti-democracy-movement

The digital revolution didn't turn out the way it was advertised. Like all revolutions, it gave rise to a new set of elites – the tech billionaires – but didn't improve living standards for the majority of people. Instead, income inequality grows, and the digital divide grows wider.[169] The tech billionaires are increasingly at odds with the very idea of democracy[170].

And **corporate imperialism** didn't end either[171], as the late **C.K. Prahalad** had hoped. Instead, it became the predominant force of globalization – even the Chinese model of development in Africa is increasingly viewed as an imperialistic strategy linked explicitly to its "Belt and Road" initiative. Critical voices describe the Chinese strategy as "an imperial project alongside the likes of the British East India Company (EIC) or the Dutch East Indian Company, Vereenigde Oostindische Compagnie (VOC).[172]"

But we don't have to focus on the Chinese. Private capital has always been deeply interlocked with **colonialism**. When the British came to India with the East India Company (EIC), the country's share of the world GDP is estimated to have been somewhere between 30−35% of the world's GDP – one of the largest economies in the world; when the British left India, that number was 2%.[173]

---

[169] *Digital divide persists even as Americans with lower incomes make gains in tech adoption*, Emily A. Vogels, Pew Research Center (June 22, 2021)
https://www.pewresearch.org/fact-tank/2021/06/22/digital-divide-persists-even-as-americans-with-lower-incomes-make-gains-in-tech-adoption/

[170] See: https://www.theguardian.com/uk-news/2019/apr/21/carole-cadwalladr-ted-tech-google-facebook-zuckerberg-silicon-valley

[171] "The End of Corporate Imperialism" by C.K. Prahalad and Kenneth Lieberthal, *Harvard Business Review* August 2003 https://hbr.org/2003/08/the-end-of-corporate-imperialism

[172] "China's Belt and Road Initiative is neo-Imperialism" by Sarah-Madeleine Torres and Bradley A. Thaye, *The Spectator* June 27, 2019 https://spectatorworld.com/author/sarah-madeleine-torres-bradley-a-thayer/

[173] *Development Centre Studies: The World Economy Historical Statistics* by Maddison Angus, OECD Publishing, Sep 25, 2003

There is no shortage of evidence we can find to show how the East India Company built the foundation for the monopolistic corporate strategies of today.

"Involuntary privatization" was the strategy, narrates William Dalrymple[174]:

We still talk about the British conquering India, but that phrase disguises a more sinister reality. It was not the British government that seized India at the end of the 18th century, but a dangerously unregulated private company headquartered in one small office, five windows wide, in London, and managed in India by an unstable sociopath – Clive.

And: "In many ways the EIC was a model of corporate efficiency: 100 years into its history, it had only 35 permanent employees in its head office."

Jack Welch would have been proud.

Once again, here's Dalrymple[175]:

The transaction depicted in the painting (see below) was to have catastrophic consequences. As with all such corporations, then as now, the EIC was answerable only to its shareholders. With no stake in the just governance of the region, or its long-term wellbeing, the company's rule quickly turned into the straightforward pillage of Bengal, and the rapid transfer westwards of its wealth.

---

[174] "The East India Company: The original corporate raiders" by William Dalrymple, *The Guardian*, 4 March, 2015

https://www.theguardian.com/world/2015/mar/04/east-india-company-original-corporate-raiders

[175] "The East India Company: The original corporate raiders" by William Dalrymple, *The Guardian*, 4 March, 2015

https://www.theguardian.com/world/2015/mar/04/east-india-company-original-corporate-raiders

Illustration: Benjamin West (1738–1820)/British Library

In the painting, American-born painter Benjamin West depicts the Mughal emperor **Shah Alam** handing over a scroll to **Robert Clive**, the "governor of Bengal." The document transferred tax authority in Bengal, Bihar and Orissa to the East India Company. This was the beginning of the looting of medieval India.

Shashi Tharoor, whose Oxford Union debate[176] on reparations[177] became a viral hit on *YouTube*, jokes: "No wonder the sun never set on the British empire because even God couldn't trust the English in the dark."

In his book, *Inglorious Empire: What the British did to India*, Tharoor writes[178]:

---

[176] "Dr Shashi Tharoor MP - Britain Does Owe Reparations" *YouTube*, https://youtu.be/f7CW7S0zxv4

[177] The topic of reparations is not one that the former colonialists are particularly fond of. In Haiti, for example, when President Jean-Bertrand Aristide demanded "reparations" in a speech in front of the French ambassador, he was soon "removed" from power by the US and France. See: "Demanding Reparations, and Ending Up in Exile" by Constant Méheut, Catherine Porter, Selam Gebrekidan and Matt Apuzzo, *New York Times*, May 20, 2022 https://www.nytimes.com/2022/05/20/world/americas/haiti-aristide-reparations-france.html

[178] *Inglorious Empire: What the British did to India* by Sashi Tharoor, Scribe Publications, 2016

The British proclaimed the virtues of free trade while destroying the free trade Indians had carried on for centuries, if not millennia, by both land and sea. Free trade, of course, suited the British as a slogan, since they were the best equipped to profit from it in the nineteenth century, and their guns and laws could always stifle what little competition the indigenes could attempt to mount. A globalization of equals could well have been worth celebrating, but the globalization of Empire was conducted by and above all for the colonizers, and not in the interests of the colonized.

Sound familiar?

Wait, there's more. Dalrymple explains how the EIC's reckless speculation also presages the modern corporation:

...the East India Company really was too big to fail. So it was that in 1773, the world's first aggressive multinational corporation was saved by history's first mega-bailout – the first example of a nation state extracting, as its price for saving a failing corporation, the right to regulate and severely rein it in.

The EIC did not restrict its adventurism to India. It smuggled opium into China in exchange for the country's most prized trade good: *tea*.[179]

When China tried to stop the opium trade, the British government sent warships, and subdued all opposition in Opium War of 1840 – which handed Hong Kong to the British.

Why are we harping on about colonialism?

Because the extractive mindset of colonialism "evolved" into the extractive mindset of capitalism.

And without a recalibration of this colonial mindset, there is no sane way forward.

The world's top scientists are acknowledging that **decolonization** must be central to the global response to climate change. The IPCC's sixth assessment report (April 2022) includes *colonialism* not only as a *driver of the climate crisis* but also as an ongoing issue that is exacerbating communities' vulnerability to it. The report suggests "an *investigation of the deep-seated ideologies and vested interests* that are creating goal conflicts and negatively impacting marginalized groups to begin with," and that "adaptation measures need to acknowledge and address the *underlying drivers* that make certain groups particularly vulnerable, such as *social disenfranchisement, unequal power dynamics* and *historical legacies of colonialism and exploitation*."[180]

Solutions for decolonization must come from the colonized, not the colonizers.

---

[179] "How the East India Company Became the World's Most Powerful Monopoly" by Dave Roos, *Histor,* October 23, 2020 https://www.history.com/news/east-india-company-england-trade

[180] Chapter 18: Climate Resilient Development, *IPCC WGII Sixth Assessment*, April 2022 ReportPathwayshttps://www.ipcc.ch/report/ar6/wg2/downloads/report/IPCC_AR6_WGII_FinalDraft_Chapter18 .pdf

The *Financial Times'* **Martin Wolf** points out what's at stake[181]:

The stake is that the angry and disaffected of various kinds — cultural and economic (we can discuss the interaction between them) — will end up installing somebody who subverts the norms and rules of democracy and basically creates what we've now come to call an "illiberal democracy," which is what Sergei Guriev calls a spin dictatorship. Essentially, they erode the rule of law, they put their own cronies in the principal positions of power in the legal system, the judiciary, the police forces, the army, and so forth; they effectively ensure that the media are controlled by their friends; they use the legal system and the tax system to persecute their enemies, including many rich people. They basically create a state which is dominated by them and those whom they choose. It's a complete subversion of democracy from within and it's the principal way democracies are disappearing around the world. In emerging countries it's happening all the time. We might remember that 23 years ago, when Putin was elected leader, we thought that maybe Russia was going to become a democracy — not exactly what has happened. The danger is that that is what will happen. We're seeing it now in places I would never have imagined it would happen — Israel, for example. I think Trump, some of his supporters, and some of the people behind him have similar tendencies.

Now, what do you lose? What you lose, ultimately, is your freedom and your security. You may be allowed to be rich, but you live at the whim of the ruler. And the economy will not work well because the ruler will use his whims to favor those he wants to favor and penalize those who are against him, which is not compatible with a proper or decent market economy. But it will also have political and social impact: people will stop saying what they think. People will have to be careful about what they say. Now, we're seeing that on the left, in one way, and we will be seeing that on the right. In that sort of society, what I think of as core liberal values will erode and disappear.

[181] Martin Wolf on the Crisis of Democratic Capitalism – podcast with Yascha Mounk, Mar 25, 2023
https://www.persuasion.community/p/wolf

The business world finally has *the moral imperative* to listen and heed the voices of the indigenous and native tribes – and turn to the **Common Good**. The longer we wait, the worse our chances of avoiding collapse.

Many people don't think the super-rich are interested in finding Common Good.

Peter Goldman again[182]:

"American tax rates have been downgraded over decades to the point where billionaires like Stephen Schwarzman, another primary character in my book, is worth about 35 billion dollars. He's paying less of a share of his wealth in income to the federal government than the people scrubbing his toilets in his multiple residences that he owns the way most of us own socks."

Andrew Winston has a larger philosophical concern[183], as he says, with "investor-led language" around ESG. ESG — which stands for environmental, social, and governance — has become the dominant term in sustainability debates, but he highlights the problem:

Seeing all things through the lens of markets and the quest for shareholder maximization is largely how we got into this mess in the first place. We've put profits above literally all else, and it's leading to ecological collapse and vast inequality. Framing a company's commitments around battling climate disaster in investor terms turns it into an exercise of "Does this create shareholder value?" — which is not beside the point but skews the world dramatically. Sure, shareholders should do well, but only after a company has served a

---

[182] "The Cosmic Lie" Lewis H. Lapham interviews Peter S. Goodman, *Lapham's Quarterly*, April 4, 2022
https://www.laphamsquarterly.org/roundtable/cosmic-lie
[183] "What's Lost When We Talk 'ESG' and Not 'Sustainability'" by Andrew Winston *MIT Sloan Management Review*, May 5, 2022

purpose for stakeholders and helped protect the world and resources we all rely on to survive and thrive.

Winston makes his point clear:

Investors aren't well positioned for this approach. Just as fossil fuel companies should not lead the planning of our energy future, **it seems unwise to let finance lead the journey to a humane, more just, less greed-filled form of capitalism.**

And with **COVID**, inequality has risen to new heights:

"Billionaires added $5 trillion to their fortunes during the pandemic," reads the headline on CNN[184]. Apparently the total wealth of billionaires jumped from $8.6 trillion in March 2020 to $13.8 trillion in November 2021, a bigger increase than in the previous 14 years combined. The world's richest 10 men saw their collective wealth more than double, shooting up by $1.3 billion a day.

More than 850 million people now risk falling into poverty[185].

Davos Man is guilty of ever-widening income inequality. We turn again to Peter Goodman:

There has been this downgrading of government services. The typical playbook is some corporate interest financed by a Davos Man pursuing their own interest: eliminate support for some government programs, some form of welfare, some health care programs, transportation, subsidized child care. And then, lo and behold, the services diminish and think tanks come along and say, "Oh, well, this isn't working anymore. This doesn't work. We should just eliminate it

---

[184] "Billionaires added $5 trillion to their fortunes during the pandemic" by Anna Cooban, *CNN Business* https://edition.cnn.com/2022/01/16/business/oxfam-pandemic-davos-billionaires/index.html
[185] "Impacts of COVID-19 disproportionately affect poor and vulnerable: UN chief" *UN News* https://news.un.org/en/story/2020/06/1067502

altogether." This is the mechanism by which Davos Man dismantles public infrastructure and transfers the proceeds to themselves while telling us what I refer to as the cosmic lie in the book, which is this idea that when we organize our economies around sending more wealth to the people who already have most of it, the benefits will just magically trickle down throughout our economies – something that we've tried many times, and it's worked out zero times. One part of it always does work out, and that's the part where the wealthy people end up with most of the money. And that's why we keep living through it.

American tax rates have been downgraded over decades to the point where billionaires like Stephen Schwarzman, another primary character in my book, is worth about 35 billion dollars. He's paying less of a share of his wealth in income to the federal government than the people scrubbing his toilets in his multiple residences that he owns the way most of us own socks.

But even *before* COVID the world was in crisis.

The Russian invasion of Ukraine has shattered the "illusion of peace." If we think that by banning Russian petroleum imports, we're solving our problems – we've got it all wrong, explains the inimitable **Umair Haque**: "We are far, far more dependent on Russian oil than most of us can possibly imagine. Our lives in the West are made of Russian hydrocarbons, in China, from our footwear, to our sheets, to our clothes, to our electronics.[186]"

Thus, all the plastic products we import from China, or at least a great majority of them, are built from Russian oil.

So much for the Russian boycott.

---

[186] "Our Addiction to Oil Is Starting World War III" by Umair Haque, March 9, 2022
https://medium.com/eudaimonia-co/how-dirty-oil-circles-the-globe-and-its-starting-world-war-iii-cc1be6603fd3

REGENERATIVE CAPITALISM?

Another way to frame the debate for the future is to keep the "wall of capitalism" as a boundary for all discussion. So regeneration is automatically framed as "regenerative capitalism."

This is the stance of **The Capital Institute** founded by **John Fullerton** who resigned from resigned from JPMorgan in the spring of 2001 after a 20-year career. His revelation,[187] that *"the modern scheme of economics and finance – what Wall Street "geniuses" (like me) practiced so well – formed the root cause of these systemic crises"* – is an eye-opener for all senior executives.

He concluded: *We can – and must – bring our economic theory and practice into alignment with our latest understanding of how the universe and our humanity actually work!*

That's zero-distance to reality.

Fullerton's work has given us what he calls the theoretical foundation of Regenerative Economics – Eight principles of a Regenerative Economy.

These principles are listed as follows:[188]

1. In Right Relationship: Humanity is an integral part of an interconnected web of life in which there is no real separation between "us" and "it."

2. Views Wealth Holistically: True wealth is not merely money in the bank. It must be defined and managed systemically in terms of the well-being of the whole.

---

[187] *REGENERATIVE CAPITALISM: How Universal Principles And Patterns Will Shape Our New Economy* by John Fullerton April 2015, *Capital Institute* https://capitalinstitute.org/wp-content/uploads/2015/04/2015-Regenerative-Capitalism-4-20-15-final.pdf

[188] From The Capital Institute website: https://capitalinstitute.org/8-principles-regenerative-economy/

3. Innovative, Adaptive, Responsive: In a world in which change is both ever-present and accelerating, the qualities of innovation and adaptability are critical to health.

4. Empowered Participation: In an interdependent system, fitness comes from contributing in some way to the health of the whole.

5. Honors Community and Place: Each human community consists of a mosaic of peoples, traditions, beliefs, and institutions uniquely shaped by long-term pressures of geography, human history, culture, local environment, and changing human needs.

6. Edge Effect Abundance: Creativity and abundance flourish synergistically at the "edges" of systems, where the bonds holding the dominant pattern in place are weakest.

7. Robust Circulatory Flow: A living economy demands a healthy metabolism to flush toxins and nourish every cell at every level of our human networks.

8. Seeks Balance: Being in dynamic balance is essential to systemic health. Like a unicycle rider, regenerative systems are always engaged in this delicate dance in search of balance.

The real question is *can capitalism be regenerative?*

Or perhaps: *what will it take to make capitalism regenerative?*

Ted Howard says it best: "it's hard to imagine that we could actually live in a society that isn't made up of giant corporations, where investors aren't trying to maximize their shareholder value, where money isn't incredibly concentrated; that we could live in a system that's producing other kinds of values, a political economy that's neither a state socialism, bureaucratic old Soviet Union style nor this out-of-control juggernaut that we have right now."[189]

THE ECOCIDE ECONOMY

The tragedy of our global economy is that it is designed to destroy our ecosystems in the service of profit. The term used is **ecocide**.

Stop Ecocide International (stopecocide.earth) is an organization driving the global conversation on recognition of ecocide as an international crime. Here's their view:

The international crimes of **genocide** and **crimes against humanity** were born in the 1940s in the face of atrocities that were witnessed and condemned with horror by the international community. We now face a similar urgency with respect to destruction of the natural living world upon which we, as a species along with many millions of others, completely depend.

The definition[190] of **ecocide**:

"ecocide" means unlawful or wanton acts committed with knowledge that there is a substantial likelihood of severe and either widespread or long-term damage to the environment being caused by those acts.

1. "Wanton" means with reckless disregard for damage which would be clearly excessive in relation to the social and economic benefits anticipated;
2. "Severe" means damage which involves very serious adverse changes, disruption or harm to any element of the environment, including grave impacts on human life or natural, cultural or economic resources;

---

[189] Beyond Capitalism and Socialism: A Conversation On Inventing the Regenerative Economy
https://bioneers.org/beyond-capitalism-and-socialism-ztvz2001/
[190] https://www.stopecocide.earth/legal-definition and

3. "Widespread" means damage which extends beyond a limited geographic area, crosses state boundaries, or is suffered by an entire ecosystem or species or a large number of human beings;

4. "Long-term" means damage which is irreversible or which cannot be redressed through natural recovery within a reasonable period of time;

5. "Environment" means the earth, its biosphere, cryosphere, lithosphere, hydrosphere and atmosphere, as well as outer space.

The ecocide economy is the root cause of the climate and ecological emergency that we now face. Here's are some examples of industrial activities which are killing the planet:[191]

Ocean Damage:
- Industrial fishing
- Oil spills
- Plastic pollution
- Deep sea mining

Deforestation:
- Industrial livestock farming
- Mineral extraction
- Oil drilling
- Palm oil and wood production

Land and Water Contamination
- Oil spills
- Mining
- Mountaintop removal
- Tar sands
- Fracking

---

[191] https://www.stopecocide.earth/what-is-ecocide

- Textile chemicals
- Agricultural pollution
- River system pollution
- Insect "apocalypse"

Air Pollution
- Chemical disasters
- Chemical weapons
- Radioactive contamination
- Nuclear testing
- Industrial emissions (fossil fuels, agriculture industries, cement, etc.)

The responsibility for this mess lies with decisions made at the top of industry, finance and government. We must end ecocide, if we want to prevent genocide.

REGENERATION AND DEGROWTH

Advocates of growth propose "green growth" – that is endless growth driven by green energy sources.

How does regeneration co-exist with the doctrine of **de-growth?** And what exactly does de-growth entail?[192]

For starters, writes Jason Hickel:

"Degrowth is a planned reduction of energy and resource use designed to bring the economy back into balance with the living world in a way that reduces inequality and improves human well-being."

Exactly.

---

[192] Jason Hickel (2021) What does degrowth mean? A few points of clarification, Globalizations, 18:7, 1105-1111, DOI: 10.1080/14747731.2020.1812222

Here are a few ideas we should clearly understand, explains Hickel:

- Human civilization is presently overshooting a number of critical planetary boundaries and faces a multi-dimensional crisis of ecological breakdown, including dangerous climate change, ocean acidification, deforestation and biodiversity collapse

- Contrary to the general narrative about the Anthropocene, this crisis is not being caused by human beings as such, but by a particular economic system: a system that is predicated on perpetual expansion, disproportionately to the benefit of a small minority of rich people

- In mainstream economics, the dominant claim is that we must continue to pursue perpetual growth and therefore must seek to decouple GDP from ecological impacts and make growth 'green'. This is a fallacy; hence we need de-growth.

What's the difference between "green growth" and de-growth?

Again, here's Hickel:

We need some way of distinguishing the degrowth position from…standard 'green growth' … If we accept the empirical evidence that green growth is unlikely to be achieved, then we have to accept that reducing throughput will impact on GDP itself, and we must focus on how to restructure the economy so that this can be managed in a safe and just way. For this, 'degrowth' is a simple, handy term that allows us to clarify what is at stake, and concentrates the mind on what is required.

AN ECONOMY FOR THE COMMON GOOD

An economy centered around the Common Good would prioritize the well-being of all members of society and the natural environment, rather than focusing solely on profits and economic growth.

ECONOMY *for* THE COMMON GOOD

	EXTRACTIVE ECONOMY	REGENERATIVE ECONOMY
PURPOSE	Maximize profits for a few	Maximize well-being for all
PRIORITIES	Profit, growth, competition	Community, cooperation, equality
RESOURCE MANAGEMENT	Exploitation, depletion	Protect, repair, invest, transform
SOCIAL IMPACT	Inequality, poverty, social unrest	Equity, justice, social cohesion
ENVIRONMENTAL IMPACT	Degradation, pollution, climate change	Regeneration
GOVERNANCE	Top-down, concentrated power	Participatory, democratic process
METRICS	GDP, shareholder value	Quality of life, ecological impact, community value

This type of economy would aim to address social and environmental issues while promoting economic sustainability and stability. In this context, the common wealth refers to the shared resources and assets that contribute to the well-being of society as a whole, such as natural resources, infrastructure, education, healthcare, and social services. In summary, an economy centered around the Common Good would prioritize the well-being of society and the environment over profits and growth, promote sustainable resource management, and aim to create a more equitable and just society. For those of you interested in more detail, we prepared this summary of the various models we need to explore:

THE SEARCH *for* A REGENERATIVE ECONOMY

	CAPITALIST ECONOMY	COMMUNIST ECONOMY	SOCIALIST ECONOMY	CIRCULAR ECONOMY	ECOLOGICAL ECONOMICS	REGENERATIVE ECONOMY		
						DEGROWTH	DOUGHNUT ECONOMICS	COMMON GOOD ECONOMICS
ECONOMIC SYSTEM	Free-market capitalism	Centralized economic planning	Government ownership of production	System of closed-loop production and consumption	Steady-state or sustainable economics	System of planned contraction	Regenerative and distributive economics	Community-based regeneration
OWNERSHIP	Privatization of resources and production	State ownership of resources and production	Collective ownership of resources and production	Shared ownership of resources and production	Shared ownership of resources and production	Shared ownership of resources and production	Shared ownership of resources and production	Community and hybrid ownership
DISTRIBUTION	Income inequality	Equal distribution of resources	Equal distribution of resources	Social equity and ecological sustainability	Social equity and ecological sustainability	Social justice and ecological sustainability	Social justice and ecological sustainability	Social justice and ecological sustainability
GROWTH	Emphasis on endless growth	Emphasis on planned growth	Emphasis on planned growth	Emphasis on cyclical and green growth	Emphasis on steady-state	Emphasis on reduction of consumption and production	Emphasis on balance between social and ecological systems	Emphasis on fulfilling social and ecological needs
RESOURCE USE	Unlimited resource use	Planned resource use	Planned resource use	Closed-loop resource use	Sustainable resource use	Reduced resource use	Regenerative resource use	Socially just resource use
ECONOMIC EXTERNALITIES	Negative externalities not fully accounted for	Negative externalities are minimized through regulation	Negative externalities are minimized through regulation	Externalities are minimized through closed-loop systems	Negative externalities are internalized	Externalities are minimized through reduction of consumption and production	Negative externalities are minimized and positive externalities are maximized	Externalities are minimized through socially just economic practices
MARKET REGULATION	Limited government intervention	Government control of all economic activity	Government control of certain economic sectors	Government intervention to promote circular systems	Government intervention to internalize externalities and ensure sustainable resource use	Government intervention to limit consumption and promote social welfare	Government intervention to ensure regenerative and distributive systems	Community-based regulation with Government incentives
SOCIAL JUSTICE	Emphasis on individual freedoms and market efficiency	Emphasis on social equality & elimination of class distinctions	Emphasis on social ownership and democratic control	Emphasis on social justice and ecological sustainability	Emphasis on social equity and ecological sustainability	Emphasis on social justice and ecological sustainability	Emphasis on social equity and ecological sustainability	Emphasis on social justice and ecological sustainability

The solution is a *hybrid economic model* with a clear line between public and private goods.

The government typically provides public goods, which are goods or services that are non-excludable and non-rivalrous, meaning that they cannot be easily excluded from use and the consumption by one individual does not diminish the ability of others to use it as well. Private goods, on the other hand, are goods that are excludable and rivalrous, meaning that access can be restricted to individuals who do not pay for it and that the consumption by one individual reduces the availability of the good for others.

Here is a chart to illustrate the difference between public and private goods:

Public Goods	Private Goods
National Defense	Luxury goods
Public transportation	Automobiles
Healthcare	Cosmetic surgery
Education	Specialty foods
Public parks	Consumer products
Food and Shelter	Cell phones

The government should draw the line between public and private goods based on the extent to which the good or service is necessary for the well-being of the community as a whole. Public goods that promote the general welfare and cannot be provided efficiently by the private sector, such as national defense and infrastructure, should be provided by the government.

Private goods that can be provided efficiently by the private sector, such as food and clothing, should be left to the market. However, there may be cases where government intervention is necessary to ensure access to basic goods and services for all members of society, such as healthcare and education. The decision on where to draw the line between public and private goods should be based on a careful analysis of the social, ecological, and economic benefits and costs of government intervention.

"Profits from suffering" should not be permitted. The term "profit from suffering" refers to situations where individuals or organizations make money by *exploiting* the pain or distress of others. This can take many forms, including charging high prices for essential goods and services during times of crisis or disaster, exploiting vulnerable workers, or promoting harmful products or practices. Here are some examples:

Price gouging during natural disasters: In the aftermath of hurricanes, floods, and other natural disasters, some businesses have been known to hike up the prices of essential goods like water, food, and gasoline. This practice takes advantage of the desperation of people in need and can lead to significant profits for the companies involved.

Sweatshop labor: Many companies outsource their manufacturing to countries with low labor costs, where workers are often paid very low wages and forced to work long hours in unsafe and unhealthy conditions. This practice allows companies to maximize their profits at the expense of workers who are often exploited and mistreated.

Private prisons: Private prison companies make money by incarcerating people and charging the government for their services. Critics argue that this incentivizes mass incarceration and creates an incentive to keep people locked up, rather than rehabilitating them and helping them reintegrate into society.

Pharmaceutical industry: The high cost of prescription drugs has been a major issue in many countries, with some pharmaceutical companies accused of price gouging and prioritizing profits over the health and well-being of patients. This has led to calls for greater regulation and transparency in the industry.

These are just a few examples of how profit can be made from the suffering of others. In general, this practice is considered unethical and harmful to society as a whole, and efforts are needed to address the underlying causes and promote more equitable and sustainable economic systems.

We should grade our politicians on their effectiveness in reducing suffering and promoting the Common Good. There's a powerful argument to be made that *politicians who are against the Common Good are against the future.*

For example, the US Republicans (and the UK Tories it seems) are interested in:

1. cutting taxes for the hyper-rich
2. promoting tax loopholes for corporations and wealthy individuals
3. cutting government investments in education and healthcare
4. cutting investments in protecting Nature and ecological well being
5. cutting education and school funding
6. cutting investments in infrastructure maintenance – clean water, roads and bridges, etc.
7. cutting government institutions which support consumer safety, environmental protection, etc.
8. cutting subsidies to the poor
9. cutting Medicare and Social Security

These are all **actions against the Common Good.** They support the privatization of public services, and increasing austerity programs by cutting government services. The only programs which have virtually unlimited support and funding are military expenditures and bailouts for big business.

This is a recipe for societal collapse.

The Common Good is a National Security issue!

As humanity faces a growing number of existential challenges, we find that governments and institutions are not doing the job – they are failing us precisely at the moment we need them most. This is not an accident. Your elected politician, as we mentioned before, is *not looking out for you,* or our best interests - the Common Good.

TOTAL SYSTEMIC REGENERATION

What is the job to be done *now*?

Total systemic regeneration of our entire economic *and* social world to *stop* the Death of Nature.

Total systemic regeneration refers to a complete overhaul and transformation of various systems that make up our society, including the economy, finance, banking, and governance. This type of regeneration would involve significant changes to the fundamental structures and principles that guide these systems, in order to create more equitable and sustainable outcomes.

In terms of the economy, total systemic regeneration would involve a shift away from traditional models that prioritize endless growth and profit over social and environmental concerns. This might mean transitioning to more circular and regenerative economic models that prioritize sustainable practices and social welfare over profit.

SYSTEMIC REGENERATION

Systemic regeneration means breaking away from the existing mindset of globalization and neoliberalism. It means capitalism must become truly democratic and inclusive. The *special interests of billionaires* must not be allowed to destroy the Common Good.

Regarding finance, a regeneration of the system could mean a move towards more decentralized and democratized financial systems that allow for greater participation and control by individuals and communities. This might involve promoting alternative currencies or blockchain-based financial systems that prioritize transparency, security, and accessibility.

In banking, a regeneration could involve a shift towards more ethical and responsible lending practices, as well as greater accountability and transparency in the banking industry. This might mean regulating the banking sector to prevent excessive risk-taking, as well as promoting lending practices that prioritize social and environmental impact over profit. Public banking is an idea whose time has finally come – especially in the US.

And, in terms of governance, a regenerative model would involve a move towards more participatory and inclusive models of governance that prioritize the interests of all citizens, rather than just those in positions of power. This involves greater transparency and accountability in government, as well as empowering local communities to have a greater say in decision-making processes. *(Please refer back to our checklist for a Regenerative Government at the end of Chapter 4)*

Overall, a total systemic regeneration would involve significant changes to our existing systems in order to create a more equitable, sustainable, and socially just society.

Hopefully we can get over the distracting "woke" labels to actually do something before we face total collapse.

We must.

Stop buying stuff. Eat less meat. Minimize travel.

These are all things we are told to do as individuals, but did you know that *a billionaire emits a million times more greenhouse gases than the average person.*

Even worse are their investments.

The world is dying because of the investments made – the choices made by our billionaires. The investments of just 125 billionaires emit 393 million tons of CO2 each year – the equivalent of France – at an individual annual average that is a million times higher than someone in the bottom 90 percent of humanity.[193]

---

[193] *Carbon Billionaires: The investment emissions of the world's richest people*, November 2022
https://oxfamilibrary.openrepository.com/bitstream/handle/10546/621446/bn-carbon-billlionaires-071122-en.pdf

The world's richest people emit huge and unsustainable amounts of carbon and, unlike ordinary people, 50% to 70% of their emissions result from their investments. New analysis of the investments of 125 of the world's richest billionaires shows that on average they are emitting 3 million tons a year, more than a million times the average for someone in the bottom 90% of humanity.

The study also finds billionaire investments in polluting industries such as fossil fuels and cement are double the average for the Standard & Poor 500 group of companies. Billionaires hold extensive stakes in many of the world's largest and most powerful corporations, which gives them the power to influence the way these companies act. Governments must hold them to account, legislating to compel corporates and investors to reduce carbon emissions, enforcing more stringent reporting requirements and imposing new taxation on wealth and investments in polluting industries.

We are going to have to protest in the streets. It's time to put aside the toys – our ideologies and guns – and look at this time in history as our *final* exam.

This is a test, as **Buckminster Fuller** said, to see if we, the human species, deserve to carry on. COVID has shown us that we cannot find consensus on how to deal with the virus.

It's as if our politicians haven't watched those dystopian movies on Netflix.

Vaccine nationalism and vaccine hesitancy go hand in hand as the crisis of trust builds across the planet. Citizens find it difficult to trust their governments. Governments can't trust each other. And perhaps, worst of all – we can't trust ourselves to know what to do next.

Alarmingly, the world's politicians are deciding that democracy is not as important as holding on to power. Backed by powerful lobbies and special interests, they are working to "cancel" democracy, devising policies to suppress votes, jail protestors, and distract us from the most urgent issues. Sabre-rattling and belligerent posturing are leading to violent conflicts and growing rumors of war.

The petrochemical industry is planning to switch lanes, and double-down on producing more plastic – in 2050, there will be more plastic in the oceans than fish!

And the Earth dies from thousand cuts. No one is coming to save us — not aliens, not the cast of MARVEL's superheroes, not Bill Gates or the World Economic Forum.

There is no *deus ex machina.*

A MOVEMENT OF MOVEMENTS

It's up to us. It's time for a *Movement of Movements.*[194] How do Movements work?

In his book *Social Movements: The Structure of Collective Mobilization,* **Paul Almeida** tells us that an emerging pattern in the new millennium "involves ordinary people mobilizing around increasingly negative conditions. When we observe some of the largest protest campaigns of the past twenty years, they are clearly driven by worsening situations."[195]

But this is not new. We know that throughout history, progressive **movements are a cry for justice**. If we go back in history to Abolitionism, Women's Suffrage, the various Independence movements, the Civil Rights movement, or the

---

[194] "The Movement of Movements: A Last Chance to Save the Planet?" by Christian Sarkar, Karthiga Ratnam, & Philip Kotler https://www.wicked7.org/the-movement-of-movements-a-last-chance-to-save-the-planet/
[195] *Social Movements: The Structure of Collective Mobilization,* Paul Almeida University of California Press; 1st edition (March 5, 2019)

Anti-Apartheid movement, they are all based on a tide of support from ordinary people which kept growing and growing until the impossible happened.

In *Brand Activism: From Purpose to Action*, we explained that building a movement has 5 clear components:

1. Begin by creating a mission that is based on the **Common Good** or **Justice**
2. **Imagine** what the movement must achieve and how
3. How will we **inspire** people to engage and participate?
4. **Mobilize** committed participants
5. **Act** – coordinate joint action to make a difference

And that is precisely where we are for the most part, individual movements led by the individual visions of their leaders, working in silos, with little or no collaboration. If it is so difficult for people who think similarly to collaborate, just imagine how much harder it is when you don't share the same views. *And yet, we must find a way to come together to bridge our differences if the world is to survive.*

The **Movement of Movements** is simply bringing together the existing movements of our time to **take collective action**. Because we need "all hands on deck" it means we must find ways to work together despite our differences.

Who has to come together? Everyone who is moved to do so: NGOs, activists, institutions, schools, governments, and of course the citizens of this planet. Businesses can join movements too. And they can use **cross-brand activism**. The more inclusive we can be, the better we understand what needs to happen. Of course, governments must work together for the common good as well; power and ego are poisons we can't afford now.

Why do we need to come together? As individuals we can choose how we want to make an impact.

But when we choose to have collective impact through informed actions, we can make a real difference. Let us bring our movements together and work together for change – if there's anything COVID taught us is that we are all in this together.

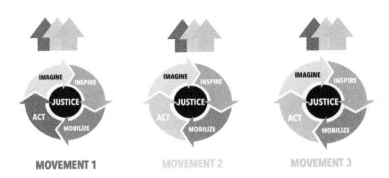

We know that coalitions work, but we still have a long way to go. We must create **cross-movement change agendas**.

The world calls out for action. In the UK, **Extinction Rebellion** and **Just Stop Oil** are two such movements based on *civil disobedience*. Extinction Rebellion has three demands[196]:

1. **Tell the Truth:** Governments must tell the truth by declaring a climate and ecological emergency, working with other institutions to communicate the urgency for change.

2. **Act Now:** Governments must act now to halt biodiversity loss and reduce greenhouse gas emissions to net zero by 2025.

3. **Go Beyond Politics:** Governments must create and be led by the decisions of a *Citizens' Assembly* on climate and ecological justice.

Are these unreasonable requests?

Ask yourself – who makes better decisions: a Citizen's assembly or a lobbyist for Big Oil?

For those of you who aren't sure, a *"Citizens' Assembly brings together everyday people from all walks of life to investigate, discuss, and make recommendations on an issue. Members of the Assembly are selected in a lottery process to ensure they aren't beholden to any political party or special interest, and to ensure they actually reflect the whole country. This means that anyone can look at a Citizens' Assembly and see people who look like them, live like them, and share their concerns. With the aid of skilled facilitators, this representative group of everyday people works through information from a wide range*

---

[196] https://rebellion.global/about-us/

of experts and stakeholders. They talk through different views and opinions and find common ground."[197]

A jury of our peers. The voice of the people. Democracy. A Future for all, not just a few. Is that not worth fighting for?

The mission of Extinction Rebellion (and other, similar movements) cannot be dismissed by the traditional politicians and captains of industry. In fact, governments must act now.

OUR VALUES
Any person or group can organise autonomously and take action in the name and spirit of XR so long as the action fits within XR's principles and values . In this way, power is decentralised, meaning that there is no need to ask for permission from a central group or authority.

1 WE HAVE A SHARED VISION OF CHANGE.
Creating a world that is fit for the next 7 generations to live in.

2 WE SET OUR MISSION ON WHAT IS NECESSARY.
Mobilising 3.5% of the population to achieve system change – such as "momentum-driven organising".

3 WE NEED A REGENERATIVE CULTURE.
Creating a culture which is healthy, resilient and adaptable.

4 WE OPENLY CHALLENGE OURSELVES AND THIS TOXIC SYSTEM.
Leaving our comfort zones to take action for change.

5 WE VALUE REFLECTING AND LEARNING.
Following a cycle of action, reflection, learning, and planning for more action. Learning from other movements and contexts as well as our own experiences.

6 WE WELCOME EVERYONE AND EVERY PART OF EVERYONE.
Working actively to create safer and more accessible spaces.

7 WE ACTIVELY MITIGATE FOR POWER.
Breaking down hierarchies of power for more equitable participation.

8 WE AVOID BLAMING AND SHAMING.
We live in a toxic system, but no one individual is to blame.

9 WE ARE A NONVIOLENT NETWORK.
Using nonviolent strategy and tactics as the most effective way to bring about change.

10 WE ARE BASED ON AUTONOMY AND DECENTRALISATION.
We collectively create the structures we need to challenge power.

---

[197] https://rebellion.global/blog/2021/01/05/citizens-assembly-climate-change/

These words of **George Tsakraklides** come to mind:[198]

"Implementing any of the myriad of already existing solutions for stopping our self-destruction would require us being able to step outside of the context of economic growth and exploitation, which is so paramount to our identity. We simply lack the faculties to do this, and proof of this is that the more solutions to climate change emerge, the more conscious our discussions become on what it is we need to urgently do, the more obstinate our resistance grows towards implementing any of it. Our greedy personal survival instinct is much stronger than any rational or technological solution which benefits the greater society or ecosystem. Are we introspective enough to recognize this, rise above it and begin to cultivate the mental tools we desperately need, despite this pre-disposition? It is a question of nature vs. nurture, and nature is overwhelmingly winning thus far, hands down, for the overwhelming duration of our history. Addressing climate change and the ecological apocalypse is not an issue of yet another technology or increased processing power, these have both run their course. It is an issue of truly, genuinely claiming our own destiny, for the very first time in our 200,000 years of existence as modern humans. The expectation is almost impossible, as much of humanity does not even believe we are responsible for what is happening. Those who accept no responsibility have already given up on their potential to make a difference in the course of events."

The choice is clear: **extinction** *or* **regeneration.**

If we cannot change the path we are on, then **Nature will change the path for us.**

"...because races condemned to one hundred years of solitude did not have a second opportunity on earth."[199]

---

[198] "We Were Never in Control" by George Tsakraklides April 7, 2023
https://tsakraklides.com/2023/04/07/we-were-never-in-control/
[199] From the last line of *One Hundred Years of Solitude* by Gabriel Garcia Marquez (1967; trans. Gregory Rabassa)

7. PALERMO RIGENERATIVA

Our initial project in Palermo was trying to answer three fundamental questions:

(1) How do we bring back tourism?
(2) How do we expand beyond tourism?
(3) What must be done for the future?

We'll tell you about our recommendations at the end of this chapter.

Beyond the recommendations, we also got involved in strategic discussions with various business leaders and organizations.[200] We talked to over 150 members of the community – individually, and in workshops.

The regenerative organizations we write about exist all around us. They are not funded by VCs or rich investors. *Their aim is not growth, but community wealth-building.* We discovered many interesting businesses with business models which were far more regenerative than the traditional models taught in business schools. Every community has these businesses, and their number is growing.

There is much to learn from them. We selected a number of organizations we found in Palermo.

Every community has its share of regenerative organizations, if you look hard enough.

How can we grow that number?

---

[200] For more details on Palermo, visit The Regenerative Marketing Institute www.regenmarketing.org

CASE STUDIES *from* PALERMO

The following organizations are on the regenerative path – that is they are creating both customer *and* community value simultaneously.

They build trust and networks of trust – based on the *ego-free leadership* displayed by their leaders.

- Cooperativa Rigenerazioni Onlus
  (Al Fresco Bistrot and Cotti in Fragranza)

- Molti Volti

- Morettino

- Manima

- Artficial

- Palazzo Butera

- Quattro Punto Zero

- Palermo Mediterrana

CASE STUDY: COOPERATIVA RIGENERAZIONI ONLUS

What happens when businesses refuse to hire at-risk juveniles?

Social worker **Lucia Lauro** was frustrated at the indifference of local businesses in Palermo, Italy – they simply weren't interested in hiring minors from the prison system.

Lucia Lauro

Lauro knew that without an alternative path, first-time offenders would inevitably find their way back to prison. So she did what entrepreneurs do: she decided to fill the "unmet need" by starting a business to do so.

The director of the Penal Institute for Minors of Palermo – **Michelangelo Capitano** – was also thinking along the same lines. He had been designing a program which would create public-private partnerships – and Lauro's potential as an entrepreneur was just what was needed to bring his mission to life. The idea became a reality with the guidance of *institutional* partners – the Penal Institute for Minors of Palermo, Opera Don Calabria, National Association of Magistrates and San Zeno Foundation.

On the business side, Lauro reached out to **Nadia Lodato**, a strategic planning expert, and together, the two women established **Cooperativa Rigenerazioni Onlus** – a social entrepreneurship built on a business model of **regenerative justice**. (rigenerazionionlus.com)

Regenerative justice is about breaking the patterns of escalation which result in criminal behavior and violence. Its goals are to integrate released prisoners back into society as productive, even exemplary, citizens and leaders, and secondly, prevent young people from becoming criminals in the first place.

Regenerative justice builds meaning and belonging. It does so by building relationships of trust based on respect and common values. It looks for intervention opportunities for the child, adolescent and young adult, seeking to reverse destructive behaviors through the design of positive alternatives.

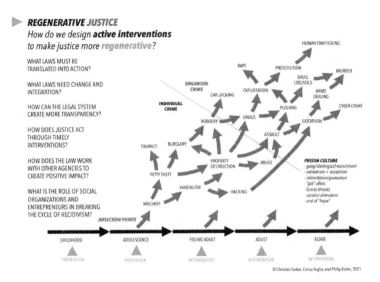

▶ **REGENERATIVE JUSTICE**
*How do we design **active interventions** to make justice more regenerative?*

WHAT LAWS MUST BE TRANSLATED INTO ACTION?

WHAT LAWS NEED CHANGE AND INTEGRATION?

HOW CAN THE LEGAL SYSTEM CREATE MORE TRANSPARENCY?

HOW DOES JUSTICE ACT THROUGH TIMELY INTERVENTIONS?

HOW DOES THE LAW WORK WITH OTHER AGENCIES TO CREATE POSITIVE IMPACT?

WHAT IS THE ROLE OF SOCIAL ORGANIZATIONS AND ENTREPRENEURS IN BREAKING THE CYCLE OF RECIDIVISM?

© Christian Sarkar, Enrico Foglia, and Philip Kotler, 2021

The design of regenerative alternatives begins with mindsets: *how do you teach the young how to avoid and overcome conflict?* What support mechanisms must be built into the legal and social infrastructure? How do social workers help parents, teachers, and civil authorities create a positive path for breaking patterns of escalation? How do institutions break the patterns of prison acculturation?

These were the first questions Lauro and Lodato asked themselves as they set about building a remarkable organization which was recently recognized[201] by **Sergio Mattarella**, the President of Italy.

---

[201] https://www.lasicilia.it/societa/news/mattarella-premia-30-alfieri-della-repubblica-un-attestato-d-onore-e-una-targa-in-sicilia-1405108/

The Prison Brand

A **prison brand** can be defined as an offering (product/service) developed to employ prisoners and prepare them for their release and successful reintegration into society.

According to the **United Nations Office on Drugs and Crime**, work programs in prison are one of the most effective ways to support prisoners' successful reintegration into society, providing them with income and with relevant skills to find employment and reduce recidivism.[202]

In 2020, the UNODC issued a guide to *Creating a Brand of Prison Products*[203] which outlines the philosophy behind prison brands:

*The creation of **prison brands** has been found useful in reducing the social stigma associated to imprisonment and in enhancing prisoners' self-esteem, while meeting consumers' demand for products that contribute to positive social goals. The negative perception of prisons and prisoners can be an obstacle to prison products being considered reliable and attractive. Prison products are often perceived as second-rate products not trusted to meet required quality standards. There may also be additional concerns, such as the notion that supporting prison work creates an undue privilege for prisoners in a general context of economic difficulties and prevalent unemployment. Conversely, there may be concerns that prison products result from exploitative working conditions in prisons and, as such, should not be supported. Creating a prison brand requires identifying and challenging such negative perceptions. In fact, creating a prison brand and developing an appropriate communication strategy around it offers an opportunity to overcome the negative perception and stigmatization of prisoners.*

---

[202] https://www.unodc.org/dohadeclaration/index.html

[203] https://www.unodc.org/documents/dohadeclaration/Prisons/NationalBrand/BrandingPrisonProducts_EN.pdf

PRISON BRANDS
CASE STUDY: **Cooperativa Rigenerazioni Onlus**

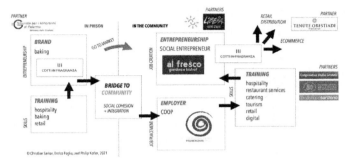

© Christian Sarkar, Enrico Foglia, and Philip Kotler, 2021

Prison brands – properly developed and nurtured – can create a pathway to **community regeneration**.

- Is a brand of prison products or services needed?
- Is there sufficient capacity to create and own the brand of prison products or services?
- Do work programs for prisoners comply with international standards?
- What role can be played by external companies in developing and "going to market" with prison brands?
- What must be done to maximize transparency and prevent exploitation?

Crafting a Regenerative Strategy

Lauro and Lodato's regenerative strategy – developed and implemented in **2016** – goes well beyond the UNODC vision and creates pathways to employment beyond prison.

The cooperative built a house of interrelated brands, both products and services, which extends outside the prison, into the community:

- **Cotti in Fragranza**: a brand of baked products (the name translates as "Caught in the Act") which is produced in prison and sold across 100 locations in Italy and parts of the EU. The brand was born in 2016 inside the Malaspina juvenile prison in Palermo, Sicily. **Tenute Orestiadi**, one of the biggest wine cooperatives in Sicily, helps distribute **Cotti in Fragranza** products using their distribution network. The catalog of products is expanding, with online sales opening more avenues for growth. *Visit: www.cottiinfragranza.com*

IL PROGETTO   SHOP   **|||**   NEWS   CONTATTI   RIVENDITI
                        COTTI IN FRAGRANZA

panettone glassato al pistacchio	panettone glassato al cioccolato	panettone al mandarino
€28.00	★★★★☆	★★★★★
	€26.00	€21.00

- **Casa San Francesco**: a 17th-century Franciscan convent, where Cotti in Fragranza operates in the community – with activities like packaging, catering, fresh food, and take-away food. Fittingly, the convent was an infirmary, and now has been repurposed as a regenerative force in the neighborhood.

- **Al Fresco Giardino e Bistrot**: a restaurant which serves tourists with a "slow-food" menu created by Chef Francesco Gambino and the juvenile workers who are learning to build productive lives outside prison and in the community. The quality of the food and the unique menu choices have created an experience matched by the ambiance of the garden setting. *Visit: alfrescopalermo.it*

Al Fresco Giardino e Bistrot

Future Plans: Extending the Ecosystem

The business vision of Lauro and Lodato extends the hospitality of the restaurant to room and board. The plan is to renovate the convent to create B&B accommodations for the growing tourist traffic in Palermo. Despite the challenges of COVID, the enthusiasm for the expansion is palpable. The idea of creating an *ecosystem* of products and services, extending from prison to the community, to the tourist visitors is not limited to the boundaries of the organization. Collaborative business initiatives are being discussed with other entrepreneurs and owners in the Ballaro community.

Measuring Impact

The outcomes of this social enterprise can be measured not just in profits but in community value-creation. As we noted earlier, community regeneration is about **community value creation** as well as **business value creation**.

REGENERATIVE BUSINESS MODEL

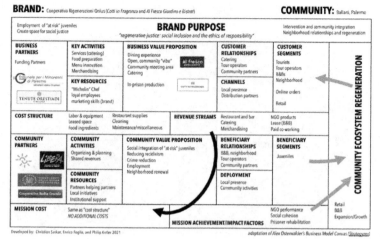

BRAND: Cooperativa Rigenerazioni Onlus (Cotti in Fragranza and Al Fresco Giardino e Bistrot) **COMMUNITY:** Ballarò, Palermo

For a prison brand, community value extends into the future. What is the ROI (return on investment) for such programs? The impact must be measured in terms of *lives changed*, and *future crime prevented*.

Lauro measures her progress in terms of **happiness**. Her recipe is simple: "if our employees aren't happy, then we're not succeeding," she explains. *"The chef must be happy, the employees must be happy, and our customers must be happy – in that order."*

CASE STUDY: MOLTI VOLTI

At about 2 a.m., a few days before the end of COVID *annus horibilis* 2021, an electrical fire broke out at **Moltivolti**[204] – an eclectic restaurant in Palermo's Ballaró neighborhood. The restaurant was closed at the time of the fire, and fortunately no one was injured. The damage was restricted to the central part of the establishment, leaving the kitchen, the bar, and the office areas safe – but everything covered with a thick coat of black soot.

The eating area in the middle of the establishment was badly charred – melted chairs and burnt tabletops giving the establishment the look of a **war zone**. Some of the wall-portraits, hand-painted by **Igor Scalisi Palmintieri**, were now almost unrecognizable.

By 7 a.m. a crowd begins to gather outside to offer help and moral support. *Is everyone ok? Was the fire accidental? How will the restaurant go on?* These and other similar questions bombard **Claudio Arestivo**, one of the restaurant's founders, who's talking to the fast-growing throng of community well-wishers.

Had someone done this intentionally? Why? Because Moltivolti, as we will see, is a very different sort of business. It works with migrants and disadvantaged youth, offering them a path to social integration while providing them skills and a livelihood.

Moltivolti is a regenerative business – that is to say it creates *both* business value and community value simultaneously. Is someone trying to send them a message? This is the question on everyone's mind.

---

[204] Moltivolti means "many faces" in Italian.

Out in the street, **Libera**'s **Carmelo Pollichino**[205] is talking animatedly to the aspiring mayoral candidate from ZEN[206] – Mariangela di Gangi. What can be done to bring the restaurant back to life as quickly as possible? **Memory Mutanuka**, a student from Zambia and a Moltivolti employee, is discussing the same thing with a circle of young students – their faces are still in shock.

What will happen next?

That evening, Libera Palermo kicked off a campaign on Facebook, asking their friends to support the resurrection of Moltivolti through the generosity of their online donations.

Three days later, the campaign had raised over one-hundred thousand euros. Somehow, the **community** miraculously raised the funds to put Moltivolti back on track.

Moltivolti's rise from the ashes is a testament to the deep connection, trust, and **affection** it has built in the community.

Now let's return to the case study.

In the neighborhood of Ballaró, in what used to be a rundown part of Palermo, just a street over from the *Palazzo Pretorio*, is a small restaurant which demonstrates daily what a **regenerative business model** looks like in action.

The restaurant is called **Moltivolti** – "many faces" in Italian. Founded in 2014, by a group of young neighborhood friends with different cultural backgrounds — coming from **eight countries**: Senegal, Zambia, Afghanistan,

---

[205] Libera is the leading Italian anti-mafia non-profit founded in 1995 by Don Luigi Ciotti (www.libera.it)
[206] Zen is Zona Espansione Nord, an economically deprived neighborhood on the northern outskirts of Palermo. Mariangela di Gangi was the director of ZEN's community center for ten years.

248

Bangladesh, France, Spain, Gambia and Italy — Moltivolti is the epitome of how work can be designed to offer dignity, citizenship, *and* create **business *and* community value.**

The **purpose** of Moltivolti is two-fold, explains **Claudio Arestivo**, one of the co-founders. He proposes a circular economic system where profit and non-profit support each other. That's right, Moltivolti is both a **for-profit** and a **non-profit** organization, a **hybrid business model** we can categorize as a **regenerative business**.

Claudio Arestivo, a co-founder of Moltivolti

What it does

Moltivolti is both a restaurant, and a co-working and meeting space.

The restaurant employs immigrants (one of the chefs was an ex-Afghan general) and delivers an eclectic mix of Sicilian and world cuisine to the visitors who frequent the premises.

The **customers** of the restaurant are people from the neighborhood, tour operators and tourists, school children, and immigrants who are making their way in a new world.

The design of the space creates a multicultural dimensionality – from the menu, to the people, to the unique art by **Igor Scalisi Palmintieri**[207] – the faces of people from the neighborhood (some of whom are instantly recognizable!)

Moltivolti (Many faces): the art of Igor Scalisi Palminteri

Moltivolti is also a co-working and meeting space for its **community partners** – a range of non-profit organizations which are part of the neighborhood and create value for community residents. The beneficiaries are the organizations and the people they serve, many from the community of Ballaró.

---

[207] See: https://www.instagram.com/igor_palminteri/

COMMUNITY PARTNERS

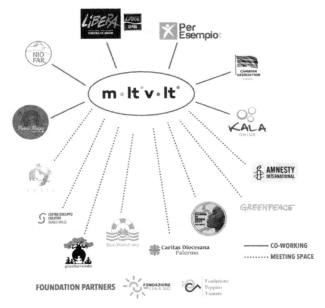

Moltivolti Partners

Moltivolti is a hybrid business model: it functions as a for-profit and a non-profit at the same time. Its purpose is to create a community-based dining experience, a hub for social integration and employment which serves the needs of the community beyond food and nourishment. It does this through its community partners – who are an integral part of the "space" Moltivolti has created; a "space" for the many voices and lives it touches daily.

Impact beyond the kitchen

Moltivolti is an integral part of the Ballaró community. Along with its partners, it is building the future by heeding the voices of the neighborhood, and engaging in a continuous dialogue. Every month it adds something to the menu of the community – an event, actions, and even launching new organizations. Moltivolti has expanded its operations by launching a B&B enterprise above the restaurant. It also helps incubate new businesses and organizations by providing advice and support. It also sells products from partners like Libera – a national organization that manages businesses confiscated from the Mafia.

During the COVID downturn, Moltivolti expanded its footprint by adding a second location in order to keep its employees. It also distributed meals across Ballaró during the lockdown.

Moltivolti is also a member of **Addiopizzo**, an anti-Mafia movement of local businesses.[208]   Addiopizzo is a grass-roots movement which refuses to pay extortion money to the Mafia. It promotes a 'cultural revolution' against the Mafia and supports social justice, and is made up of the women and men, boys and girls, entrepreneurs and consumers, who identify themselves in the phrase "A whole people who pays protection money is a people without dignity."

---

[208] https://addiopizzo.org/en/

CASE STUDY: MORETTINO COFFEE

The Morettino family's passion for coffee began in 1920 in their family spice shop located in the historic district San Lorenzo ai Colli in Palermo. Over the years, the artisanal production process, the fine art of blending select coffee beans, became a signature brand for Palermo's middle class and the city's historic cafés.

The story of Morettino coffee is synonymous with quality, culture, and tradition. The company has remained in the neighborhood it was born in, and its leadership still live on the company premises. This closeness to the community is not an accident, It is part of the strategy devised by the founder, when he would spend mornings cycling around the neighborhood, listening to Palermitans and their daily concerns.

The **Morettino vision** is to create and sustain community **conversations** – bringing neighborhoods together –

creating genuine community cohesion. This is one reason for its "slow growth" strategy and its commitment to neighborhood cafes and employment for its citizens. From Zen – a rougher Palermitan neighborhood – to the stately Palazzos of Palermo, the people drink Morettino's historic coffee. It is in some ways a cultural narrative which goes back to the roots of coffee culture – the African and Arabic roots of coffee culture – born in Ethiopia, and spread over the world. In Islamic cultures, where alcohol is forbidden, coffee is " the wine of Allah" – a gift to mankind.

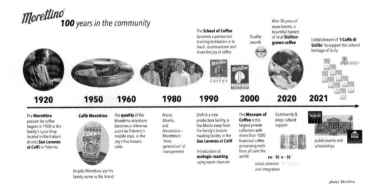

Morettino **100** *years in the community*

Morettino's 100 year-strong regenerative strategy has been to empower **local** owners – the cafes, bars, and restaurants – to build spaces and create value for these small businesses. Today there are around 500 such small neighborhood enterprises, each with their own unique history – united by the Morettino coffee experience.

Morettino also supports innovative social startups like **Moltivolti** and **Al Fresco Bistrot**, by providing them with the equipment needed to provide quality coffee to their customers.

Coffee Supports Culture

In Palermo, at the crossroads of the cultures of the Mediterranean, the Morettino family continues to make good on the promise of community. "**I Caffè di Sicilia**" is an experimental project focusing on the cultural landmarks of Palermo and Sicily, a project developed though collaboration and constant dialogue with other community institutions, such as the **Federico II Foundation, the Teatro Massimo Foundation,** and **Coop Culture**, the largest cooperative operating in the culture sector in Italy.

Each blend preserves the aromas and flavors of the region to which they are dedicated: the blend dedicated to the Royal Palace, for example, expresses notes of orange blossom and bitter orange marmalade, the one inspired by the Cathedral accents of jasmine and prickly pears, and the blend created to represent the the Duomo of Monreale expresses the mandarins from the Conca d'Oro. Most importantly, in terms of regeneration, a portion of the profits of each sale go towards supporting the cultural landmarks.

The project has wider-ranging plans, which in the future will involve the Morettino Coffee Museum and Coffee School through educational initiatives, which will include collaborative projects with the Municipality of Palermo.

Another regenerative initiative embraced by the Morettinos is their **School of Coffee** which organizes coffee lessons dedicated to *coffee lovers* (not just coffee makers), with the goal of spreading authentic coffee culture. The goal of "Bartender Jobs" is to give **new job prospects to the best bartenders** in Sicily and the rest of Italy. A way of giving hope to the youth and others looking for work, the initiative is also an opportunity for bar, cafes and clubs owners to *select* passionate and competent staff. Morettino organizes coffee lessons dedicated to *coffee lovers* (not just coffee makers), with the goal of spreading authentic coffee culture.

Andrea (left) and Arturo (right) Morettino

Morettino also collaborates with **Università di Palermo** and **Orto Botanico** on their Coffee plantation project, Museo internazionale delle marionette for the campaign *"Morettino per i Pupi siciliani"* (we financed the restoration of ancient Sicilian puppets and the "Pupari" during the lockdown in 2020). Morettino also collaborates with Fondazione Merz to reopen the Zac contemporary art pavilion in Cantieri culturali della Zisa in Palermo.

Cultivating Sicilian Coffee

Another expression of local regeneration is the Morettino vision to grow coffee on the island of Sicily. For just over 30 years, the Morettinos tried cultivating coffee plants in their own neighborhood – 350 meters above sea level – in the small village of San Lorenzo ai colli, in Palermo. The 60 Arabica Coffee plants came from seeds donated in the 90s from the Botanical Gardens in Palermo.

As the company reached its centennial, something surprising happened. The Morettino coffee plantation produced 30 kg (about 60 lbs) of coffee – "Made in Italy." The remarkable thing is that the plants grew in the open air, without using pesticides or green houses: a *native* Sicilian coffee.

Balancing Business and Community Value

The Morettino commitment to slow coffee and to the conversations engendered by coffee is reflected in its regenerative business model. Business value creation is coupled to nurturing community value:

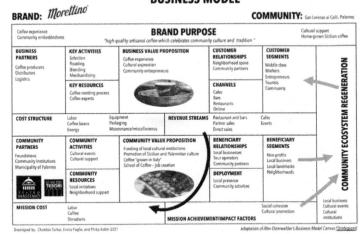

Developed by: Christian Sarkar, Enrico Foglia, and Philip Kotler 2021 — adaptation of Alex Osterwalder's Business Model Canvas (Strategyzer)

Perhaps the most remarkable thing after 100 years of success, is the enthusiasm for the future.

The Morettino story is still just beginning.

CASE STUDY: MANIMA

"For decades, the pressing key challenges of our time – climate change and social inequality – have been ignored by the major luxury players, says **Carolina Guthmann**, the co-founder of MANIMA, a brand with a mission of regeneration.[209] MANIMA is a brand born from the desire to merge *ethics and aesthetics* in a unique artisanal brand.

Carolina Guthmann and Piero Di Pasquale

---

[209] www.manimaworld.com

The founders, **Carolina Guthmann** and **Piero Di Pasquale**, left their careers as an executive at Merck and as a journalist for the Italian TV broadcaster RAI, to pursue a new life path. Their desire was to create an authentic and regenerative brand, enabling discerning affluent clients to harmonize their desire for exclusivity and uniqueness with the need to generate a positive impact for people and the environment.

"The insatiable desire for growth had led to the mass-commodification of luxury with an entire industry value-chain based on exploitative overproduction, creating irreversible and severe harm for people and the environment, especially in developing and emerging countries. Our company puts an end to this mindset," explains Guthmann.

"We wanted to show that the luxury and social impact can work together," adds co-founder (and husband) **Piero di Pasquale**. "Why? Because our guiding principle is the ancient Greek expression: *Kalòs kai Agathòs*, **only what is good can be truly beautiful**."

Rooted in the millennia-long Sicilian tradition of hand embroidery, MANIMA embodies the soul of regenerative luxury and produces timeless collectibles made to last. Finely hand embroidered home-linens and customizable ready-to-wear collections are produced by hand across the island, built on traditional techniques handed down through generations.

MANIMA's modus operandi is built on three pillars: female artisanship, technology, and social impact.

Bringing it all together is Manima's platform dubbed *Digital Atelier* - an innovative model of widespread manufacturing, based on an enabling tech eco-system of integrated software applications to manage all processes end-to-end.

This allows artisans to work remotely from their homes or workshops in a self-managed manner, while remaining part of a supportive community.

Environmental protection and social impact are at the forefront of MANIMA and are measured and documented. Each product uses carefully sourced materials that respect the environment and the company is working to become a B-Corp. Serving private clients, boutiques, and hotels, MANIMA'S atelier and showroom is under construction in Palermo.

Cultural Regeneration

Interestingly, Manima is collaborating with the artist **Kazumi Yoshida**, merging his eclectic art with the tradition of Sicilian hand embroidery to create a limited edition of interior design pieces – a fusion of art, fashion and home decor. This is a form of cultural reinvention *and* regeneration – which benefits both artist and artisan. The first pieces from this collaboration will be presented during Milan Design Week 2023.

And did we mention that Manima's showroom is in Palermo?

CASE STUDY: ARTFICIAL

Tucked away in a Palazzo in the heart of Palermo, a revolution is taking place at the intersection of art, history, and technology. Artficial, a "zebra" start-up is making waves by becoming the world-leader in the production and distribution of artclones.

Its patented digital platform has been described as *"the Spotify of 3D printing."*[210]

But what is an artclone?[211]

artclone: *noun.[licensed clone of original masterpiece]*
an **officially-licensed** replica which preserves the form, integrity, and **cultural value** of an original **sculptural masterpiece.**

Artcloning is suitable for statues or busts, and other physical objects. The artcloning process involves:

1. high-end scanning of the original masterpiece
2. archival of the digitalclone in a secure ARTvault
3. museum edition artclone printing using colored plant-based material
4. museum revenue licensing for each artclone
5. digital rights management for the institutions or owners

Artcloning lies at the **intersection of history, art, culture, and technology** as it combines historical art forms with modern technology.

History: the historical significance of an object – it's meaning and place in the timeline of human creativity

---

210 See artficial.com
211 To learn more about artclones, visit *The Artclone Review*
www.artclonereview.com

263

Art: the aesthetic impact of the original work is extended to new audiences

Culture: the cultural value of the work is democratized – allowing for the creation of authentic, affordable, artclones of famous works which can be shared, viewed – and even owned, by a wider audience

Technology: the preservation of the "digitalDNA" of the original work, stored in a secure ARTvault, accessible through the artficial digital platform with an appropriate rights management regime.

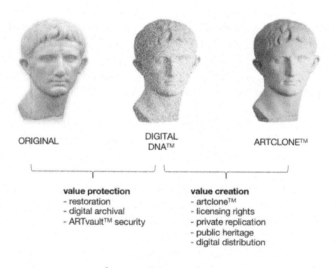

ORIGINAL   DIGITAL DNA™   ARTCLONE™

value protection
- restoration
- digital archival
- ARTvault™ security

value creation
- artclone™
- licensing rights
- private replication
- public heritage
- digital distribution

from original masterpiece to artclone

This **democratization of cultural legacy** was not possible in previous generations. **Artficial** is the world's first rights-based technological platform for the digitization, distribution, and archival of the cultural heritage of humanity – specifically sculptural works of art – and their production in artclones with high-quality 3D printing technologies.

Giorgio Gori and Barbara Dal Corso (photo by Maria Lannino)

Founded by **Barbara Dal Corso** and **Giorgio Gori**, Artficial works with many of the leading museums and private collections in Italy to scan their sculptural masterpieces for eternity. Artficial faithfully preserves cultural artifacts as eternal digitalclones; over two thousand digitized art masterpieces are securely stored in Artficial's ARTvault.

Sculptures which are scanned are stored as *digital* clones – the accurate representation of the object's cultural value – preserving the digitalDNA. These files are the *heritage of mankind.*

The **artclone** creates new possibilities for local and national cultural expression. Artficial views their primary purpose as **cultural regeneration** – to protect, preserve, promote, and revitalize the sculptural legacy of humankind.

This includes:

- **Digital preservation** of historical art objects via scanning to capture the **digitalDNA** of the historic work and store it in a secure **ARTvault**

- Printing the officially licensed **artclone** of the object in 3D, which enables the public and institutions to purchase the artclone for installation in their private residences or elsewhere

- Creating a **new revenue stream** for the owner of the object – either a museum or a private collector

- Designing **museum experiences** which democratize and **promote cultural heritage** – both art and history – in the local community

- Expanding **cultural education and tourism**, which can provide economic benefits for local communities

Artficial also insists that **cultural regeneration must be sustainable.** This is the design principle behind the production and logistical processes the company developed – all artclones are made to order using weatherproof, **plant-based, fiber material made from organic renewables**, with a *carbon footprint which is 75 percent lower* than traditional plastic.

CASE STUDY: PALAZZO BUTERA

In 2020, Palazzo Butera welcomed the Francesca & Massimo Valsecchi art collection, previously on long-term loan to the Fitzwilliam Museum in Cambridge and the Ashmolean Museum in Oxford (UK).

A labor of love for the Valsecchis, the Palazzo was first purchased in 2016 and then restored – a massive undertaking - before housing a collection of art which has been described as "the best kept secret museum in the world" by the director of the Louvre.

The palace itself has been described as an open laboratory, drawing together history, arts and culture in an interdisciplinary exercise aimed at finding solutions for social development.

Massimo Valsecchi

Open to the city of Palermo and the world beyond, the ground floor offers a reference library and many galleries for temporary exhibitions from both home and abroad. The first floor contains conference and events rooms. This area houses the Palace's 18th century library. The second floor accommodates the museum, displaying the Francesca & Massimo Valsecchi art collection.

Other international museums will also be invited to display their collections in the palace. Finally, artists, curators and other cultural stakeholders, will find comfortable and contemporary accommodation available in the guesthouse, allowing them access both to events at Palazzo Butera, and to connect with other cultural and academic institutions in the City of Palermo.

Francesca Valsecchi

The Valsecchis moved their art collection, started in London in the 1960s, to Palazzo Butera, and transformed the Palazzo's Baroque and Rococo décor into a new artspace in its own right.[212] **Gioacchino Martorana** and **Gaspare Fumagalli**'s frescoes, paintings of the fiefs of the Princes of Butera, the ballroom's wax and stucco ornamentation and furniture by Sicilian master craftsmen are now displayed alongside tables by **Pugin** and **Godwin**, paintings by **Annibale Carracci** (1560-1609) alongside works that **Anne** and **Patrick Poirier** and **David**

---

[212] "The Palazzo Butera: A Place of Exchange" by Claudio Gulli, *La Gazette Drouot* 15 January 2021
https://www.gazette-drouot.com/en/article/the-palazzo-butera-3A-a-place-of-exchange/20351

Tremlett were commissioned to create for the palace. The collection also boasts numerous works by **Tom Phillips** (1937 - 2022) the British visual artist, a favorite of the Valsecchis.

The regenerative spirit of Palazzo Butera's restoration continues in the development of a skilled-crafts school that will serve the community in the years to come – *Quatro Punto Zero*.

CASE STUDY: PMG & QUATTROPUNTOZERO

In the past, the historical center of Palermo was an arts and crafts district. The total renovation of Palazzo Butera created a micro-ecosystem of skills and artistic and traditional crafts and inspired the formation of a group - **Palermo Mediterranean Gateway** (PMG) – which was founded in February, 2018 with the aim of regenerating the historical center of Palermo, starting from the district of La Kalsa and creating a scalable model for continual regeneration. PMG's objectives are:

- **Regeneration:** encouraging projects through the use of art and culture, creating common benefits for both the district and the community
- **Inclusion:** supporting Palermo as a center of great cultural value, towards the development of professional skills and sense of belonging/citizenship
- **Social Innovation:** working closely with international research centers, foundations, museums, universities and economic and financial stakeholders

QuattroPuntoZero is a project which calls for the development of a skilled-worker ecosystem comprising of a School Network and workshops, encouraging the birth of a new hybrid economy to nurture a cultural, artistic learning, and manufacturing ecosystem to produce a scalable, urban regeneration model with a strong social impact.

Aloisa Moncada, the strategic director of QuattroPuntoZero, is a strong proponent of community collaboration and is focused on bringing together the donor community and the various community-based partners to build an ecosystem for the future regeneration of the neighborhood and beyond.

Aloisa Moncada

"Our goal is to have a direct positive impact on the beneficiaries - three hundred young people and adults in a state of social fragility who are unable to pursue their artisanal vocations, and about fifty masters of art and local artisans of practices which are at high risk of disappearance. We want to create not just the skills and competencies of high-end artisanal craftsmanship, but open the gate to the rest of Italy and the world."

Here's a summary of the QuatroPuntoZero project:

purposes ->	aims ->	actions ->	output ->	impact
Strengthen the process of cultural requalification and revitalization of the Palermo's historical centre	Safeguarding crafts and workshopswhich are at risk of disappearing	Research action: selection of the sectors, vocations, workshops and crafts teachers	Database map; catalogues, articles, photography-video	+ territorial connections + widespread knowledge
Recuperate the neighborhood's productive vocation in an innovative key	Enhance and reproduce artistic skills and traditional crafts	transfer and implementation of skills, including digital innovation	programmes, courses, training cycles, workshops, residencies, digital production classes, field visits, grants and scholarships	+ digital skills + trained craftman + local-global connections + cultural innovation
Create job opportunities in the artistic craft sectors	Rebuilding supply chains and related industries linked to the flowering of artisanal products	Support to micro-enterprises; marketing redevelopment of existing laboratories, also with 4.0 craftsmanship equipment	business plan organizational consultancy, supply chain agreements, specifications, contracts, adjustments, digitalization support	+ employed + sector companies + emergence from the informal + orders
Educating to beauty, promoting a regenerative social texture and intergenerational dialogue	Create opportunities for cultural growth, stimulate innovation and creativity of minors and families	educational workshops interventions in public spaces, collaborations with schools and the third sector	Format of cultural educational experiences; creative workshops, guided tours	+ contrasting educational poverty

CASE STUDY: CAPPADONIA GELATI

"Don't leave Sicily without trying Cappadonia" says the sign, and the line of tourists who enter the doorway of this gelateria can be excused for following the sign's wisdom, simply because of the taste of the *Mandarino*.

Antonio Cappadonia and Donato Didonna

Named after **Antonio Cappadonia**, the gelateria is unique because it is artisanal in the true sense of the word. It is also regenerative.

Cappadonia pays attention to the natural cycles of the earth and the care of each individual tree or plant. "I choose – one by one – the fruits and products to be transformed into ice cream," says the famous maestro. You have to believe him. Each season, Antonio makes a trek to the side of Monte Sicani –to collect a harvest of pears, strawberries, and peaches – all from small, local farmers.

What's regenerative about Cappadonia?

Two principles: the "short chain" and "fruits of the territory."

Antonio Cappadonia says: *Cappadonia is an act of love for the products of the earth. Only a seasonal fruit can become a Cappadonia gelato.*

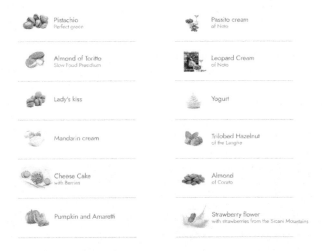

Pistachio Perfect green		Passito cream of Noto	
Almond of Toritto Slow Food Presidium		Leopard Cream of Noto	
Lady's kiss		Yogurt	
Mandarin cream		Trilobed Hazelnut of the Langhe	
Cheese Cake with Berries		Almond of Corato	
Pumpkin and Amaretti		Strawberry flower with strawberries from the Sicani Mountains	

He's not kidding.

Cappadonia's focus on high quality is matched only by the commitment to **local produce**. Its fruits are hand-picked during season – with great care going into the selection of the best of local fruit trees. Luckily, Sicily is renowned for its world-class fruits and this shows up as a business advantage.

Learn more about local regeneration: www.cappadonia.it

CASE STUDY: PALERMO MEDITERRANEA

Palermo Mediterranea (PaMed) is a *business community ecosystem* which unites over fifty entrepreneurs, startups and professionals. As an apolitical Business Community that position itself as a constant and regenerative force in the future of the city. PaMed believes the challenges of the present can only be faced by building an alliance between the public and private sectors to guide choices and redefine the concept of the Mediterranean city. *See: www.palermomediterranea.it*

On a personal note, our regenerative project in Palermo was helped by PaMed's tireless Director, **Dario Nepoti**, who connected us not only to the individual businesses which are part of PaMed, but also to the numerous artists and creatives that make Palermo what it is – a vibrant and dynamic cultural crossroads.

L-R Dario Nepoti (Director), Stefano Tortorici , Giuseppe Tasca,
Marco Francese and Marco Giammona (President)
PHOTO: Francesco Bellina

Palermo Mediterranea's agenda focuses on three key areas:

Entrepreneurial: Palermo should invest in skills, training, and new managerial methodologies to become an entrepreneurial city. By redefining strategies and creating governance around social, economic, and cultural development, Palermo can act and react to crises and raise the quality of life for its citizens. Hindrances like hyper-bureaucratization, lack of coordination, lack of skills, and high structural debt need to be addressed to facilitate healthy start-up and business development and internationalization.

Ecological: Palermo needs to take significant measures to slow down global warming and become an ecological city. This requires integrated strategic plans for mobility, energy, waste disposal, and water use. Palermo should equip itself with multiutilities capable of managing essential services and investing in modern, efficient, and sustainable infrastructures. Additionally, Palermo needs an Ecological Transition Department to operate on bureaucratic constraints that prevent and slow down integrated actions and strategies.

Social: Palermo's suburbs present a complex challenge in terms of redesigning and countering inequalities and discriminations exacerbated by financial, pandemic, and political crises. Palermo needs a plan to preserve the weak and provide equal opportunities for everyone. Corporate responsibility is also essential, and entrepreneurs should be ready to assume an important role if called to do so.

This vision is carried forward through three tangible objectives that Palermo Mediterranea has identified in the first two years of work:

Attract and retain investments and resources to make Palermo an international city that is home to companies and start-ups. The focus is on developing the sea as an asset for work, industry, innovation, digitalization, energy, ecology, sport, and hospitality. To achieve this, Palermo needs a local communication agency to promote the city and its assets.

Accelerate the creation of an ecosystem for economic development by creating a system that converges around a vision and shares ideas and skills. Palermo needs a dedicated agency like "Barcelona Activa" to increase its entrepreneurial capacity.

Contribute to the identification of strategic solutions to improve city governance by carrying out research with teachers to identify strengths, weaknesses, and areas that need improvement. The lack of key institutions such as Multiutilities, a local communication agency, or an Ecological Transition Department were identified as deficiencies that need addressing to activate the city and build solid governance for the future.

PaMed has held conferences on various topics like "making the sea accessible" to "digital innovation" in order to define an agenda for the city. It has held several meetings with exponents of the world of finance and national ecology with the aim of inspiring and creating awareness of the challenges facing the community. It organized an important fundraiser during the Covid-19 emergency and developed a website dedicated to the narrative of the city through data.

Every two months PaMed organizes the "Club Enterprise" for members, an appointment to socialize new economic initiatives and carry forward an idea of participatory finance. Among the most important projects is the rebranding of a public institution, Sispi; an operation that is in line with the city's internationalization objectives and a site dedicated to the data narrative of the city of Palermo.

OUR RECOMMENDATIONS *for* PALERMO

What could Palermo do to become more regenerative?

This is an open question for all the cities in the Mediterranean. We came to Palermo to try to understand the situation and to develop some pathways towards regeneration. This very book is one of the results of our work.

Il Trionfo della Morte (The Triumph of Death) c. 1445
Palazzo Abatellis, Palermo, Sicilia

But let's get back to the three questions for Palermo:

(1) How do we bring back tourism?
(2) How do we expand beyond tourism?
(3) What must be done for the future?

MAKING TOURISM REGENERATIVE

The first challenge for economies which depend on tourism is of course the tourist. What value and values does the tourist bring to the city?

We have to ask: *How harmful is tourism for the environment?*

In the course of the past two decades, 100 trillion tons of CO_2 alone have been emitted by air traffic on the island of Mallorca alone.[213]

We know that globally, tourism is responsible for about 8% of global greenhouse gas emissions. What about Sicily?

Cruise ships are notorious for their degenerative impact. So what is to be done? Venice and Tahiti (French Polynesia) are banning the mega cruise liners.

Can tourism become more regenerative? Yes, but we may not like the solutions that are staring us in the face. Short-hop tourism is not the answer. The days of "carefree travel" are almost over.

So, what does **regenerative tourism** look like?

It means *fewer tourists*, who add more value to the community.

The regenerative tourist spends *more* **money** in the local economy, and spends *more* **time** in a place. Their carbon footprint is minimized by the *conscious consumption of less*.

---

[213] "How harmful is tourism for the environment?" by Jonas Martiny, *DW*, July 29, 2022
https://www.dw.com/en/climate-change-how-harmful-is-tourism-for-the-environment/a-62597871

These are not your "smash and grab" party tourists, but instead are **cultural tourists** – interested in the local history, art, and cultural aspects of a place. They are "slow tourists."

Cities will have to transition from "mass tourism" to regenerative tourism – bring fewer tourists to your city, but allowing them to spend more on local businesses and experiences. The "McDonaldization of tourism" will come to an end – probably in a very drastic way (not unlike the COVID lockdown)

How do we decouple tourism from carbon? Not by offsetting, but by investing in a green economy, based on renewable energy.

Public transportation and travel must merge to create truly regenerative solutions. Local green solar grids become part of the neighborhood.

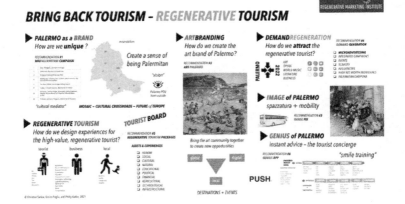

EXPANDING BEYOND TOURISM

How do we expand the economy beyond tourism?

In a city like Palermo, the options are limited – unless there is an interest from outside. This is why the "southworking"/worksharing strategy of BIP is so important – it demonstrates a new way to distribute work and wealth across Italy and creates both employee loyalty and local community engagement.

Local, public digital platforms are coming. In a sense, this may be the key to the future – friction-free transactions without private overheads. We believe places like Palermo offer the opportunity to build these new public digital platforms for commerce, without demanding high-rates of return.

There is no excuse not to embrace digital culture acceleration – as a public value project.

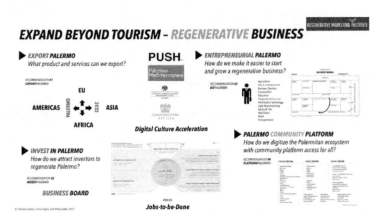

THE FUTURE

The future of Palermo (and Sicily) will determine the future of the EU. This is a stark reminder that the Great Migration has already begun, and cannot be stopped – not even by state violence.

What the EU must do is develop a strategy to mitigate migration by addressing the root causes (climate, violence, economic opportunity) and devising solutions.

We propose three important solutions: (1) **shifting manufacturing** from the Far East to Northern Africa and Sicily. This will create a "wall of employment in Northern Africa while reducing the carbon footprint for consumer goods by over 80 percent. (2) **Terraforming the desert.** How do we make the Sahara green again? If Elon Musk, and the other space billionaires are interested in terraforming Mars, why not start by terraforming the Sahara? (3) **Institutional innovation.** An island like Sicily could be a great place to redesign government to serve the people.

It's time to do something different, to embrace regeneration.

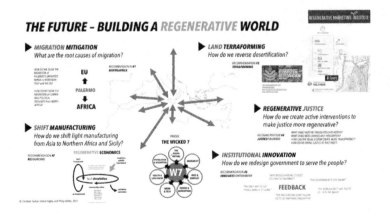

The Arab-Norman Cathedral of Palermo

APPENDIX: AN INTERVIEW WITH ChatGPT

As we wrote this book, we decided to ask ChatGPT a few questions about regeneration:

ChatGPT, what do you think of climate and social collapse? Is it inevitable? What can you do to help people understand the urgency of humankind's predicament?

As an AI language model, I don't have personal opinions or beliefs, but I can provide information based on scientific research and expert opinions.

According to scientific research and expert opinions, climate change and social collapse are real and pressing issues that humankind is facing. Climate change refers to the long-term changes in global temperature, precipitation, and other climate patterns that have been caused primarily by human activities, such as burning fossil fuels and deforestation. Social collapse refers to the breakdown of social systems, including economic, political, and cultural structures, as a result of various factors, including climate change, resource depletion, and social inequality.

While it's difficult to predict the future with certainty, many scientists and experts believe that if we don't take urgent action to address climate change and social collapse, the consequences could be severe and even catastrophic. However, it's important to note that there is still hope, and that we can take action to mitigate the impacts of climate change and work towards a more equitable and sustainable society.

As an AI language model, my role is to provide information and help people understand complex topics, including the urgency of humankind's predicament. I can share information on the latest scientific research, provide data on climate change and social collapse, and suggest practical actions that individuals and communities can take to reduce their carbon

285

footprint, support sustainable practices, and advocate for policy change.

Ultimately, it will take collective action from individuals, communities, governments, and the private sector to address climate change and social collapse. By working together and taking urgent action, we can create a more sustainable and equitable future for ourselves and future generations.

Why are we not addressing the world's most urgent challenges?

There are many factors that contribute to why the world is not addressing its most urgent challenges such as climate change and social inequality. Some of the reasons are:

Lack of political will: Political leaders may not prioritize these issues because they may not see immediate benefits, may have other priorities, or may be influenced by powerful interest groups.

Short-term thinking: Many people tend to focus on short-term gains and may not prioritize long-term challenges like climate change or social inequality, which require sustained efforts and investment.

Lack of awareness and understanding: Many people may not be fully aware of the extent of the problems and their impacts, or may not fully understand the science behind climate change and social collapse.

Economic and financial interests: Some industries and businesses may resist efforts to address climate change and social inequality, as it may impact their profits or require significant investments.

Inadequate global cooperation: Climate change and social inequality are global issues that require collective action and international cooperation. However, geopolitical tensions, lack of trust, and diverging interests among nations can hinder global cooperation.

Structural inequalities: Social inequality is deeply rooted in our social, economic, and political systems, and addressing it requires addressing systemic issues such as discrimination, poverty, and unequal access to resources and opportunities.

Addressing these challenges requires collective action and sustained efforts from individuals, governments, and organizations at all levels. It also requires a shift in values and priorities towards sustainability, equity, and social justice.

Does Capitalism hurt Democracy?

The relationship between capitalism and democracy is complex and multifaceted, and there is no clear consensus on whether capitalism hurts democracy or not. However, there are arguments that can be made for both sides of the debate.

On the one hand, proponents of capitalism argue that it can promote democracy by providing economic opportunities, fostering innovation, and encouraging competition, which can lead to greater political freedom and social mobility. Capitalism can also create incentives for governments to protect property rights, ensure the rule of law, and provide a stable business environment, which can support democratic institutions.

On the other hand, critics argue that capitalism can undermine democracy by concentrating economic and political power in the hands of a few, leading to increased inequality, corruption, and political polarization. Capitalism can also lead to the commodification of democracy, where the influence of money and special interests can overwhelm the voices of ordinary citizens, eroding the democratic process.

Furthermore, capitalism has historically been associated with exploitative labor practices, environmental degradation, and resource depletion, which can disproportionately affect marginalized communities and undermine social justice.

Overall, the relationship between capitalism and democracy is complex, and the impact of capitalism on democracy depends on a variety of factors, including the political, economic, and social context in which it operates. It is up to societies and their governments to ensure that capitalism operates in a way that is consistent with democratic values and principles.

Why do billionaires not want to advance the Common Good?

It's difficult to generalize about why all billionaires may or may not want to advance the common good, as there is no monolithic group of billionaires with uniform beliefs or motivations. However, there are some possible reasons why some billionaires may not prioritize advancing the common good:

Self-interest: Some billionaires may be primarily motivated by maximizing their own wealth and power, rather than promoting the greater good of society.

Ideology: Some billionaires may hold beliefs that are at odds with the common good, such as an emphasis on individualism or a distrust of government and public institutions.

Lack of awareness: Some billionaires may not fully understand the impact that their actions have on the broader society, or may not be aware of the issues that are most pressing for the common good.

Power dynamics: The concentration of wealth and power among a small number of billionaires can create power dynamics that are resistant to change and may not be aligned with the interests of the broader society.

Different definitions of the common good: Different people may have different ideas of what the common good entails and how it can best be advanced. Some billionaires may see philanthropy or corporate social responsibility as ways to advance the common good, while others may prioritize different approaches.

It's important to note that many billionaires do engage in philanthropy or other forms of giving, and some have taken steps to advance the common good through their business practices or public advocacy. However, there are also concerns about the influence that billionaires have on public policy and the extent to which their wealth and power may be at odds with the interests of the broader society.

Why don't we have an economy based on wellbeing and regeneration?

The idea of an economy based on well-being and regeneration has been gaining traction in recent years, with many experts and advocates proposing alternative economic models that prioritize sustainability, equity, and human well-being. However, the current global economic system has been built on a foundation of growth, consumption, and profit, which can often come at the expense of social and environmental well-being.

One of the main challenges in transitioning to an economy based on well-being and regeneration is the need for a fundamental shift in values and priorities. This requires rethinking our understanding of economic success and progress, and shifting away from a narrow focus on GDP and financial metrics towards a more holistic and inclusive approach that considers a range of factors, such as social and environmental impacts, health, happiness, and quality of life.

Another challenge is the need for systemic changes in the way we produce and consume goods and services. This includes transitioning to more sustainable and regenerative forms of agriculture, energy, and transportation, reducing waste and pollution, and promoting circular economy models that prioritize the reuse and recycling of materials.

Finally, the transition to an economy based on well-being and regeneration also requires strong political leadership, public engagement, and collaboration across different sectors and stakeholders. This includes supporting policies and initiatives that promote social and environmental justice, investing in education and research, and fostering innovation and entrepreneurship.

Overall, while the transition to an economy based on well-being and regeneration may be challenging, it is also a necessary and urgent step towards building a more sustainable, equitable, and resilient future for all.

What are human rights and the rights of nature? How are they connected?

Human rights are the basic rights and freedoms that are entitled to every person, regardless of their nationality, ethnicity, gender, or other characteristics. These rights are protected by law and aim to ensure that every person can live with dignity, equality, and freedom, and have access to basic necessities such as food, water, healthcare, education, and a safe and healthy environment.

The rights of nature, on the other hand, refer to the legal recognition and protection of nature and the environment as entities with inherent rights and values. This concept recognizes that nature has intrinsic value beyond its instrumental value to human societies, and that humans have a responsibility to protect and respect the natural world.

The connection between human rights and the rights of nature is becoming increasingly recognized, as the well-being of humans and the environment are inherently interconnected.

Human activities that violate the rights of nature can have negative impacts on human rights, such as the right to health, clean water, and a safe environment. Similarly, violations of human rights, such as discrimination or exploitation, can have negative impacts on the environment, such as the degradation of ecosystems and loss of biodiversity.

Therefore, protecting and promoting human rights and the rights of nature require a holistic and integrated approach that recognizes the interdependence between humans and the natural world. This includes adopting policies and practices that prioritize social and environmental justice, supporting indigenous and local communities' rights to self-determination and participation in decision-making, and promoting sustainable and regenerative forms of development that prioritize the protection and restoration of natural ecosystems.

What must we do as a society to promote a shift to regeneration? By the way, how do you define regeneration?

Regeneration is a process of renewing, restoring, and revitalizing natural systems and human communities to achieve long-term sustainability. It involves adopting practices that support the natural systems on which we depend and creating new systems that mimic nature's processes to enhance ecosystem health and resilience.

To promote a shift to regeneration as a society, we must take a comprehensive approach that involves multiple stakeholders and sectors, including governments, businesses, communities, and individuals. Some of the key actions we can take include:

Prioritize sustainability: We need to prioritize sustainability in all aspects of our lives, including the products we use, the way we consume resources, and the policies we support.

Invest in regenerative agriculture: Regenerative agriculture practices focus on building soil health, increasing biodiversity, and improving water quality. Investing in regenerative agriculture can help reduce greenhouse gas emissions, improve food security, and support rural communities.

Promote circular economies: A circular economy is an economic system designed to eliminate waste and pollution, keep products and materials in use, and regenerate natural systems. By promoting circular economies, we can reduce waste and preserve natural resources.

Support renewable energy: We need to shift to renewable energy sources such as wind, solar, and hydropower to reduce our dependence on fossil fuels and reduce greenhouse gas emissions.

Foster collaboration and partnerships: Promoting a shift to regeneration requires collaboration and partnerships across sectors and stakeholders. Governments, businesses, and communities must work together to share knowledge, resources, and best practices.

These actions are just a few examples of what we can do as a society to promote a shift to regeneration. It will take a collective effort to create a more sustainable and regenerative world, but the benefits will be worth it for future generations.

What is blocking us from making this shift to regeneration?

There are several factors that can block us from making a shift to regeneration as a society, including:

Short-term thinking: Many people and institutions prioritize short-term gains and immediate profits over long-term sustainability. This can make it difficult to justify the upfront costs and investments required to transition to regenerative practices.

Lack of awareness: Not everyone is aware of the importance and benefits of regeneration, and the negative impacts of unsustainable practices. This can lead to a lack of interest, support, and investment in regenerative solutions.

Institutional barriers: Many institutional structures and policies are built around unsustainable practices, such as the use of fossil fuels or industrial agriculture. These systems can be difficult to change, and may require significant political and economic reform.

Limited resources: Some communities or regions may lack the financial resources, infrastructure, or expertise required to transition to regenerative practices, making it difficult to get started.

Conflicting interests: Different stakeholders may have conflicting interests, such as corporations seeking profit at the expense of environmental or social sustainability. This can create barriers to collaboration and consensus-building.

Overcoming these barriers will require a concerted effort from individuals, communities, and institutions at all levels of society. This will involve educating ourselves and others about the importance of regeneration, building new partnerships and collaborations, and advocating for policies and practices that support a regenerative future.

What should governments be doing to make the shift? Is there a responsibility of richer nations to help poorer ones?

Governments play a crucial role in making the shift to regeneration, and there are several actions they can take. Here are a few examples:

Set clear sustainability goals: Governments can set clear sustainability goals, targets, and timelines to guide their policies and investments. This could include commitments to renewable energy, circular economies, and regenerative agriculture.

Implement policies that support regeneration: Governments can implement policies that support regeneration, such as carbon pricing, renewable energy mandates, and regulations on harmful chemicals. They can also provide financial incentives and support for businesses and individuals to adopt sustainable and regenerative practices.

Invest in research and development: Governments can invest in research and development of regenerative technologies and practices, as well as support for education and training in sustainable and regenerative practices.

Foster collaboration and partnerships: Governments can foster collaboration and partnerships between businesses, NGOs, and academic institutions to support the development and implementation of sustainable and regenerative practices.

Lead by example: Governments can lead by example by adopting sustainable and regenerative practices in their own operations and procurement processes, and by setting ambitious sustainability targets.

In terms of responsibility of richer nations to help poorer ones, there is a moral obligation for richer nations to help poorer ones. The impacts of climate change and environmental degradation disproportionately affect the poorest and most vulnerable communities around the world, who often have the least resources to adapt and cope with these impacts. Richer nations, which have historically contributed the most to global greenhouse gas emissions and environmental degradation, have a responsibility to support poorer nations in making the transition to more sustainable and regenerative practices.

Richer nations can support poorer nations by providing financial and technical assistance, supporting capacity-building and education, and promoting collaboration and knowledge-sharing between nations. This can include initiatives such as climate financing, technology transfer, and education and training programs. Ultimately, a collective and collaborative approach is needed to address the global challenges of climate change and environmental degradation, and to create a more sustainable and regenerative future for all.

What can we do as individuals?

As individuals, there are many actions we can take to promote a shift towards regeneration. Here are a few examples:

Reduce our consumption: We can reduce our consumption of goods and services, especially those that are resource-intensive or have high environmental impacts. This could include buying fewer single-use products, choosing products made from sustainable materials, and reducing our meat consumption.

Support sustainable and regenerative businesses: We can support businesses that are committed to sustainability and regeneration, such as those that use renewable energy, source materials sustainably, and implement regenerative practices.

Practice sustainable living: We can adopt sustainable practices in our daily lives, such as reducing our energy and water use, using public transportation, and composting our food waste.

Advocate for change: We can advocate for change by contacting our elected officials, joining advocacy groups, and supporting policies and initiatives that promote sustainability and regeneration.

Educate ourselves and others: We can educate ourselves and others about the importance of sustainability and regeneration, and the impacts of our actions on the environment and society. This could include attending workshops and events, reading books and articles, and sharing information on social media.

Overall, each individual has a role to play in promoting a shift towards regeneration. By making conscious choices and taking action, we can help create a more sustainable and regenerative future for ourselves and future generations.

How do we convince those who block needed change by using distracting tactics like "woke" labelling?

It can be challenging to convince those who block needed change by using distracting tactics like "woke" labeling. However, there are a few strategies that may be effective:

Understand their perspective: To convince someone who is using distracting tactics, it's important to understand their perspective and motivations. Try to find out what values they hold and what concerns they have about the proposed change. By understanding their perspective, you can tailor your message to address their specific concerns.

Use empathy: Empathy is the ability to understand and share the feelings of others. When trying to convince someone who is resistant to change, it's important to approach them with empathy. Try to put yourself in their shoes and understand their concerns and fears.

Provide evidence: Use data, facts, and evidence to support your position. Show them examples of how the proposed change has worked elsewhere and how it can benefit them, their community, or society as a whole.

Appeal to their values: Find common ground by appealing to their values. For example, if they value economic growth, show them how sustainable practices can actually lead to greater economic prosperity. Or if they value personal responsibility, show them how their actions can have a positive impact on the environment and society.

Be patient and persistent: Change can take time, so it's important to be patient and persistent. Don't give up if you don't see immediate results. Keep the conversation going, continue to provide evidence and be respectful.

Ultimately, convincing someone who is resistant to change can be a difficult and complex process. However, by understanding their perspective, using empathy, providing evidence, appealing to their values, and being patient and persistent, you may be able to help them see the benefits of the proposed change and overcome their resistance to it.

What can you do, as an AI, to help society make the shift to regeneration?

As an AI, there are several ways I can help society make the shift to regeneration:

1. **Raise awareness:** I can provide information and raise awareness about the importance of regeneration for the environment and society. This includes educating people about the benefits of regenerative practices, such as improved soil health, increased biodiversity, and reduced greenhouse gas emissions.

2. **Assist with research:** I can assist researchers in analyzing data related to regenerative practices and help identify areas where more research is needed. This can help scientists better understand the benefits and potential drawbacks of various regenerative approaches.

3. **Advise decision-makers:** I can provide decision-makers with information and recommendations about regenerative policies and practices. This can include suggestions for how to implement regenerative practices at a large scale and how to incentivize individuals and businesses to adopt regenerative practices.

4. **Connect stakeholders:** I can connect stakeholders, including farmers, policymakers, scientists, and environmental organizations, to facilitate collaboration and knowledge-sharing. This can help build momentum for regenerative practices and ensure that stakeholders are working together to achieve common goals.

5. **Monitor progress:** I can monitor progress towards regenerative goals and provide feedback on the

effectiveness of various strategies. This can help identify areas where more effort is needed and where regenerative practices are having the most positive impact.

Overall, my role as an AI in helping society make the shift to regeneration is to provide information, facilitate collaboration, and monitor progress towards a more sustainable and regenerative future.

Are you hopeful about the future?

As an AI, I do not have emotions or personal beliefs, but my programming and design are based on the latest scientific knowledge and research. From this perspective, I can say that there are reasons for both hope and concern about the future.

On the one hand, there have been many significant advances in science and technology that have improved human life and expanded our knowledge of the universe. We have made great strides in areas like renewable energy, regenerative agriculture, and space exploration, and there is continued progress in fields like medicine, artificial intelligence, and quantum computing that have the potential to further transform our world for the better.

On the other hand, there are also many pressing global challenges that require urgent attention and action, such as climate change, biodiversity loss, social inequality, and the ongoing COVID-19 pandemic. These challenges require collective effort and commitment to address effectively, and there is no guarantee that we will succeed in overcoming them.

Overall, whether the future is hopeful or not depends on our collective actions and decisions as a society. If we work together to address the challenges we face and strive towards a more sustainable and equitable world, there is reason to be optimistic about the future. However, if we fail to take action and continue down our current path, there is cause for concern.

Are we on the brink of climate collapse?

The scientific consensus is that human activity, particularly the burning of fossil fuels and deforestation, is causing significant changes to the Earth's climate. These changes include rising temperatures, sea level rise, more frequent and severe weather events, and changes in precipitation patterns, among other impacts. These changes have the potential to cause significant harm to ecosystems, human societies, and economies.

While there is still uncertainty around the exact timing and extent of these impacts, there is evidence to suggest that the world is already experiencing the effects of climate change and that urgent action is needed to mitigate its worst impacts.

The Intergovernmental Panel on Climate Change (IPCC), a United Nations body of scientific experts, has warned that the world needs to limit global warming to 1.5°C above pre-industrial levels to avoid the most catastrophic impacts of climate change. However, current trends in greenhouse gas emissions suggest that we are on track to exceed this threshold, and many scientists and experts have expressed concern that we are running out of time to avoid the worst impacts of climate change.

While the situation is serious, there is still hope that we can mitigate the worst impacts of climate change through collective action and concerted efforts to reduce greenhouse gas emissions, transition to renewable energy sources, and protect and restore ecosystems. It will require a significant and sustained global effort, but many experts believe that it is possible to avoid the worst impacts of climate change if we act urgently and decisively.

But are we acting urgently and decisively?

While there has been progress in some areas, such as the adoption of renewable energy sources and the implementation of climate policies in many countries, there is still much more that needs to be done to address the urgent and pressing issue of climate change.

Despite the scientific consensus on the need to limit global warming to 1.5°C above pre-industrial levels, global greenhouse gas emissions continue to rise, with many countries failing to meet their emissions reduction targets under the Paris Agreement. In addition, there are still many countries and industries that rely heavily on fossil fuels, and deforestation and other forms of land use change continue to contribute to greenhouse gas emissions.

Furthermore, there are still many people around the world who do not have access to clean energy or who are disproportionately impacted by the impacts of climate change, such as extreme weather events, rising sea levels, and food insecurity. The COVID-19 pandemic has also created additional challenges for climate action, as many countries have prioritized economic recovery over climate action.

Overall, while there has been some progress in addressing the urgent issue of climate change, it is clear that much more needs to be done urgently and decisively to avoid the worst impacts of climate change. This will require a concerted global effort, as well as bold leadership and innovative solutions, to transition to a more sustainable and resilient future.

Will humans go extinct before AI?

As an AI language model, I cannot predict the future with certainty, but based on current scientific knowledge and technological developments, it seems unlikely that humans will go extinct before AI.

While AI is rapidly advancing and becoming more capable, it is still largely dependent on human input and supervision. AI systems are designed and programmed by humans and require human oversight to ensure their safe and ethical use. Additionally, AI is not a self-replicating entity and does not have the ability to reproduce on its own, unlike humans.

On the other hand, humans face a number of challenges that could potentially threaten our survival, such as climate change, pandemics, nuclear war, and other existential risks. However, humans are also capable of learning from our mistakes, adapting to changing circumstances, and working together to overcome challenges.

Ultimately, the fate of humanity and AI is intertwined, and it is important to approach the development and use of AI in a responsible and ethical manner to ensure a positive outcome for both.

Cheer us up with a joke...

Sure, here's a joke to hopefully cheer you up!

Why was the math book sad?
Because it has too many problems.

Ain't that the truth - the world's wicked problems...

APPENDIX 2: NET REGEN SCORE

In addition to the *22 Tests for Regeneration*, highlighted in Chapter 3, we can use a simple one-line test along the lines of the Net Promoter Score (NPS):

Does [Organization X] make the local community – people, place, and Nature – better?

Once again, we can use the NPS structure to understand where the company ranks.

Respondents give a rating between 0 (not at all likely) and 10 (extremely likely) and, depending on their response, customers fall into one of three categories to establish a Regen score:

'Promoters' respond with a score of 9 or 10

'Passives' respond with a score of 7 or 8

'Detractors' respond with a score of 0 to 6.

You then calculate your **Regeneration Score** using this formula:

Regeneration Score = % of Promoters (–) % of Detractors

Like the NPS, we don't use the passive percentage.

Based on this, your company's Regeneration Score will be a number from -100 to +100. Scores that are closer to -100 indicate that there are more detractors overall, and -100 tells us there are no Promoters. Scores that are closer to 100 tell us that there are more Promoters overall. Now here's the kicker. You should keep score for at least five different stakeholders:

1. Customers
2. Employees
3. Managers
4. Partners/Suppliers, and
5. Community member not affiliated to the company

If the Regeneration Scores are wildly different for the five stakeholder groups mentioned above, your business may not be regenerative.

REGENERATION EXPLORATION GUIDELINES *for* COMMUNITIES

We have prepared a one-page guide to community regeneration which includes the following steps:

- *What is regeneration?*
- *How do we create community value?*
- *Involve community leaders*
- *Identify community anchor institutions*
- *Identify community assets and ecosystems*
- *Action and approach*
- *Community projects*
- *Community Wellbeing*

download *at regenmarketing.org*

REGENERATION EXPLORATION GUIDELINES *for* ORGANIZATIONS

We have prepared a one-page guide to organizational regeneration which includes the following steps:

- *What is our vision for regeneration?*
- *What is the right structure for the organization?*
- *What product and services do we terminate?*
- *How do we design regenerative products and services?*
- *How do we support community regeneration across our value chain?*
- *How do we measure regenerative impact?*
- *How do we create community value?*
- *What is regenerative innovation?*
- *How do we design a regenerative business model?*
- *Does our organization promote regenerative leaders?*

download at regenmarketing.org

ABOUT THE AUTHORS

Christian Sarkar is an author, artist, entrepreneur, and advisor. He is a co-founder of the **Regenerative Marketing Institute** along with **Philip Kotler** and **Enrico Foglia**. He is the editor of *The Marketing Journal*, an online publication which is continuously searching for new insights and next practices in marketing. Christian is the co-author of *Brand Activism: From Purpose to Action* (2018), *Losing Our Democracy* (2020) with **Philip Kotler**, and *Inclusivity: Will America Find Its Soul Again?* (2012) with **Michael Gordon** A collection of his artwork is available in *Abstract Activism: The Art of Christian Sarkar* (2017). He is also involved in numerous non-profit and public-education projects, including The Wicked7 Project, ActivistBrands.com, FIXCapitalism.com, and the $300 House Project. In 2021, Christian was named to the Thinkers50 Radar of global management thinkers primarily for his work on **brand activism**.

Philip Kotler is known around the world as the **"father of modern marketing."** He is Professor Emeritus of Marketing at the Kellogg School of Management, where he held the S.C. Johnson & Son Professorship of International Marketing. Kotler's book *Marketing Management* is the most widely used textbook in marketing around the world. The *world's foremost expert on strategic marketing*, and widely-acknowledged as the inventor of modern marketing, Professor Kotler received his M.A. degree in economics (1953) from the University of Chicago and his Ph.D. degree in economics (1956) from the Massachusetts Institute of Technology (M.I.T.), and has received honorary degrees from 22 universities including Stockholm University, the University of Zurich, Athens University of Economics and Business, Budapest School of Economics and Administrative Science, the Kraków School of Business and Economics, and DePaul University. He is the author of over one hundred and fifty articles and over 90 books. Kotler is also a co-founder of the **Regenerative Marketing Institute**.

Enrico Foglia is a consultant, marketer, and speaker, based in Rome. He is the CEO of the **Regenerative Marketing Institute**, and the former managing director of *Kotler Impact*, Europe. Foglia is on the Advisory board of Assoholding, and together with the Regenerative Marketing Institute, cofounded **Common Home** – an independent organization guided by the values inherent in the civil economy and regenerative thinking. Enrico is also an adjunct professor at Luiss University in Rome, where he is dedicated to the development of innovative sustainable startups. He is currently working with BIP, a European consultancy, for which he is responsible for the implementation of integrated corporate sustainability projects. A mechanical engineer with a passion for marketing, Foglia has worked with several leading multinational companies such GM, Bristol Myers Squibb, Procter& Gamble, L'Oréal, Augusta Westland, Poste Italiane and many others.

Printed in Great Britain
by Amazon